More Industry-Acclaim for
How to Excel in Leasing Apartments

..."*Finally—a book on apartment leasing that goes beyond the simple quick fixes. Both inspirational and practical, How to Excel in Leasing Apartments is priority reading.*"

Terri L. Norvell, V.P. Marketing
Maxim Property Management, San Mateo, CA

..."*A first rate, well-organized book of an extremely important topic. I can't think of any industry profes-sional who wouldn't be helped by reading it.*"

Frank H. Livingston, Senior Vice President
Draper & Kramer, Chicago, IL

..."*The country's leading experts tell all. 12 leasing champions share their expertise in this one-of-a-kind leasing guide.*"

Andrew M. Chaban, Executive Vice President
Princeton Properties, Lowell, MA

How to Excel in Leasing Apartments

Registered in Apartment Management Program
National Association of Home Builders
1201 15th Street, NW
Washington, D.C. 20005-2800
(800) 368-5242

This publication is designed to provide accurate and authoritative information in regard to the subject matter covered. It is sold with the understanding that the publisher is not engaged in rendering legal, accounting, or other professional service. If legal advice or other expert assistance is required, the services of a competent professional person should be sought.

- From a Declaration of Principles jointly adopted by a Committee of the American Bar Association and a Committee of Publishers and Associations.

How to Excel in Leasing Apartments
ISBN 0©9645538-0-5

Printed in the United States of America. For further information, please contact:
Registered in Apartment Management (RAM) Program
National Association of Home Builders
1201 15th Street, NW
Washington, DC 20005-2800
(800) 368-5242

"HOW TO EXCEL IN LEASING APARTMENTS"

Chapter 1: How to Develop a Winner's Mindset

Chapter 2: A Job Description, Expectations & Performance Standards for Leasing Professionals

Chapter 3: Telephone Inquiries & On-Site Prospect Qualifying

Chapter 4: Between Qualifying & Closing

Chapter 5: The Close—A Win-Win for Everyone

Chapter 6: Follow Up & Watch Your Closing Ratio Soar

Chapter 7: Selling within the Law

Chapter 8: Merchandising—Your Silent Partner

Chapter 9: Don't Wait for Traffic to Come to You— Go Get 'Em!

Chapter 10: Resident Renewals & Retention

Chapter 11: Personal Growth Messages

ACKNOWLEDGMENTS

Our combined group of contributing authors would like to convey a special thanks to the National Association of Home Builders (NAHB) and its Multifamily Council for sponsoring this work on behalf of the association's residential income property membership.

The Board of Trustees for NAHB's National Council of the Multifamily Housing Industry and the RAM Board of Governors have given us wholehearted support, encouragement, and endorsement, without which this task could not have been accomplished, timely or at all.

We each owe a special thanks to Kimberly Duty, NAHB's staff person in the Multifamily Council assigned to coordinate this ambitious project. Typical of Kim, she has done so in record time with maximum efficiency. Kim's ability to take on this assignment speaks to the team effort of the entire Multifamily Council and its leadership through Robert Corletta and Lasse van Essen.

We also owe special recognition to our legal content reviewer, Laurence A. Lasky, Lasky & Scharrer, Dayton, OH. Mr Lasky is a member of the Dayton Bar Association and a guest lecturer and consultant on fair housing and Section 8 evictions. His comments and contributions help ensure the cutting-edge quality level of the Chapter Seven, Selling Within the Law.

Simply writing a book does not guarantee its circulation, however. And we owe a warm thanks to Miller, Freeman, Inc. and the folks responsible for the Multi-Housing World Conference, who have provided such a fabulous forum and subsequent vehicle to enhance awareness and delivery of our book. Patti Mayersohn and Laura Templeton, thank you for your special efforts.

FOREWORD

This book has been a long time coming. What's amazing is that the industry got by without it for so long. Over the numerous recessions, mergers, acquisitions, growth and shrinkage in the country, many of our top professionals have taken their expertise to new fields of endeavor. Of course, these swings have taken a toll on the industry but the cleansing process hasn't been all bad either. The trick is to figure out how to ride the waves and land on your feet with as few bruises and dings as possible.

The contributing authors who were invited to share their expertise with you through this book know quite a lot about resiliency. Much like you, they have each had their share of learning experiences and are working every day at going with the flow. It all sounds familiar, doesn't it? They're survivors. And if you're taking this book seriously, you're a survivor too. But our intention here is to go way beyond that plane of existence and leap onto a higher level of satisfaction, reward, and career fulfillment. It's a wonderful experience to discover joy and excitement in what you do and the way you do it.

While this book is full of various perspectives and techniques on leasing apartments and developing winning attitudes and productive mindsets, it also presents some controversy and counter-viewpoints. It isn't our intention to confuse you but to present various ways of achieving objectives by working with the personalities and innate characteristics that distinguish each of us. Most of you will be comfortable relating to each of us some of the time but not all of the time. Nor do you need to agree with everything one of us says about a given approach. Education and acquired knowledge are all about choices. We hope to give you lots of those.

To get the most out of this book, read it from front to back in sequence. Then, return to those areas that appeal to you most at this time. The answers to your specific issues of concern aren't likely to be contained in one chapter or in any particular author's viewpoint on a stated subject.

Most of us have woven our concepts over several chapters. Gems of thought and action pop up in the most unlikely places. Were you to be searching chapter headings only to resolve certain issues, you might miss the tidbits of wisdom that could escort you to where you need or want to be. And at different times in your life and career path, you will need to revisit chapters and concepts that didn't appeal to you at other times, simply because you weren't ready for them.

How to Excel in Leasing Apartments is your personal companion and resource guide to accompany you on your journey. We're glad to be travelling in such good company.

Carol Ann Cardella, RAM, MIRM, GRI
Chairperson

INTRODUCTION

In the spring of 1994, the National Association of Home Builders' (NAHB) Multifamily Council convened a meeting of the leading experts in multifamily leasing to explore a training and certification program for the often overlooked leasing professional. Support for the idea among those present was unanimous. So unanimous, in fact, that within a month, NAHB had committed to the project under its Registered in Apartment Management (RAM) program. One year later, **How to Excel in Leasing Apartments** became a reality.

How to Excel in Leasing Apartments is a companion to a national training program that leads to a designation as a Certified Leasing Professional (CLP). This program would not be possible without the continued support of the National Council of the Multifamily Housing Industry (NCMHI) Board of Trustees and RAM Board of Governors, as well as the hard work of the CLP Committee Chair, Carol Ann Cardella, and each of the authors who contributed to this book. Their combined expertise and years of producing training materials have created a book unique to the industry.

What are **NAHB** and **NCMHI**?

The National Association of Home Builders is a national trade association representing the housing industry with over 170, 000 members in more than 800 state and local associations nationwide. The multifamily industry is represented through the NCMHI.

NCMHI is the fastest growing network of multifamily professionals in the nation and represents 25,000 firms, including builders, developers, owners, managers, and related professionals. NCMHI provides its members with a comprehensive array of services such as training programs and seminars, valuable industry publications, legislative tracking, and a variety of "how to" information.

What is the RAM Certification Program?

The RAM Certification program is the oldest residential property management certification program in the U.S. RAM provides a series of training and certifications at various levels of expertise to property managers of multifamily rental, condominium, cooperative, subsidized, and market-rate housing throughout the industry. Our certifications include:

▶ Registered in Apartment Management (RAM)
▶ Advanced RAM
▶ Certified Leasing Professional (CLP)

The RAM designations distinguish qualified multifamily housing professionals from those who do not meet national standards of experience and competence. By holding one or more of the RAM designations, you say to your peers and prospective employers that you are a qualified individual committed to promoting professionalism in the multifamily housing industry. For more information on how to become a RAM, please contact NCMHI at (800) 368-5242.

Certified Leasing Professional Certification

How to Excel in Leasing Apartments is a companion and required reading for the national Certified Leasing Professional course curriculum. The CLP builds on the foundations presented in this book and provides industry professionals with an affordable means to develop their skills and productivity level. Candidates who successfully complete the CLP course curriculum are granted the CLP designation.

The CLP course is available to the industry through a variety of options:

- ▶ Intensified regional workshops conducted by nationally recognized trainers are brought to metropolitan areas servicing active apartment markets around the country.
- ▶ The "standard" curriculum is offered by local HBAs, Multifamily Councils, colleges, and universities, and as the program develops, educators are trained locally.
- ▶ A home study program is available to those NAHB and NCMHI members whose properties and site personnel are not located in a metropolitan area.

For more information on certification or to find out about course offerings in your area, contact NAHB at (800) 368-5242.

MEET THE AUTHORS

CAROL ANN CARDELLA, RAM®, MIRM®, GRI®

Carol Ann is president of her own consulting firm, established in 1972, and specializes in sales training, organizational development, marketing strategies, and troubleshooting problem properties. Carol Ann's career began in the apartment marketing industry in 1969, since which time she has learned to overcome the various cycles plaguing apartment owner/developers by providing remedies to assist them through the inevitable and foreseeable cycles.

Carol Ann enjoys the reputation of a dynamic, informed, nationally recognized speaker, author, and facilitator/trainer. She resides in Cincinnati, Ohio, and travels throughout the United States and Canada to problem solve for her clients.

She has served NAHB as a Governor on the RAM Board and as a Trustee for the National Sales & Marketing Council. She is also a Charter Member of the Institute of Residential Marketing.

Contact Information:
Carol Ann Cardella
Cardella & Associates, Inc.
2104 Alpine Place
Cincinnati, OH 45206
(513) 851-8010

or contact NAHB's National Council of the Multifamily Housing Industry at (800) 368-5242, ext. 215.

DOUGLAS D. CHASICK, CPM®, RAM®

Doug is an accomplished speaker and author and is the former editor of *NOI NEWS*, an apartment management newsletter. A favorite of property management professionals across the country, Doug is known for his incisive, action-based presentations that are jam-packed with common sense, easy-to-use information, and humor. Over the past 10 years, Doug has spoken at numerous local and state apartment association events.

Doug's approach extends from his hands-on experience, gained over 18 years in on-site, supervisory, consulting, and executive positions, such as director of property management. He began his career as a resident manager for a 524-unit apartment property, and has since been responsible for the portfolios of over 28,000 apartments and more than 8 million square feet of commercial, retail, and industrial properties.

Contact Information:
Doug Chasick
National Realty Management, LP
7800 East Kemper Road
Cincinnati, OH 45249
(513) 489-1990

or contact NAHB's National Council of the Multifamily Housing Industry at (800) 368-5242, ext. 215.

TONI BLAKE CLINE

Toni Blake Cline has become one of the nation's leading motivational humorists with her "laugh while you learn" philosophy. Toni has worked her way to the top through her drive for excellence and high performance. Toni epitomizes the American entrepreneur. She is the owner of Blake Cline Productions, Inc., and is the president of Innovative Marketing and Consulting Services.

Toni has studied in Europe, speaks four languages, and has completed extensive research in communication and human behavior. Her syndicated column, "Tips from Toni," is published in more than 30 trade magazines across the country. Toni is recognized as an expert in customer service, sales, and marketing. Originally an on-site leasing agent, she knows property management from real experience. She captivates audiences with her down-to-earth approach to business and with her humorous stories depicting the personal side of the industry. Toni's clients include a variety of industries: apartment associations, apartment management companies, hotels, and banking, real estate, investment and management firms. She travels to over 80 cities annually, educating and entertaining audiences with seminars, workshops, and keynote presentations.

Contact Information:
Toni Blake Cline
Blake-Cline Productions, Inc.
2239 S. Alkire Ct.
Lakewood, CO 80228
(303) 980-5997

or contact NAHB's National Council of the Multifamily Housing Industry at (800) 368-5242, ext. 215.

KAY GREEN, MIRM®

Kay Green is a nationally recognized leader in the field of interior design. She founded Kay Green Design + Merchandising, Inc., in 1975. The company has since become one of the nations's most respected design firms. Based in Orlando, Florida, the firm performs merchandising services for builders and developers throughout the United States, as well as interior design services for private clients throughout Florida.

A nationally recognized speaker on design and building trends, Kay is regularly featured at national and regional builder conferences. She is also an instructor for the NAHB Institute of Residential Marketing qualifying courses. She serves as design columnist for *Southeast Homebuilder & Remodeler* magazine, and her byline appears often in other publications. In 1991, Kay was inducted into the NAHB's prestigious Society of Honored Associates. She was also selected to serve on the Board of Trustees of the NAHB'S National Sales and Marketing Council.

Contact Information:
Kay Green
Kay Green Design & Merchandising
327 Ernestine St.
Orlando, FL 32801
(407) 648-4622

or contact NAHB's National Council of the Multifamily Housing Industry at (800) 368-5242, ext. 215.

NICKI JOY, MIRM®

Since 1971, Nicki Joy, president of Nicki Joy and Associates, Inc., in Washington, D.C., has trained and motivated leasing and sales professionals nationwide. Nicki energizes and educates her audiences with her insightful training courses and powerful speaking programs.

Nicki, a member of the Institute of Residential Marketing, also holds a Senior Housing Marketing designation. She is a member of the board of advisors for numerous industry organizations, a columnist for several publications, including *The New York Post*, and the author of an exciting new book on sales.

Contact Information:
Nicki Joy
Nicki Joy & Associates
19816 Meredith Drive
Rockville, MD 20855
(301) 963-0700

or contact NAHB's National Council of the Multifamily Housing Industry at (800) 368-5242, ext. 215.

CYNTHIANN KING, RAM®

As the president of C King Unlimited, Cynthiann provides a comprehensive menu of innovative marketing and training services to meet the needs of industry organizations and associations.

She has a winning combination of professional training and business marketing experience. Cynthiann has 10 years of hands-on experience in the management field and 7 years' experience as a professional educator, and is a frequent presenter and seminar leader at apartment association meetings, conferences, and conventions. Her list of clients includes prominent management and development firms located throughout the nation. She is a CAM candidate with the National Apartment Association and a RAM with the National Council of Multifamily Housing Industry. She is the author of numerous articles for industry trade magazines and journals.

Contact Information:
Cynthiann King
C King Unlimited
1036 E. Meadowlake Drive
Palatine, IL 60067
(708) 776-8696

or contact NAHB's National Council of the Multifamily Housing Industry at (800) 368-5242, ext. 215.

DANIEL R. LEVITAN, RAM®, MIRM®, SHMS®

Daniel R. Levitan is senior vice president at The Greenman Group, Inc., where he is responsible for the research, analysis, and creation of all real estate development and marketing strategies for properties throughout the United States, Canada, and the Caribbean. He also directly supervises implementation of these strategies for selected clients across the nation, with hands-on involvement and direction in community planning, product design, administration, marketing, merchandising, promotion and sales/leasing, and he provides customized consulting.

Daniel is a member of numerous industry associations and is serving as the 1995 Chair of the NSMC's Builder/Realtor Relations Committee. He is a noted speaker, lecturer, trainer, and author in the shelter industry.

Contact Information:
Dan Levitan
Levitan & Associates
P.O. Box 16022
Fort Lauderdale, FL 33317
(305) 473-4244

or contact NAHB's National Council of the Multifamily Housing Industry at (800) 368-5242, ext. 215.

BRENDA McCLAIN, Advanced RAM®, CPM®

Brenda McClain is a noted national speaker, trainer, and consultant with 18 years of property management experience who specializes in teaching the skills and techniques of training and development with authority and impact.

Brenda is the founder of Brenda McClain & Associates, which was established to promote specialized quality training and further the professional development of the multihousing industry. She gained her knowledge of property management from being a "hands-on" senior divisional manager responsible for 2,000 units in seven states. She is a member of many training associations and was named the "1994 Woman of the Year" by the American Biographical Institute. Brenda has developed curricula and published numerous management articles for periodicals including the Journal of Property Management, RAM Digest, and Habitat. With her expertise in management issues, Brenda is a favorite speaker at many training sessions, meetings, and banquets. Brenda was honored as the first woman to receive the coveted RAM of the Year award in 1986 from the National Council of the Multifamily Industry (NCMHI).

Contact Information:
Brenda McClain
Brenda McClain & Associates
5120 Autumncrest Dr.
Greensboro, NC 27407
(919) 632-0909

or contact NAHB's National Council of the Multifamily Housing Industry at (800) 368-5242, ext. 215.

Paula -
wow! what an
achiever. your results oriented
attitude is very
refreshing. warm wishes -
Jennifer A. Nevitt
August 1995

JENNIFER A. NEVITT, RAM®

A strategic planner by inclination and experience, Jennifer has spent her career in marketing and training, primarily in multifamily property management. She also has a strong interest in development, especially of one-of-a-kind communities.

While she was national marketing director for a midwestern company, she was responsible for 20,000 multifamily units and for training all property managers and their staffs within a 12-state area. An accomplished speaker, she has presented seminars and speeches at Multi-Housing World Conferences, for the National Apartment Association, and at the annual conventions of the NAHB. Jennifer is the author of articles on marketing strategies including what she has dubbed "stack marketing," an innovative way to get maximum results from minimum dollars, and is the creator of marketing and operations seminars covering marketing plans, competitive rent analysis, waiting list strategies, time management, budget preparation, and financial statement analysis.

Contact Information:
Jennifer Nevitt
Bravo Strategic Marketing
PO Box 40142
Indianapolis, IN 46250
(317) 290-3757

or contact NAHB's National Council of the Multifamily Housing Industry at (800) 368-5242, ext. 215.

SHIRLEY A. ROBERTSON, RAM®, ARM®, CPM®

As a Certified Property Manager and an Accredited Residential Manager, Shirley is director of Professional Development & Training for Southern Management in Vienna, Virginia.

She has published articles in numerous industry magazines, has been a seminar leader for Multi-Housing World Conferences for the past 7 years, and also shares her expertise through participation in several association committees in the property management industry.

Over the past 18 years, Shirley has demonstrated a special management talent in leasing and marketing both assisted and conventional rental properties that has propelled her through the ranks from on-site manager and property manager to corporate training and supervisory positions. Shirley has helped train and certify over 600 RAMs over the years. Imaginative methods of communication have made Shirley an effective instructor of high school and college students, as well as skilled professionals. Shirley's skills as a motivational speaker, educator, and trainer have been built on a reputation for quality and dedication.

Contact Information:
Shirley A. Robertson
Shirley Robertson & Company
12023 Twin Cedar Lane
Bowie, MD 20715
(301) 403-2175

or contact NAHB's National Council of the Multifamily Housing Industry at (800) 368-5242, ext. 215.

ANNE SADOVSKY, RAM®

Anne Sadovsky is the owner of a Dallas-based marketing consultant and seminar firm where she and associates provide services such as contract apartment leasing, consulting, seminars, and training.

She has been affiliated with multifamily housing for almost 25 years. Anne has been a member of numerous trade organizations. Her professionalism has been recognized by the National Speakers Association, which has designated her as a "Certified Speaking Professional."

Anne is a contributing editor for a variety of publications throughout the nation. Her books, 101 Thoughts to Make You Think and 101 Thoughts for Becoming the Real You, are in bookstores nationally. She is a popular guest on radio and television talk shows and has appeared on Hour Magazine with Gary Collins. Her success story has been written about in Money magazine, Ladies Home Journal, Womens Wear Daily, and Texas Business.

Contact Information:
Anne Sadovsky
Anne Sadovsky & Co.
7557 Rambler Rd, #1454 LB73
Dallas, TX 75231
(214) 692-9300

or contact NAHB's National Council of the Multifamily Housing Industry at (800) 368-5242, ext. 215.

TAMI SIEWRUK

Tami Siewruk is the chief executive officer and president of The Sales & Marketing Magic Companies, based in Palm Harbor, Florida. Her companies specialize in providing the multifamily housing industry with the most effective leasing, marketing, management training information, and seminars available.

She currently serves as the chairperson for The Multifamily Councils' Network of the National Council of the Multifamily Housing Industry of the NAHB. Tami additionally serves on committees for RAM Digest, Certified Leasing Agent, Pillars of the Industry, and Multi-Housing World. Her newsletters, Sales & Marketing Magic, NOI News, and the Extra have thousands of subscribers throughout the United States, Canada, Sweden, and Russia. Her Tools & Forms Catalog offers a wealth of sales, marketing, and management aids, all designed specifically for the multifamily housing industry. The Annual Brainstorming Sessions, hosted by Tami's companies, has become an industry event not to be missed. Tami has been a keynote speaker at many Multi-Housing World Conferences and has been invited repeatedly to present at NAHB's Builders' Show.

Contact Information:
Tami Siewruk
Sales & Marketing Magic
36473 US Hwy 19 North
Palm Harbor, FL 34684
(813) 784-9469

or contact NAHB's National Council of the Multifamily Housing Industry at (800) 368-5242, ext. 215.

how to excel in leasing apartments

CHAPTER 1

How to Develop a Winner's Mindset

"Positioning Yourself:"
What it Takes to Move into
First Place   *-Cardella*

"Winning Traits & Attitudes"
-Sadovsky

"The Characteristics of Success"
-McClain

"A Quest for Excellence"
-Chasick

"What it Takes to Succeed"
-Nevitt

POSITIONING YOURSELF: WHAT IT TAKES TO MOVE INTO FIRST PLACE
By Carol Ann Cardella, RAM®, MIRM®, GRI®

Perceptions

Who are we? How do we choose to reveal or conceal ourselves? In a business environment, and for the sake of our personal career growth, are we comfortable enough with ourselves to adopt a business image that doesn't really reflect the personality we prefer to project?

Or are we so intent on making our own statement as individuals that we override or bypass the image needed in our business life to achieve success? And, if we choose to adopt the image that will bring us closer to our goals, can we sustain that image? Or will our real self sneak out in other ways to defeat the original impression we dressed up to convey?

Senior-level management would like to think they hire people whose personal image is closely aligned with both the company image and the site image, so that the net effect is a more comfortable consumer. After all, this is what this discussion is all about—delivering a comfort zone for the consumer together with a healthy business climate for ourselves and our organization. But the reality is that personnel are often not ideally matched to the situation at hand on any given site. This is especially true in the sales field. And leasing is sales.

There are two possible scenarios that describe how a leasing agent came to be: 1) Someone at some management level decided that a "salesperson" was needed to lease apartments, and so they set out to hire a person with sales skills and a personality conducive to the objective; or 2) Someone at some management level, usually a site level, decided that they needed more help to handle the workload, consisting of paper, people, and property. And leasing is one of those elements needing handling where the budget permits a hire.

However you came to be, you need to find out if your performance and success are measured by your leasing/sales skills as evidenced by your closing percentages. If you have the title of "leasing consultant" or "rental agent," someone in upper-level management is holding you accountable for leasing effectiveness.

This book is all about leasing, and the various author/ trainers are writing under the assumption that the leasing people reading this book are doing so to enhance their performance in their chosen field. None of us are so naive as to think every reader has chosen a sales career in leasing, not permanently and maybe not even temporarily. You may have gotten the job assignment by default when you really would prefer to be doing something else—like management. Many leasing people enter the sales field as an entry-level vehicle to get into management.

If sales is not your chosen field at this time in your life, but "you took the job just to pay your bills until something better comes along...," we're here to tell you that this is a tough job to fake, or slide by or lie back in. Success or failure is almost immediate in leasing. For that reason, many sales personalities enjoy instant gratification and rewards that are not available in other fields. Leasing is a great entry-level opening into a sales, sales management, merchandising, or marketing career. The personality characteristics necessary to be a good leasing agent provide a good foundation from which to develop skills to access those fields just mentioned.

So, what does all this have to do with first impressions and how we convey ourselves? We wear and project our attitudes. If we're doing what we want to be doing, we're happy and turned on to our daily routine. It shows. And when we like what we're doing we tend to make compromises to ensure our attainment of success. Success breeds success. It's amazing to realize what we're willing to do to accomplish what's important to us.

And what's important to us, as salespeople, is delivering what's important to the consumer. We're supposed to be consumer-savvy and attuned to getting inside their heads to discover their needs and wants, and then match their needs and wants with what we have to offer. How can you accomplish all that if you have barriers getting in the way? Consumers have so much baggage of their own, especially in this time of transition in their lives, that it doesn't help to compound their baggage with more of our own.

For that reason, how we convey ourselves and what the consumer perceives is important to helping us, as individuals, achieve our sales goals. The point here is that what the consumer perceives is more important than what we prefer to project. Don't let your personality stand in the way of your success. Get out of your own way!

What the customer believes is fact, even if it's incorrect. Perception is fact for the believer no matter how untrue or distorted it is from the other perspective.

Consumer perceptions are conveyed in many ways off-site and on-site. Our telephone voice and conduct lend as much to a first impression as our physical appearance does. The environment we work in and how we use that environment, including how we use promotional materials, forms, or how we relate to others are all part of the impression. Impressions amount to "packaging."

We've all witnessed the preferred packaging of professionals to amateur packaging for products we use every day. Sometimes, we as consumers make uninformed or ill-informed decisions and rely on the packaging to influence our choices. We tend to "trust" more professional and appealing packaging when faced with decisions where we're not in our own comfort zone of knowledge. So it is with your consumer.

We know that the delivery system for perceptions relates to the five senses: taste, smell, sight, sound, and touch. And by now we also acknowledge that all-important "sixth sense": inner voice, intuition, or insight. We, as individuals, are as much a part of the customer's perception as the curb appeal of model merchandising is. Therefore, it behooves us to make adjustments in our appearance, speech, and conduct to make sure we deliver a positive experience for the customer. It gives us an edge over our competition.

After all, you can be the deciding factor when your customers are faced with what they feel are comparable choices. You can make the difference. You can tip the scale in your site's favor, simply because the customer chooses to relate more to you than to your competitor. Then there's no doubt that it paid off for you to massage the way you come across, even if you project a modified image to the one you prefer to envision for yourself. In an ideal world judgments would not be made so superficially. But then we don't live in an ideal society and we must accept reality or pay the consequences of being ineffectual. And being less good at what you do will not help you get noticed to advance your career or your rewards.

Posturing Yourself for Success

If you really want to be more effective, then you need to figure out how to come across more effectively. Why not solicit some constructive input about yourself from peers and managers in your company who are recognized and respected for their successes? And while you're out there taking a poll about yourself, why not consult some professionals for advice on wardrobe, hair, cosmetics, poise, grammar, and personal communication skills?

Those of us in the industry who are recognized professionals weren't born that way. We came up pretty much the same way you did. And most of us have been made over from time to time to massage our images, our delivery, and our attitudes. That's just a part of growing and releasing any baggage that is weighing us down. Solicit honest input from qualified people, then try the recommendations to see if they produce the desired results. You may be a little uncomfortable at first, but it's easy to get accustomed to success when it's in progress. Of course, we don't think anything is wrong with the way we look or come across. Otherwise, we would have corrected whatever appearances or behaviors gave the wrong impressions.

Specifically, pay attention to the following:

> Don't do or wear anything that will distract you or your customers. Anything extraneous could send out mixed signals or cause confusion. Don't clutter the customer's memory or recall unnecessarily. It wears them down and postpones your success.

> This is not the time to take center stage: center stage is where your customer belongs.

> Make a conscious effort not to grandstand or upstage your customer. It makes the customer feel unimportant. Your objective should be to put the customer at ease.

> If you've made your best effort to be effective, then quit worrying, stop overcompensating, and concentrate on solving the issues and concerns of the customer.

> You aren't there to "sell" or "pitch," you're there to help someone find a nice place to live that meets their needs but not necessarily all their

wants. Sometimes the customer needs guidance to become more realistic about their present situation. That could mean making some compromises by weighing the alternatives. You can be helpful in that process of elimination.

▶ With each encounter by phone or in person, even retroactive to prospects you've seen in the past, think about what the customer needs, wants, hopes for, is afraid of, wishes to be. You can't meet all their needs but you can listen, be empathetic, help them get realistic, and let the exchange be genuine communication. They'll feel better and you will have been the catalyst. It all begins with your attitude and how you come across.

▶ Looking for an apartment should be a fun, elevating experience. It won't be that way unless you create the environment and make it happen. That's what will set you apart from others. It's the path to being outstanding—get out of your "self" and get into the other person.

What Zaps or Increases Productivity Levels?

Discover (or finally acknowledge) what influences your behavior and your results. There are ways to increase your productivity level that are totally within your realm of control. Some things you add and some things you subtract to enhance your performance. Here are some suggestions, but you really need to "fess up" and create your own list.

Zaps	Increases
Insufficient sleep	Getting the right amount of sleep

Being stressed out	Creating space for downtime
Eating the wrong foods	Getting organized
Sugar	Having a routine that works
Caffeine	Eating balanced meals
Salt	Eating at regular intervals
Prescription drugs	Avoiding bad foods & beverages
Insufficient exercise	Exercising regularly
Cigarettes	Meditation or solitude
Alcohol	Reading or hobby time
Watching TV	Prudent TV time
Talking on the telephone	Prudent telephone time
Too much or too little playtime	Focusing on what you do well
Being disorganized	Being prepared and on time
Being unprepared	Revisiting goals
Certain people	Certain people

A list isn't going to solve all your problems, but awareness is the first step in modifying self-defeating behaviors and will lead you to the path of achievement and success. Your successes and failures are a matter of choice—your choice.

Action or inaction is also a matter of choice. Put yourself into an action mode and you'll realize your dreams, generally sooner than you thought possible.

Being Organized

Organized salespeople project a calm, professional image that typically elicits confidence and trust from the prospect. You will reap many rewards if you invest time in being organized. Follow these tips:

Be prepared every day. Salespeople have a habit of "winging" it because they're used to talking their way out of or around tight spots.

Be on time for work and for appointments. Salespeople are often not realistic about time and tend to overbook themselves by cramming too much into too short a time frame.

Unclutter your environment. Make it neutral territory. This enables both you and your prospects to be relatively free of distractions. It also makes the prospect feel welcomed and have a sense of belonging.

Focus your attention. Unclutter your head. Give 100 percent of your time and attention to the encounter. Don't answer phones, pop up and down to handle others, or do anything to make the prospects feel they're intruding.

Know your product by walking your ready-to-show apartment every day. Know which apartments are coming up soon and start thinking in advance about which locations or apartment types would suit prospects on file.

Tools and resources should look sharp and be accurate. Have a product and community information book with you whenever you show. Have your facts on hand in an orderly, professional manner. Make sure your forms and promotional materials are in good condition and collated for use.

Have a daily routine and stick to it. Include the things you like to do as well as things you don't like to do. Make sure you accomplish your daily routine and then work on your weekly and monthly objectives. Recognition and success come with a series of mini-successes. Working on accomplishing your daily objectives will help you meet your overall objectives.

Getting through a chapter with an unexciting title is a measure of success. If you got the message, one or more self-defeating behaviors will be replaced with more productive ones that will bring you closer to your destiny, one day at a time, one success at a time. I hope I have presented enough thought- and action-provoking suggestions here to cause you to revisit the chapter whenever you need a shot of self-discipline or when you're on the grow again.

Most of the resources you need to be successful in sales come from within. All you need to do is to figure out how to tap into your own reservoir.

WINNING TRAITS AND ATTITUDES
By Anne Sadovsky, RAM®

Clients often ask me what makes a successful leasing consultant. If only answering that question were simple. Before listing winning traits, let's examine why we work in the first place.

Several college studies have asked employees why they work and what keeps them motivated. The answer may surprise you if you think that money is the main factor. In fact, several other factors are always listed before monetary compensation. Each survey indicated that employees want to make a contribution, to be in on what is happening, to develop friends who care about them, and to feel important and needed. Money is around fifth on the list!

To become a successful, productive, and happy employee, you need to develop and/or improve the traits listed below.

Desirable Traits

Appearance

One doesn't have to be handsome or gorgeous. Just do the best with what you've got. Personal grooming, proper attire, and a willing smile go a long way.

Product Knowledge

Where did you get yours? Most of us probably learned to do our job by doing our job! Knowing your product is more than just knowing how to do your job. Study your competition, read the real estate section of your local newspaper, pay attention to what is happening with interest rates and single family homes. All these areas impact your property. Next, really study your floor plans and amenities. Plan responses to objections about certain features, or the lack thereof. Make a list of the best-selling features of the property and how those features benefit the customer, to go with each floor plan.

Friendliness

The initial greeting of the client, the boss, and the residents carries a lot of power. All of us want to be acknowledged and received by a friendly face. Perceived indifference by employees is the cause of most lost business. Walk in the clients' shoes, and treat them the way you want to be treated.

Sincerity

Don't be phony. Today's consumer is extremely savvy. They can pick up insincerity a mile away. You must be genuinely interested in them and their needs.

Confidence

Where does confidence come from? Knowledge! The more you know about what you're doing, the more confident you are.

Caring and Understanding

If you have all the other traits, but not this one, you will lose. In today's sales environment, the development of a relationship between the buyer and the consumer is more powerful than the actual product or service or the price and value. All of us tend to do business with people we like.

Believability

The client must have confidence in the truthfulness of the salesperson. A pattern and practice of credibility builds reputations that create long-term customer relationships. Honesty is always the best policy.

Genuine Love of People

This is probably difficult to learn if it doesn't come naturally. Helping others with the sensitive decision of choosing their home requires a caring that might not be necessary in other jobs.

A Desire to Serve

Problem-solving skills, a cool head under pressure, and the ability to calm others are necessary requirements for dealing with renters.

Most of the traits above are behaviors that can be improved with effort. If you see areas where you can improve, start working on them now. It is never too late to be the best you can be.

Attitude

A person's attitude shows in everything they do, including work, personal relationships, parenting, and so on. So let's establish right up front that the way you act, the way you treat others, the way you live, and whether you win or lose are determined by your attitude.

Can a negative attitude be turned into a positive one? If so, how? A great deal of study has gone into understanding how attitudes are formed and how to improve them. Here are some tips based on some of those studies and on common sense.

- ▶ **Be Realistic about Yourself**

  Is a negative attitude impacting your life in an unfavorable way? The first step to change is to realize that it is needed. Watch for denial. If you aren't sure whether a poor attitude is affecting you, ask for an honest appraisal from your closest friend.

- ▶ **Be Aware of Childhood Conditioning**

  Like many behavioral traits, attitudes are often learned from childhood conditioning. Give some thought to how you came by some of your negative attitudes.

- ▶ **Count Your Blessings**

  Our society tends to focus on the negatives in our lives rather than the positives. Make a list of everything you are grateful for, for example, good health, people who love you, a promising career, and anything else you can think of that brings you joy.

- ▶ **Make a Contribution**

  Volunteer to help others. Remember the old cliché, "I wept because I had no shoes, then I met a man who had no feet." What a sense of accomplishment comes from helping someone in need. It can't help but improve your attitude.

How You React Is What Counts

You own your attitude. Because you are in charge of you, you can choose your thoughts and behaviors. It really doesn't matter what other people do, it only matters how you respond to what they do.

Improving a negative attitude isn't easy. But little that is really worth having comes easily. Sometimes we get up, only to have something or someone push us down. The secret lies in getting up one more time. Here's an analogy to give you hope:

> *Pretend that you are a rough chunk of stone, just delivered to the polisher. If a stone can feel, polishing is probably pretty painful. Getting the corners and sharp edges off has to hurt. Yet the finished stone is beautiful, shiny, and polished. Life's challenges are a test. We are being polished, tested, and taught. And when we complete the test with lessons learned and a positive attitude, we pass.*

THE CHARACTERISTICS OF SUCCESS
By Brenda McClain, Advanced RAM®, CPM®

There should be no doubt in your mind at this point in your career that you are a salesperson. Sales, as it relates to property management, can be summed up in three simple words, *"RENTING IS SELLING."* And as a salesperson, you should know that there are particular personality traits and attitudes that can improve your likelihood of succeeding.

Many students ask why we should take time away from studying sales techniques to study such things as personalities. The answer is that your personality can affect your success far more than your knowledge of sales techniques. Studies have shown that 20 percent of a person's success is due to what she/he knows about their job and industry, but 80 percent is due to their personal characteristics. We can assume that many prospects make the decision whether or not to lease based not on the knowledge of the leasing professional, but rather on the personality of that individual. For that reason, and because the properties you represent are probably worth millions of dollars, it seems prudent to take a look inward at the characteristics of successful multifamily managers and leasing professionals.

If you want to be successful, take a look at the personalities and characteristics of successful people in our business. Are they positive people? Do they readily accept change and challenges? Are they risk-takers? Does specialization spell success? Are they people-persons or paper-persons, or both?

The first step in learning how to be more effective is knowing and understanding your own behavioral style. Recognizing the personality traits in your customers is the next step. Identifying and understanding personalities helps you understand the true motivation behind a person's comments and actions. It also helps you minimize any hostility that might arise and gives you a better chance of resolving any conflict. A study by *Psychology Today* magazine found that a key ingredient of the successful salesperson is an ability to recognize the personality style of the prospect and immediately adapt her/his style and method to that of the prospect. When you adapt your sales presentation to "fit" the personality of the prospect, you also make each prospect feel more comfortable and increase the likelihood that they will rent from you.

Your product, the apartment community you represent, will also take on your personality. We do not sell all things to all people. We sell solutions to problems relating to individual lifestyles. If not, we end up with a product that has no personality of any kind. What personality does your product represent? "Come live with us," "This is a great opportunity to live where you can meet people," "We are the best value for the money," or "We have all the answers to your problems."

The Personalities of Leasing Consultants

According to the Personality Profile System, there are four major classifications of personalities. The first type is a decisive individual who wants immediate results. Another type enjoys group action, verbal contact, and is a personable salesperson. A third type wants stability and approaches each situation in a slower, more planned manner. The final type wants accuracy, acts carefully, and is precise, reserved, and concerned. According to this system, one of these four characteristics is usually the primary one in a person's personality pattern, and she or he draws most behavioral characteristics from that factor.

This system can provide us with valuable information about ourselves. It can also be used by management companies to help motivate their employees. Frank Basile, Senior Vice President of the Gene B. Glick Co., offers the following observation based on his firm's personnel survey:

> *"We believe that identifying the specific personalities of our employees may help us better understand their emotions, how they judge other people, what their potential value to the organization is, what their strengths and weaknesses are, how they like to behave under pressure, what they fear most, and, as a result, what we can do to increase their effectiveness to the organization and themselves."*

As you develop your personal plan for success, keep in mind that the key principles of a winning personality are:

▶ Understand and accept yourself.
▶ Understand and accept your job requirements.
▶ Understand and accept others.

Discover your natural strengths and capitalize on this knowledge to maximize your effectiveness at work, in the community, or with your family. Study your personality through reading or through individual self-study personality profiles. Analyzing and evaluating oneself, and doing it properly, is a difficult job. We tend to see ourselves in the best possible light, even seeing our failings as somehow attractive. Are you willing to take the risk?

Successful Habits of Effective Leasing Personnel

How effective leasing consultants will be in performing their job cannot be predicted by the degree they hold or the number of years of experience they have. Neither of these traditional yardsticks measures effectiveness. Rather, the key determinant is whether a leasing consultant will acquire the skills to develop effective habits. Webster defines the word "habit" as: "the prevailing disposition or character of a person's thoughts and feelings; mental makeup." The question then becomes: What habits must you learn to move up the organization ladder in property management?

First, you must adopt quality as one of your daily habits. Do the job the very best way you can and do it right the first time.

Second, if you want someone to "buy" something from you, develop effective listening and follow-through habits. Most sales are lost because you didn't listen to the customer when he told you exactly what he wants. Effective communication will be covered in depth in another section. Examine each failed sale to try and determine why the prospect did not buy from you. What you learn can be invaluable in your success with future sales.

Finally, you must try to understand the job of property management as a whole, not just the piece of the equation you represent. Recognizing how the various functions of the organization depend on one another, and how changes in any one part affect all the others, will enhance your effectiveness and success rate.

> The key to becoming successful is knowing your own personality and how it relates to the sales function. You can begin that process by asking yourself the following questions:
>
> 1. What are the most significant accomplishments in your job?
> 2. Describe some of the tough problems you encounter in your job.
> 3. What personal attribute or ability do you have that contributes most to the success of your job?
> 4. What attribute or characteristic do you have that you wish you did not have?
> 5. How much did you progress during your last job?

Attitude

How is your attitude? There are only two: positive and negative. Has anyone told you lately that you have a positive attitude? Do you believe you have a positive attitude? If not, you need to begin working on one immediately, because no pessimist has ever excelled in sales. Successful salespeople have optimistic attitudes and are "try and try again" people. Henry Ford said, "Whether you believe you can...or cannot, you're right." Your success lies within yourself.

Although there are many different kinds of negative attitudes, employees with negative attitudes do have one thing in common. They tend to believe that every change directed by management is directly aimed at them and their happiness. One type of negative attitude is indifference. Indifferent employees simply never learned to care about their work and have to be dragged through their jobs with threats and cajolery. Another type is hostile anti-authoritarianism. These people resent being told what to do and show it. The last type is the temperamental employee who is easily wounded by any type of criticism. None of these belong in the sales arena.

What kind of attitude do you have? Use the following test to find out.

- What do you like best about your job?
- What do you not like about your job?
- What do you feel about your boss?
- Is there anything about the company or the way it does business that you do not like?
- What do you consider the ideal job for you?
- Under what type of supervision do you work best?
- What bothers you most about your co-workers?

Take a minute to honestly answer these questions and then come up with possible ways to make your attitude more positive. A positive mental attitude will help you handle the short- and long-term pressures of apartment leasing without becoming discouraged.

Enthusiasm must also be incorporated into your attitude. Never underestimate the fact that enthusiasm sells! You are the representative of your property and community, and if you are not excited about it, prospects will notice. People lease from leasing personnel they like and respect. Your enthusiasm will make them feel welcome and confident they picked the right place.

Proficiency

One quality that should never be overlooked is the salesperson's ability to do the job with a great degree of proficiency. For decades people have argued over whether sales is a science or an art. The answer is that it is both. It takes an artist to acknowledge the level of detail needed to do a job well and a scientist to figure out how to get the rest of the job completed efficiently. The ultimate proficiency test is doing your job well enough to be recognized and promoted.

Communication

Are you a good communicator? To evaluate how good your communication skills are, ask yourself, "Am I a good listener?" Most of us should answer no. We prefer to do the talking. And if we're not actually talking, we are thinking about what we are going to say next. Listening, however, is the most important skill a salesperson can have.

Listening can help you succeed in sales. Renting is selling and listening is the vehicle for closing as well as the basis for quality customer service.

Are You a Good Listener?
Test Yourself (*and be honest*):

1. Does your attention slip while you are listening to what the other person is saying?

2. Do you avoid eye contact with the speaker?

3. Do you stop listening if the speaker is uninteresting?

4. Do you feign attention while you are thinking about something else?

5. Do you stop listening when you are offended by something the speaker has said?

6. Is it possible your own biases color your interpretation?

7. Do you interrupt the speaker?

8. Are you easily distracted by the speaker's appearance or physical gestures?

9. Are you easily distracted by outside interruption and other stimuli?

10. Are you missing important content in the speaker's words because you are thinking ahead about your next comment?

If you answered "no" to eight or more questions, you are a rare breed—a natural listener. If you answered "no" to at least six of these questions, you are a good listener. Four or fewer "no" answers means that some work on your part could generate instant benefits in the form of increased sales.

A QUEST FOR EXCELLENCE
By Douglas D. Chasick, CPM®, RAM®

People who succeed in multifamily leasing do so for two reasons. First, they have a thorough understanding of what their job is and what it means to work in sales. Second, they possess the personality traits and professional habits that lead to success in any field.

Although most job titles contain the word leasing, for example, leasing agent, leasing consultant, leasing counselor, or leasing manager, our job is SELLING. Many people hear the word "sales" and think of pushy, high-pressure people selling cars and insurance—a negative connotation unfortunately often based on personal experience for them. But sales is not a dirty word, it's what all of us do, every day, regardless of our job title.

When someone has a need for a product or service, they want to buy, but they don't want to "be sold." Being sold implies that you don't have control or, worse yet, you've "been taken." Yet if someone has a need or a problem, and you can fill that need or solve their problem, they will be not only be grateful, but they will also want to buy what you offer.

To be successful as a leasing professional (salesperson), we must view selling in a new light—a positive light. Our job is not about tricking anyone or getting them to buy something they don't want. Our job is to assist them in solving their problem within their budget. (What's their problem? Well, if they were happy living in their current apartment, why are they standing in YOUR OFFICE?) And that's what selling is all about: creating a relationship with someone, identifying their needs and/or problems, and offering them a solution.

Create and Maintain Enthusiasm

While there are many areas we must focus on to be successful as leasing professionals, the most important is attitude. It has been said that the formula for success is 80 percent attitude and 20 percent technique. This is especially true in selling. If we don't create and maintain an enthusiastic attitude, no technique in the world will be effective. That's right, I said, CREATE AND MAINTAIN. Attitude is not something that "happens" to us, although many people would argue that assertion. How many times have you heard someone say "Oh, I'm just not in the mood today" or, "I don't feel like it." What would it take to get them in the mood, or make them feel like it? If we're not responsible for our attitude, who is? Our spouse? Our boss? Our friends? The answer is simple: WE MAKE OUR OWN MOOD!

Every day, in every situation, we always have a choice: We can be the victim of our circumstances, and react accordingly, or we can rise above our circumstances and be in whatever mood we declare. If you observe people who are successful, you'll notice they are always "up," regardless of what kind of day they're having. That's because they understand that not being in the mood really means not producing any results. They constantly generate enthusiasm, instead of waiting for it to happen to them.

Once we master creating our attitude, and maintaining it regardless of our circumstances, we can examine how we choose to act. Most people limit themselves because they believe themselves to be a "certain type of person." How many times have you heard someone say, "I'm not that type of person" or "I'm not like that"? The fact is that those statements are untrue—we can be whatever way we want to be, because we always have a choice in the matter.

The problem with acknowledging that we can be however or whoever we want to be is that we then become 100 percent responsible for our actions. When someone "isn't that type of person," they aren't responsible for their actions—some outside factors must be forcing them to be "that way." When we realize and acknowledge that we are always in control of how we are, we become accountable for our actions—and sometimes that can be pretty scary!

Whether we talk about cold-calling for prospects, or asking a minimum of seven closing questions, we must dig deep to find the true reason for our discomfort or unwillingness to proceed. Just saying "I can't do that" or "I'm not that aggressive" is insufficient, because those reasons don't allow us to confront and conquer the source or the real reason for our reluctance to perform the task at hand—those reasons merely allow us to escape and blame someone/something other than us for our inability to act.

Learn New Habits

All of our actions are based on habits that we learned at some point in our lives. Many of the habits that we learned years ago in response to a specific circumstance are no longer appropriate to our current circumstances, yet we often operate on "automatic pilot," reacting with our old habits.

The easiest way to overcome an ineffective habit is to learn a new habit. It's said that you can learn a new habit by repeating the behavior you'd like to learn for 21 consecutive days. This new habit will then replace the old habit, and allow you more freedom in your actions.

Successful salespeople are not the victims of their circumstances; rather, they are the architects of their lives, using their circumstances to their advantage. As the old saying goes,

"When all you have are lemons, make lemonade." So do the successful salespeople follow their plans and achieve their goals, even when all they encounter is lemons.

So, how can we stay committed and enthusiastic hour after hour, day in and day out? The easiest way is to remember why we got out of bed in the morning: We want to achieve our goals, feel good about ourselves, and make some money! If you think you got out of bed so you could complain about your job and your life, you probably should have stayed in bed. If you don't have a purpose and direction, a set of goals to pursue and achieve each day, you'll have to settle for whatever you get—you'll be a victim of circumstances.

Set Specific Goals

Once you've established your new habit of creating an enthusiastic attitude, you're ready to set your goals. Goals are essential to successful selling because they enable you to see where you're going and establish a plan to get there—your roadmap to success. To be effective, you must follow several guidelines:

▶ Goals must be in writing. When you have goals in mind, but don't put them in writing, they're not really goals, they're wishes.

▶ Goals must be specific and measurable. If your goal is "to be rich," how do you measure your progress and determine if you've achieved it? If your goal is "to have $500,000 in long-term certificates of deposit," you can easily measure your progress and clearly determine when you've achieved it.

▶ Goals must have a deadline. Using the example above, "to have $500,000 in long-term certificates of deposit," if we add "by January 1, 1998," you can measure your progress

and make corrections as needed. If you don't put a deadline on each goal, you have no reason to create urgency
to achieve the goal.

▶ Goals must be achievable. The only thing you'll achieve
by setting an unreasonable goal is frustration! Yet, if you
make the goal too easy, you won't feel challenged, and
your sense of accomplishment is diminished. When setting
your goals, be realistic about what you know you can
achieve, within the deadline you set for yourself, and then
"push it" a little.

After you've identified your goals and written them down,
identify each step required to achieve your goals. If you work
backwards from your ultimate goal, you'll end up with a plan
that is workable.

For example, if your goal is to lease 30 apartments next
month, what needs to happen for you to achieve that goal?
First of all, make sure you have 30 vacant apartments to rent!
The next step is to calculate your average closing ratio: How
many qualified prospects must you see to write one lease? If
you need to see four qualified prospects, your closing ratio is
25 percent. Now we know that you must see 120 qualified
prospects to write 30 leases. (Four qualified prospects multiplied by 30, or 30 divided by 25 percent; both ways of
calculating equal 120.)

How do you get 120 qualified prospects to your property?
Analyze the traffic reports for the past few months to determine what percentage of your total traffic is qualified. If half
of your traffic is qualified, you'll need to generate 240 traffics
that month. If 30 percent is qualified, you'll need to generate
400 traffics (120 qualified prospects divided by a 30 percent
factor (.30) equals 400).

After you come up with an advertising and marketing plan
to generate the amount of traffic you need, break your goals

down into weekly and daily amounts: Each day, I need X number of traffic, Y number of qualified prospects, and Z number of leases. By breaking your monthly goal down into daily goals, you can track your results on a daily basis, and make adjustments and corrections to your plan quickly. Always ask yourself, "What's next?" and reduce your goals to their lowest common denominator—what has to happen EACH DAY, or EACH HOUR—to accomplish your goals. Only by working one day at a time can you make changes that allow you to stay on course.

Motivational Factors

Most companies spend lots of time and money inventing programs to motivate people. Yet most experts on human behavior agree that motivation comes from within, not from any outside source. As Peter Glen said, "Nobody can motivate you but YOU. The word MOTIVATE means "to move," and nobody can make you move except you."

There are certain factors that must be present to create an environment for people to motivate themselves. First and foremost are specific goals to work toward. Once goals have been agreed on, the element of trust must be present. If there is no trust, we tend to "hold back" our full efforts, keeping something in reserve in case things go wrong. Trust also allows open and honest communication. We must be willing to give and receive candid feedback and constructive criticism so we can correct or improve those parts of our presentation that aren't working.

Support, on-going training, and frequent performance appraisals are essential to creating an environment where people motivate themselves. Without these components, we are forced to rely on our own sense of how we are doing, and we tend to use trial and error in the absence of training.

Recognition and reward are the final factors we need to continue to motivate ourselves. Everyone likes to be told when they've done a good job, and I've yet to see anyone give back a bonus!

Another characteristic of successful people is that they are effective communicators. Effective communication is not just the ability to speak clearly and persuasively, it's also the ability TO LISTEN and TO HEAR what the other person is saying. Some of the common problems we encounter when communicating include:

▶ Poor timing—Don't assume someone is ready to receive your communication. Make certain that the other person is not busy and that this is a convenient time before you begin speaking.

▶ Suspicion and mistrust—This is especially true with prospects, because most of them have "heard it all before." If someone doesn't trust you, how much of what you say will they hear? Establish a rapport and a comfort level before beginning any sales conversation.

Tips for Effective Communication

1. Every communication should have a clear, specific purpose. Organize your thoughts in a logical sequence before you communicate.
2. Choose the proper time and place.
3. Speak quietly, clearly, and slowly.
4. Always be a professional. Losing your temper or your patience is a sure way to sabotage any communication.
5. Look for feedback, both verbal and nonverbal. Ask questions frequently.
6. Find and refer back to a common ground during the conversation.
7. Remember that emotions can be as powerful as facts to many people.
8. Take notes that you can refer back to later.

▶ Insufficient explanation—This can make the other person feel frustrated or even incompetent. Make certain that you are clear, concise, and understandable. Don't use jargon, and get feedback from the other person to make sure he or she is keeping up with you.

▶ Not taking the other person's point of view into account— A very common problem, especially in selling. Most of us are concerned with how any given situation or product will benefit Us. If you want to communicate successfully, address the other person's point of view—speak in terms of "you," not "me."

Another common characteristic of successful leasing professionals is that they LOVE what they do. Most of us didn't wake up one morning and choose property management as our career; we just sort of "happened into it!" The people in our business who are successful are the ones who have a genuine passion and enthusiasm for serving people. Stay in touch with why you first entered this business, and let your passion show in everything you do.

In any business, attention to detail makes a huge difference. Speed and quantity will never take the place of quality work. Today's consumer hears about "commitment to excellence" so frequently that the absence of excellence becomes obvious. Attention to detail will separate you from the people who are just trying to get through their day.

I've often said that there are two kinds of workers: list makers and list takers. The distinction has no bearing on a person's job title, since I've known porters who were list makers and company presidents who were list takers. List takers rely on other people to tell them what to do; list makers are self-generating: They constantly look for what needs to be done and then get it done, without being told. Which type of person do you think is the most successful—the list taker or the list maker?

Taking personal responsibility for producing results is another characteristic of successful salespeople. They don't complain about a lack of traffic, they start calling from old guest cards. They don't complain about a market-ready apartment that isn't, they make it market-ready. In short, they know they are responsible for the results they produce, and if they don't achieve their goals, they don't blame someone else or their circumstances.

Finally, appearance and grooming play a vital role in our success. It's often said that "we have seven seconds to make a favorable first impression." Seven seconds is long enough for someone to give us the "once-over." It's also said that "87 percent of the information people receive is visual." Put those two factors together, and you see why all property managers are obsessed with the curb appeal of the property. But what about the curb appeal of the staff?

Each property has a unique personality based on its location, resident profile, amenities, and rent range. Wearing a wool suit at a resort-themed community in Florida in August might not be the best presentation you could make! Dress appropriately for your property and your clientele. Pay attention to detail in both your grooming and your clothing. Loose threads, scuffed shoes, worn heels, and those tiny stains that we don't think anyone will notice will get noticed—and the prospect will never say a thing to us. But what do they think? If the prospect buys us before they buy the apartment, what do they think about the apartment after seeing us?

Successful salespeople integrate all of the aforementioned factors into themselves, and constantly monitor their results to determine what areas need adjustment or correction. Success is not a static condition that, once achieved, remains forever in place. Success is a moving target we aim at every day, striving to be the best we can be.

WHAT IT TAKES TO SUCCEED:
By Jennifer A. Nevitt, RAM®

When you wake up every morning, you make choices. You choose what to wear, what to eat, and which route to take to work. But the choice that makes the biggest difference in your daily work and your success throughout your career is a simple one: You can choose to do an exceptional job.

It Takes Effort

There are days when you aren't going to feel like making the extra effort that must become second nature to an effective leasing professional. Everybody has those days. A long-time resident decides to move out and the latest ad for your community did not make the newspaper. The water lines burst in a second-floor apartment. You show four apartments and no one gives you a deposit. The people on the administrative staff take too long a lunch break and leave you with the phones, which are ringing nonstop. The big things and the little things add up and you're on edge. What do you do?

> *True professionals do their jobs, even when they don't feel like it.*

So that's what you do. You speak calmly into the phone as you answer the calls one by one. Rather than rush through a call, you ask to return it. Instead of feeling martyred because your colleagues took too long, you smile warmly and ask them if they enjoyed the break. Then you divide the work according to the system in your office, and you all get back to business.

As for the four attempts without a signed lease, instead of blaming anyone or anything, you take a look at your own performance. Were you polite and interested? Did you anticipate and answer all objections? Did you show a product that was market-ready? If you find any weakness in your presentation, you begin correcting your mistakes immediately, and you promise yourself to do better with the very next prospective resident. And you will, because you have chosen to succeed.

Personality Counts, But a Solid Work Ethic Is More Important

There are people who seem to have been born knowing how to relate to other people. They are "people-people." To the rest of the population, the others of us who enjoy people most of the time but who sometimes feel awkward or ill-at-ease, the "people people" seem to be blessed with the best of all gifts.

No question, they are fortunate, but with some effort, you can become more like them. You can cultivate confidence and knowledge, which will put you at ease. You can remind yourself that your job is to help people find the right place to live and to represent your employer professionally while doing so. These skills can be learned by anyone willing to put in the necessary time and effort. No matter your level of education or experience, you can develop yourself while you build your career—understand that it is a career, not a job.

In business, owners want results. So, results-oriented people are noticed. Do you stick with a problem or question until you have solved it or answered it? You are already building your success.

Every Client Is an Opportunity

Every person deserves to be treated with dignity and shown respect. This basic principle goes beyond financial worth, the kind of clothing one wears, or what kind of car one drives. Do you appreciate the opportunity that a client is giving you by calling or coming to the property? Or do you make judgments and assumptions based on first impressions? Resist the temptation to do so. If we use assumptions and observations to build understanding and help us to communicate, good. If we use them to build walls and make harsh judgments, we help no one, least of all ourselves.

Self-improvement Is Crucial

Suppose that you don't know everything there is to know about grooming, etiquette, proper use of the English language, how to dress, how to close a sale, or any other basic and useful skill necessary to your business. Find out. Choose a role model from among your colleagues or a professional group and cultivate a friendship. If possible, find a mentor, a person further along in your chosen career who can act as a guide. Learn from others.

This necessarily calls for taking a hard look at yourself and making an honest—though not overly critical—assessment of your best and worst attributes. Keep in mind that knowing the worst is not as bad as fearing the worst. Make your appraisal, decide what to work on first, then get going. Just by taking this first step, you will have made a major improvement, and your confidence should begin to show it. This in turn will improve your work.

Take Responsibility for Your Own Success

In addition to making a commitment to ongoing self-improvement, taking responsibility for your own success means that you don't wait for someone to tell you that a job needs to be done, nor do you wait for someone to suggest more training. You don't wait for someone else to evaluate your sales techniques. Instead, you look for opportunities to add to your knowledge formally and informally. You continually evaluate your own performance and come up with better methods.

The Goodness Factor

Goodness is an old-fashioned idea that, applied daily and conscientiously, can change the way your work and live. By being a good person, you set yourself up to succeed. Goodness, by itself, will not guarantee business success. But goodness and its partner, thoughtfulness, can give meaning and value to your working days as well as to your personal life.

Here's the gist of it: If,

- with every action you make an effort to be kind and thoughtful,
- you make a conscious effort to invest every act, no matter how mundane, with care and presence of mind, and
- you do everything with great attention to the moment,
- then, no matter how common or ordinary your day is, you have invested it with uncommon and extraordinary value. And people will notice.

Not only will you elevate every task you do, you will elevate yourself as well. People are drawn to those who are happy, at peace with themselves, able to give of themselves to others, and willing to make an effort, people who are, in a word, good.

Etiquette 101: The Basics

"Please" and "thank you" and "you're welcome" have never gone out of style. Stand when a client enters. Offer to shake hands. Make eye contact and smile. Remember the opportunity this client is giving you, and behave accordingly.

"I'm sorry" and "I apologize" are often used interchangeably, but they are not the same thing. The distinction is important. When you make a mistake or intentionally do wrong (such as not returning a phone call), say "I'm sorry." If the problem is not something for which you were personally responsible, or you did not intentionally cause harm or disappointment, say, "I apologize." For example, the Smiths in #407 have called to tell you that the dishwasher has not been fixed as promised. You say, "I apologize...." and you say what you will do, such as call it to the attention of the maintenance supervisor immediately. Then do it. If you personally messed up, then you say, "I'm sorry." And you make amends as soon and as thoroughly as possible.

Send notes. Thank people who have been kind to you. Drop a line to the resident in C-3 who gave you cookies and the vendor who rushed an order. Send birthday and anniversary cards and notes when you know there is a special day approaching. Acknowledge other people's helpfulness and remember their special days, and they will remember you.

Grooming 101: The Basics

The old adage about dressing for success remains true: Dress for the position you want, not for the position you're in. Anything about your appearance that could mark you as unpolished or unprofessional needs to be changed immediately.

In addition to basic cleanliness, a professional who intends to excel pays attention to details. Shoes are polished—no run-down or discolored heels. Polished nails are smooth and chip-free—no ragged cuticles or splits. If shirt collars and cuffs are frayed, replace the shirt. Check for spots on ties, scarves, and jackets.

Hair should be clean and neatly styled. "Big hair" looks unprofessional. Control it during business hours and enjoy its wilder nature after hours. As a guide, observe the way professionals at levels above your own have their hair cut and styled.

Stand straight and tall. Not only will you feel better, but you also will look confident and professional, and this will help your clients have confidence in your presentation.

Avoid perfume and strong-smelling aftershave. Scent can be annoying to some people and a health hazard to those who are allergic. Don't risk offending a client by wearing an overwhelming scent.

In short, anything you can do to help others (including clients and your employer) to see you as confident, well-prepared, and thoroughly professional will help you to advance.

Winning Work Habits

Successful people tend to be ambitious, enthusiastic, and self-confident. They have learned how to set priorities. They plan the work that must be done and how it fits into their day. Then they work their plan.

Successful people write almost everything down. They take notes when talking on the phone, looking for information that can help them build a relationship or fill the needs of a client.

Successful people are responsive. They return phone calls promptly. When taking messages, they include details such as first and last names, date and time of day, and what the caller has requested. They also answer their mail.

Successful people are resilient. A setback for them is only temporary because they make a deliberate decision to move forward. Then they match their actions to that decision.

Use Standard English

Your language—spoken or written—tells people more than the content of your words. Make certain that the message conveyed about you is a positive one. Use standard English when speaking and when writing. If you can't spell or speak correctly, people will notice. This will be seen as a flaw in your presentation and, possibly, as a flaw in the property you represent. Clients may perceive a lack of quality.

Use more than a computerized spell checker to proof written materials. A spell checker can only catch errors that are misspellings. It cannot tell you that "form" should be "from." If you are uncertain about proofing your own letters and reports, find someone who can proof them for you. Even if you get help, continue to proof your own work and over time you will develop the ability to spot problems.

Dependability: Without it, You Won't Go Far

Even if you do everything else you should, and even if you have the best personality of all time, if you don't follow through, you won't succeed. Clients, colleagues, vendors, and employers have to know that they can count on you and that you mean what you say. For example, you're going to be late, and it means you won't be able to honor a commitment. The dependable person takes the time to call the person and explain. If you're going to be late, you owe a telephone call, an apology, and a willingness to go out of your way to reset the meeting.

You are set apart
not by what you
say you'll do,
but by what you do.

If you find that you're often running late, ask yourself: Am I overextending myself? Not allotting enough time is a warning sign that your schedule needs to be reworked. It is vital that you allow enough time to ensure that you will be dependable, because dependability and credibility are so closely linked.

What it Takes to Win

On a small white slip of paper wedged inside a fortune cookie were the ultimate words on what it takes to succeed:

None of the secrets
of success will work
unless you do.

The strongest combination of personal characteristics and winning habits—goodness, a strong work ethic, initiative, enthusiasm, and a professional appearance—works best when you make the effort, day after day.

Habits and Personality Traits for Success

Here's a quick list of some of the habits and personality traits that will make you become successful:

 ▶ Mind that every person deserves to be treated with dignity and shown respect.
 ▶ Smile warmly and with genuineness. (This is easy if you believe that every person deserves to be treated with respect.)
 ▶ Listen conscientiously. Pay attention to what is not said as well as what is said.

- Always be well-groomed and well-manicured. Go beyond clean.
- Dress for the position you want, not for the position you're in.
- Stand tall.
- Focus on the job at hand. Do not allow distractions to keep you from being effective and efficient.
- Write everything down.
- Prioritize. Plan your work and then work your plan, every day.
- Evaluate your work habits and take steps to correct any deficiencies.
- Be enthusiastic.
- Use good, standard English. If you can't spell a word, look it up.
- Hold in high regard the owner's trust in you.
- Do more than you have to do to get by.
- Make a deliberate, conscious decision to succeed. Then match your actions to that decision.
- Follow through. Do what you say you'll do.

What Kind of Personality Do You Have?

There are numerous companies that have developed personality profiles you can employ to find out what kind of person you are. With these profiles, you can also learn how to sell to other personality styles. The test results, given in laymen's terms, offer enlightenment on the subject of one's own personality as well as how to be empathetic to the needs of others. Visit your local library or contact your human resources department to find out more.

What Impacted Me Most about this Chapter:

_____

_____

_____

_____

_____

_____

_____

_____

_____

_____

What I Need to Work on:

_____

_____

_____

_____

_____

_____

_____

_____

_____

My Strengths Discovered in this Chapter:

_____

_____

_____

_____

_____

_____

_____

_____

_____

A Job Description, Expectations & Performance Standards for Leasing Professionals

"A Winning Daily Routine for Leasing Reps" -*Cardella*

"The Leasing Consultant's Job Description" -*McClain*

"Sample Job Description" -*McClain*

"Time Management: What to Do When You're Not Leasing Apartments" -*Nevitt*

"The Organized Leasing Consultant" -*Robertson*

A WINNING DAILY ROUTINE FOR LEASING REPS

By Carol Ann Cardella, RAM®, MIRM®, GRI®

Ho-hum. (Zzzz...)

No, it's not time for a snooze. If you snooze, you lose.

But...but routines are boring! (Especially for sales types.)

Then you're on the wrong routine. Routines will launch you. They're fail-safe if you follow them consistently. The right routine will increase your productivity level and help you get noticed and stay ahead of the pack. A routine—your routine—will become your comfort zone. A safe haven.

A routine is a little bit of structure to help shape your day and ensure that you'll complete each day with a sense of accomplishment. Even when things go wrong, your routine will go right. It'll be there for you to assure you that you're on the right track. All you'll need is a little more time to turn situations back around again. A good routine will empower you.

A daily routine is all about developing good work habits that will carry you through difficult or trying times and slow business cycles. These are the enemies that plague any naturally energetic sales personality. Because you can't rely on other people to pull you "up" and keep you "up," you need to learn how to do this for yourself.

How you choose to fill your time determines how successful you will be. Too frequently we fill our time with busy, non-income-producing things that will not enable us to achieve our goals. We also tend to fill our minds with emotional clutter and attitudes that stand in the way of our success. We have to leave behind the excess baggage so we can move ahead.

There's another aspect of daily routines: They shape your future. But it's tough to think about and take action for the future when it seems so far away from where you are right now. And besides, there are always pressing needs now, so postponement is easy to rationalize.

A sales-type personality responds better to instant gratification and rewards. That's probably one reason why it's so hard to do things today for which you may or may not reap any benefits until some undetermined time in the future. In contrast, it's so easy to energize and get into the spirit when the results will impact your immediate future.

When you're turned on, you light up the world around you; you are a positive influence. When you're turned off, idle and flapping around aimlessly, you cast a black cloud over your world; you're a negative influence. Don't fight having a routine because it lays a foundation for your future business success.

The following are routine behaviors that any prudent employer would be pleased and proud to endorse:

1. Dress for "company" every day. You're not only representing yourself, you're representing your community, all the residents, and the entire organization supporting you. You make the first all important and lasting impression. Show your best self at all times in your business environment.

   Make sure your clothing, hair, cosmetics, jewelry, auto condition, nails, etc., are well groomed and subdued for a non-offensive business impression. Nothing about you should distract the prospect or you during your encounter. Make a conscientious effort not to upstage your prospect or your product by your appearance or conduct.

   Pay attention to your grammar, manners, and the signals you send out. This is not the time to be cute, sexy, macho, or on center stage. No chewing gum, no smoking in the office or in the presence of customers. I recommend allowing the customer to smoke in the office or wherever the customer sits to fill out the paperwork. The objective is to make the customer feel comfortable and "at home." For the same reason, you should serve seasonal beverages and snacks hospitably.

Be prepared for all weather conditions: Keep on hand large golf umbrellas for rain, boots for icy or snowy conditions, and wear a coat when it's sensible to do so or keep an extra coverup in the office or car so you aren't caught by rapidly changing weather conditions.

2. Always carry your "presentation" or "product" book with you at all times during a prospect encounter. It should consist of a loose-leaf, three-ring binder that includes the following handy reference information:

   a. blank guest cards for you to fill out for prospect encounters;

   b. a neat site plan with vacant, ready-to-show product highlighted and marked with price and apartment type or floor (update daily; do a fresh map weekly; color code if multiple plans exist);

   c. floor plans for each apartment type with net interior square footage and room dimensions for reference;

   d. standard features list;

   e. neighborhood facts: schools, bus stops, churches, shopping, nearby recreational amenities, distance to employment centers, etc.;

   f. your up-to-date available inventory; and

   g. any other data that you need to refer to when out showing.

If you always carry this book as part of your showing routine, you will be prepared at all times, which in turn will reinforce consumer confidence. It will give both you and the customer a greater comfort zone.

So you say, "Oh, I know where everything is. I don't need a book to tell me." What if a soon-to-be-resident pops in and wants to show a friend or relative his new place? Once there, he has second thoughts and decides to see something else. But you don't have your inventory sheet, which you didn't think you'd need and left back in the office. When you return to the office there are new people waiting, but you can't help them because you're stuck running back and forth reselling someone you thought was sold. You unnecessarily lost time by having to retrieve what should have been in your possession all along.

Or, you're out showing some product to a prospect who wanted to see a one-bedroom for immediate occupancy. The prospect changes her mind and asks to see another floor plan with a cute little window and view of a creek. You can't resolve anything because you don't know if you have product in that building on notice to vacate unless you go back to the office and check your reports. When you get back to the office where the facts are, the customer remains indecisive. She goes away to think about it instead of making a decision this visit. And she might get snagged by the complex down the street because when she gets there, she might immediately forget what she thought she liked at your place.

3. Arrive at work 15 minutes before the advertised opening time. Before you go into your office, go to your model, if you have one, and turn all the lights on, not by the circuit breaker but by each switch and lamp.

This is how you discover which bulbs need to be changed and what new problems may be in any particular room, such as a leak or dead flies or little rolly-poly bugs that you need to clean up. Use only 100-watt bulbs in your table lamps. They help expand space. Turn on the lamps even if it's a bright, sunny day because the light conditions will vary during the remainder of the day. Make sure the plants are tended—pluck dead leaves.

Make sure the temperature controls are set properly for customers—their comfort is your primary concern. Set it at 72° in summer and 68° in winter. This may not be your ideal comfort zone, so you may need to make some clothing adjustments. In warm climates, customers often wear less than salespeople, and they're in the heat much of the day. So a temperature that is just a little cooler than the outdoors is a pleasant experience. In winter climates, the customers are in coats most of the day and often while sitting inside with you. This is why you keep the model and office cooler than what would be comfortable for you without a coat on.

4. Open up your ready-to-show apartments by turning all the lights on, flushing toilets, checking the place over, and making notes of needed repairs for your manager. Leave the lights on all day. Open up windows when practical. You might dress up the bare space with potted flowers or bath towels and matching fluffy rugs, or light a dark corner with a rented free-standing lamp. Move these items as soon as you rent this apartment.

5. Pick up any trash or litter along your "show path." Pick any dead blooms off flowers near the model and target ready-to-show inventory. Report any problems you see along the path to your manager. Do this in writing and

put dates on the memo, retaining a copy for follow-up. Water the flowers or turn on the hoses.

6. Open the rental office and common recreation area. If you use music in these areas, make sure it really is background music suitable for all ages and not music of your personal preference. It should be soft enough not to be a distraction to customers.

7. Prepare hospitality items to serve attractively to customers—fresh coffee, iced tea, or have a tea kettle simmering for hot tea or hot chocolate. For a change, offer some herbal teas, iced or hot. Provide a few cookies or pretzels or popcorn, as well as some good quality hard candies, individually wrapped, in an attractive dish. Remember that everything should be "home-like."

   Get into the spirit of various holidays in your hospitality offerings. Make sure the kitchen area is immaculate at all times.

8. Take your messages off your machine.

9. Check to see what changes took place since you last worked. Make those adjustments in your presentation book.

10. Begin making telephone calls to follow up on all prospects. This is not the time to make judgments and weed out who you should call. Call everyone in your guest card file. You never know what changes or conditions may have affected their housing needs since you last saw them.

    Write notes to prospects from the previous day if you didn't do so immediately following their visit.

11. Scan the local newspapers to send warm notes and invitations to visit your property to newly engaged

couples, new parents, and recently promoted
employees.

12. Handle new telephone inquiries and one-on-one prospect visits. Fill up your guest cards with everything you
learned about your people. Details are memory trig-
gers. You can make the prospect feel important and
special because you remembered those little things at
a later date.

13. Work on some special events program that will be sponsored by your community in the future. Work on the
community newsletter.

14. Plan time to visit area employers and local businesses
to get referrals. Make sure you get to at least two each
week. Send notes and whatever special goodies your
property offers to people who have referred someone,
even if they didn't lease.

15. Is it time to contact your competition and get updated
information? When was the last time you visited the
competition? Are you relying on telephone impressions? Your customers shouldn't know more than you
do about your competitors.

16. Clip your ads daily if your company advertises in the
newspaper. Check out your competition's ads each day.
See what's new. Scan the papers for leads to referrals
or information about area employment. Be informed.

17. Do any and all paperwork pertaining to applications
and leases you have in progress. Process these promptly
and notify applicants of management decisions to accept
or reject them. Establish move-in appointments.

18. Brainstorm new and better ways of generating qualified
prospects.

19. Before you close for the evening, reverse your opening procedures. Make sure your kitchen area is clean and ready for the next day of business.

20. Review what you did today to accomplish your objectives and decide what you need to do tomorrow. Determine to do what is good for you for the balance of your personal day to refresh yourself and re-energize so you can put your best foot forward tomorrow. Remember that your reward for having a good day today should not include railroading yourself tonight and getting yourself off to a bad start tomorrow.

Do what is good for you. Don't postpone your success.

THE LEASING AGENT'S JOB DESCRIPTION AND ROUTINE WORK HABITS

By Carol Ann Cardella, RAM®, MIRM®, GRI®

A leasing rep's job description will vary from company to company, depending on each company's expectation of what leasing agents should do when not otherwise occupied by prospects. Some companies vary their leasing job description based on the size of the property and the traffic volume. Consequently, there is no such thing as a uniform job description from site to site within a company or even within the industry.

At a site where there is not a lot of turnover or prospect traffic to warrant leasing people having the sole responsibility for "sales," the leasing rep may be expected to function as an assistant manager who also "shows and leases" apartments. The leasing person may also be the "manager" who is the only site employee able to handle administrative affairs.

Regardless how many roles you play, if your company has given you the title or role of a leasing person, then your performance is largely measured by your ability to lease apartments and to handle the many details that impact the leasing function. It's important for you to clarify and fully understand what constitutes a "good" leasing person from your company's viewpoint, although sometimes supervisors don't always have a clear understanding of upper management's or ownership's objectives related to leasing and property merchandising.

In the overall scheme of life and personal growth, your first obligation is to yourself. In your personal life and in your career, you are accountable for both your successes and your failures. You must not allow yourself to be victimized or put into a position where you cannot be successful, feel rewarded, or enjoy the gratification of a job well done. Your future depends on what you do today and how well you do it. Success breeds success. Happiness breeds happiness. A positive, can-do attitude brings positive results. A negative or lackadaisical attitude postpones or prevents desired results.

Whatever You Pay Attention to Will Bring More of the Same.

That's why you need to pay attention to whatever you need to do to accomplish what is expected of you. And if you want to get noticed and move ahead of others, then you need to achieve more than what is expected of you. The choice is yours.

Most of us get what we want if we really want it badly enough to take risks, go against all odds, maintain a positive focus, and concentrate on the results. The point is: You need to pursue your own goals, objectives, and rewards. Nobody is going to do it for you. They may help you get there faster or sooner than you could on your own, but you make it happen. Put the right amount of energy behind your thrust and make sure you have a clear understanding of where you want to go—you'll get there.

It's amazing to see how your positive energy and results impact others. Whenever you succeed, you take others along with you. There's a wonderful ripple effect that generates an excitement and momentum of its own. You could benefit others. That makes you a very important and valuable person in your career world. It can also open up new opportunities for you. But it all begins with what you do today and how well you do it. The degree of your commitment determines the degree of your success. Feel empowered.

In general, the leasing rep's job description will include:

a. Renting vacant apartments and townhomes to qualified prospects;

b. Preleasing occupied apartments that are on notice to be vacated;

c. Processing applications, leases, credit reports, landlord and employment verifications, and whatever other forms are part of your company's lease transaction package;

d. Opening and closing the model(s) each day by making sure it shows as intended at all times;

e. Maintaining the ambiance intended for the clubhouse or common area facilities, including making sure work orders and service needed are completed satisfactorily and on time;

f. Checking on ready-to-show inventory daily and making sure it shows according to optimum management standards, including the "show path";

g Following up on past and current prospects daily by phone and by notes;

h. Contacting business and industry in person, by mail, and by phone to discover new prospect opportunities and staying in the forefront of referral sources;

i. Maintaining a daily record of advertising and promotion for your property while reviewing the same for competitors;

j. Shopping the competition periodically to stay abreast of their offerings as compared with yours;

k. Brainstorming and preparing site events and activities for residents, guests, and prospects that are geared to the market ownership wants to attract;

l. Coordinating any advertising campaign items that your company assigns to you;

m. Maintaining daily and weekly traffic and rental facts for various reports to management and ownership as

required—particularly tracking your own progress even
if it isn't required by your supervisor;

n. Working at improving your own productivity by education and exposure;

o. Maintaining the supply of brochures, handouts, and lease
package forms.

Most of us who recruit, train, and manage leasing personnel
would agree on the above list. But there are some additional
items that pertain to specific companies, market areas, or products that were not mentioned. One example is "lease renewals"
on existing residents when their lease is due to expire but
who might be candidates to stay on and renew their lease.
Some trainers in the industry include this function in the job
description of a leasing rep, a policy I do not endorse. Instead,
I assign the responsibility of lease renewals to the manager and
assistant manager (assuming the property is large enough to
warrant a full-time leasing person who is not involved with
managing the property, staff, or residents.) Generally, the property should be 200 units or larger to enjoy the luxury of
full-time leasing people who perform no other duties than the
ones itemized already. I also have a policy of separating
management functions from the selling functions, because
leasing reps should be able to devote 100 percent of their
time and attention to sales.

Of course, this system is not right for every property and
every organization. Just be aware that there's more than one
approach, and keep it in mind when it's time to evaluate how
you spend your time.

Too often we do things because, "That's the way it's always
been done." That's not a good enough reason to do anything.
Think. Be creative. Look for new and improved ways of
accomplishing your task more effectively than before.

SAMPLE LEASING CONSULTANT JOB DESCRIPTION
By Brenda McClain, Advanced RAM®, CPM®

Modern Management Company, Inc.
LEASING CONSULTANT JOB ANALYSIS

Supervisor's Name and Title:

Today's Date:

Position Function:

The leasing consultant oversees all aspects of marketing to prospects and ensures that the residents needs are met within the apartment community. The leasing consultant accurately records the number of prospects and how they found out about the property to assist the marketing department in evaluating the advertising program. Effective demonstration skills and an ability to close the sale are important.

General Description of Responsibilities:

All tasks and duties as assigned by supervisor or, in some cases, the marketing director, including, but not limited to:

1. Leasing apartments and having a thorough knowledge of the products. Must be able to meet specific sales goals.

2. Selecting qualified and appropriate applicants in accordance with Company procedure, Equal Housing Opportunity (EHO) requirements, and any applicable program regulations.

3. Conducting marketing surveys and making marketing recommendations based on an analysis of the surveys.

4. Completing traffic analysis reports on a weekly basis and any other marketing reports that may be required.

5. Walking the marketing path daily and writing up work orders accordingly. Opening and closing all models and monitoring their condition.

6. Ensuring that all vacant apartments are rent-ready and furnished with welcome packages.

7. Using the phone effectively for incoming and outgoing calls. Making follow-up calls to prospective residents (depending upon occupancy) and promptly responding to all incoming calls.

8. Continuously updating and processing lease renewals according to policy and procedures.

9. Treating all visitors consistently in compliance with Fair Housing laws.

10. Being able to explain the property's policy and procedures, services, and rate structures.

11. Processing all paperwork accurately and completely, and ensuring that all data in the resident files are kept up to date and confidential.

12. Developing contacts within the community, by means of telephone, mail, and personal visits.

13. Following up all application approvals or rejections with a phone call.

14. Following up all physical visits to the property with a thank-you note.

15. Assisting in the preparation of reports, newsletters, and security deposit notifications and planning resident activities, market surveys, etc., as necessary.

16. Attending all assigned resident activities.

17. Preparing move-in packages with local information to be included at the signing of the lease.

18. Conducting orientations of apartments and making the new residents feel welcome.

19. Following up with a personal visit within 24 hours of move-in to see if everything is all right with the resident. If not, make an appropriate notation and mark the request URGENT.

TIME MANAGEMENT: WHAT TO DO WHEN YOU'RE NOT LEASING APARTMENTS

Compiled by Jennifer A. Nevitt, RAM®
with contributions from Douglas D. Chasick,
RAM®, CPM®, Brenda McClain, Advanced
RAM®, CPM®, and Shirley Robertson,
RAM®, ARM®, CPM®

The Answer Is:

You're always leasing apartments. Even when you're not in the middle of talking to or meeting with clients, your activities should be moving you toward that constant and all-important goal of leasing the next apartment. How you handle the time between client contacts will determine, to a large extent, the outcome of those contacts.

Effective time management offers you a way to get maximum use of the time you have, even if that time seems minimal. By managing your time well, you will be able to squeeze more tasks into each workday, meet deadlines without panic, serve clients better, and spend a larger part of each day on selling and on the related activities that allow you to sell successfully.

Terms You Need to Know

When dealing with the subject of time management, there are some terms with which you need to be familiar. These include the following:

Action steps. What are the necessary processes that you must achieve, one step at a time, to complete the task? If you find

yourself feeling overwhelmed during a workday, this probably means that you're not taking the task one step at a time.

Prioritize. Rank the tasks. When 20 tasks demand attention,
a true professional sets priorities.

Delegate. This is the business management term for sharing
the load. When you supervise another person, you will be
able to give that person specific tasks to perform. You will
delegate work to that person. You may also receive work from
others when they delegate tasks to you. (You do not have to
outrank someone to delegate work to that person. However,
you may need their agreement to do so.)

Important versus urgent. To manage your time, you must be
able to distinguish between tasks that are important and those
that are urgent. Important tasks contribute to your long-term
goals. Urgent tasks scream for immediate attention. Typically,
important tasks offer you the opportunity to be proactive, to
take an action that you direct; urgent tasks are usually reactive, requiring you to react. Urgent tasks are often the result
of not accomplishing important tasks in a timely way.

Proactive. Take an action, determine the course of events,
as opposed to being reactive. Successful salespeople in any
field are proactive, decisive. For example, they do not rely on
clients to come to them, they take the actions necessary to
cultivate clients.

Goals

In the leasing profession, your ability to be productive and
feel a sense of accomplishment is based on how effectively you
reach sales goals and performance goals set either by superiors
or by you.

*The most important tasks you under-
take will be those tasks that
directly affect your long-term
goals and your ability to sell.*

One of your goals may be to put at least one person per week on your community's waiting list. Or you may have a goal to assign two of your intents-to-vacate prior to month's end.

Whatever your goals are, write each one in your notebook (on paper or on computer). If it's important enough to be a goal, it's important enough to be written onto your list of goals. You will find that if your goals are written down, you are more likely to set aside time and focus your energies toward accomplishing them.

Next, break each goal into logical steps. By breaking each goal into smaller steps, you will be able to accomplish even those that are very large and long-term.

Plan Your Work, Then Work Your Plan

To get the most out of every available minute, start with a plan. There are all sorts of time-management aids available, from notebook-style folders and worksheets to computer programs. Most are good products, but they all have one catch: They only work if you use them every day.

Each day, block out time for tasks that are urgent and for those that are important. Among the important tasks, include steps that lead to your goals (refer to your list of goals in your notebook). This will help you focus on one or more of your goals every day, day after day. If you don't include the steps that lead to your goals as part of your "To Do" list each day, you will find that you have been busy for weeks, but you have been unproductive in terms of goals. On the other hand, by including goal steps every day, you will assuredly reach your goals.

It is important to leave unscheduled blocks of time in your plan. There will also be new tasks, new information, new problems to solve, and many of them will arrive unannounced, usually when you are least able to handle them. The best way to deal with them is to expect them. By leaving some space in your plan, you will be able to take care of these new, imperative tasks—that are opportunities, often in disguise—without neglecting other tasks that are important to your goals.

A general rule of thumb is that, on any given day, you will have three unplanned, unexpected opportunities. Leave room for them.

When your three (and sometimes more) opportunities arrive, knowing that you have planned for these unknowns allows you to approach each one professionally. You will be able to remain calm and confident even while your sense of urgency is high. This positive attitude contributes to your success and to your sense of fulfillment when you have handled these hot opportunities well.

Seize the Moment

Chances are, opportunity will knock while you are busy. Unfortunately, opportunity won't wait around until you have time for it. When an opportunity walks in or calls, seize the moment. And keep in mind that some opportunities are only obvious to a person who is looking for them. Stay attuned to opportunities in marketing, resident relations, service, and sales—even if they are subtle—throughout the day. Because you are aware and ready to take action, you will be in a position to profit.

Example:

You have a client who visits your apartment community, and she happens to mention that she is part of a 10 person transfer from a regional office. If you are alert and ready to be proactive, this is a great opportunity for a corporate marketing call. Granted, a corporate marketing call was not planned into your day, but it is a great opportunity, and you're going to take it.

During the presentation to your new client, you find out that your client is staying at ABC Hotel. You also find out the name of the manager who is responsible for the transfer, and the manager's city. You call information, get the telephone number, call the number to get the fax number and address, and you send overnight to the transfer manager in charge a beautifully written letter welcoming the team to your city. You include information about your apartment homes. If you feel a real sense of urgency, you fax him or her this information. Or, if you feel it is an especially good opportunity, you send a telegram. Judge the degree of opportunity, use your experience and common sense, and act accordingly—but act.

Having made contact with the manager, you return your attention to cultivating your new client. You order for delivery to the client's hotel a salt-and-sweet snack basket, along with a note from you expressing your pleasure in showing her the apartment community.

Is your reaction to this example to say that you don't have time to do so much? You're busy already? Reconsider. If the chances are great that you could get five of the 10 transfers as new residents, this means that you could lease five apartments by expending 45 minutes worth of energy—but only if you spend the time and energy now, while the opportunity exists.

Here's another example of an opportunity, this one pertaining to resident referrals:

You return a phone call from a resident who has a question about leasing the club room for a party next month. "*(Name of resident)*, while I have you on the line, do you have any service that needs to be done on your apartment? I can write that up now." Or "*(Name of resident)*, you live in a one-bedroom. Do you have any friends looking for a one-bedroom? I have a really nice apartment very much like yours that I need a good resident for."

You don't have to set time aside to work the referrals or handle the lease renewals. If you're on top of things and open to the opportunities around you, you can integrate these and other tasks into your day, increasing your efficiency without increasing the hours you work.

Here's an example of an opportunity to integrate getting merchant referrals into your already full day:

You're on your lunch break and you need to go to the dry cleaner. You take with you some marketing materials and while you're getting two shirts, light starch, on a hanger, you discuss your community with the dry cleaner. You do the same thing with the gas station attendant, the waiter or waitress who serves you lunch, the person at the film developing counter, and the florist where you regularly order bouquets and arrangements.

Time Management Tools

You have to have your tools in order to manage time well and work confidently. Without them, you may feel paralyzed and defeated before you begin. So get your tools in order. In addition to a calendar and/or monthly planner, you may find the following helpful:

- Goal sheets
- Highlighter pens
- Colored stick-on notes to use as flags
- Computer calendar
- Dictation equipment
- Programmed telephones and fax machines (speed dial)
- Designated fax lines (a telephone line designated for your fax machine, 24 hours a day)
- Voice mail
- Card file, index, or other system for keeping track of names and numbers of contacts, suppliers, and colleagues
- Computerized mailing lists
- Computerized supplier lists

Remember, lists and files are only useful if they are up-to-date and in alphabetical order. Include updating as one of your ongoing tasks, or assign this task to a trusted assistant.

Not everyone agrees that stick-on notes are a good idea. Many time management experts recommend that you write all notes and reminders directly into your notebook on the "To Do" list. It certainly makes sense to avoid numerous loose pieces of paper and notes written on whatever is available at the moment. Without organization, it is likely that some of those loose notes and messages will be lost. However, if you find that using stick-on notes in various colors as flags to alert you to vital information helps you to get the job done effi-ciently, by all means use them in addition to your notebook or planner.

Well-Organized Files Can Save You More than Time

It is critical, absolutely critical, that the files in your office be so well organized that the flow of paper and computer information is both understood and predictable. What this level of organization gives you is ease of filing, reliable retrieval of necessary information in a minimum amount of time, and the peace of mind that comes from knowing you can put your hands on the information you need.

If the filing system in your office needs to be reworked and you do not feel competent to set up the system, delegate the task to someone who is capable of handling it. Insist that the system be simple and intuitively understood so that all in the office will be able to use it competently.

The basic system should include:

▶ Applications received
▶ Applications sent to manager for approval
▶ Lease information package, typed
▶ Alphabetically ordered designated move-in file
▶ A resident file system, by address
▶ Service tickets for work to be performed

After the system is in place, there is no need to talk about the task of filing. You will be able to pick up the paperwork or information you need at any step. This will save time and stress on you and others in the office, and it will help you to be more professional and effective.

Time Management Basics

▶ Keep your goals in mind.
▶ Know what is urgent for today and what is important. If you find that you aren't sure, ask your supervisor for guidance. Then set your priorities.
▶ Plan your work, and then use your plan every day.
▶ Stay alert for opportunities. Don't wait for a block of time in which to handle resident referrals. Work the waiting list, market the community, or perform other such tasks. Be open to ways to incorporate these into your day.

Not More Hours, More Time

Time management, even if applied consistently and with
great dedication, cannot give anyone more hours in a day.
Twenty-four is still the physical limit. What time management
can do is make your particular 24 hours more productive, less
stressful, and more rewarding. You will spend less time on
unimportant or routine tasks and have more time to spend on
what is important to you, including the leasing of that next
apartment.

When You're Not Busy with Traffic . . .

As the following list shows, there is always something useful
to do, even on a slow day, should one ever arrive. When planning your day and week, use this list to remind you of activities
and opportunities you want to include. Note the ones you
want to accomplish, in order of importance, on your "To Do"
list. Then, when you have a few minutes between calls, tackle
the next item on your list.

Work the waiting list.
- Do this every day.

Update your plan.
- Your plan may have changed since last night or this
  morning. Adjust it for maximum efficiency.
- Cross off items accomplished. (This is very satisfying.)
- Highlight, flag, or star urgent items that must be done
  today. Do one item now.

Cultivate new clients.
- Return any calls from new clients.
- Send flowers, fruit, cards, or gifts to potential corporate
  clients and special clients.

▶ Plan or revise the community's brochure or other collateral material. Send it out.

▶ Write or fax a letter to a new contact you made at your last dinner, board meeting, or club function.

▶ Go through old guest cards. Call or write and invite people back to the community.

▶ Follow up any mailing of brochures or flyers by calling potential clients.

▶ Call residents and ask two things: if there is anything they need and if they know anyone who is looking for a _____(describe it) apartment. This cements the relationship with your existing residents and helps to find qualified new residents.

▶ Call the Chamber of Commerce to obtain the names of people moving into the area.

Market the community.

▶ Update your community's marketing plan.

▶ Call or fax apartment locators with an update on available apartments. Include a brief report of one that got away— a choice apartment that is no longer available.

▶ Talk to local merchants about the community, an especially nice apartment that is now available, an event, whatever is current. Be specific if you can. Be conversational. Carry literature about the community, if feasible, and your card, at least. This is also a good time to work with the merchant to use the merchant's products, coupons, or other items as part of your effort to merchandise your apartments. (See Chapter 19 for more about merchandising.)

▶ Work on the newsletter. Be on the lookout for articles, cartoons, sayings.

▶ Update address files and mailing lists.

Work on resident retention.
▶ Call residents whose lease expires soon.
▶ Send birthday and anniversary cards.
▶ Call residents you haven't seen or heard from. Ask if they need anything. Offer to take care of it.
▶ When residents come into the office to pay rent, ask them if there's anything you can do for them.
▶ Start or update the community bulletin board.

Keep tabs on the competition and the market.
▶ Review competitive literature.
▶ Shop the competition by phone or in person.
▶ Scan publications that serve your market, including business and cultural magazines and newspapers.

Spot check the leasing center.
▶ Is the reception area clean and appealing?
▶ Check work areas for trash, clutter, inappropriate posters, toys or objects.
▶ Straighten the storage areas.

Spot check the grounds and the models.
▶ Walk the grounds and the models, picking up litter, noting areas that require repair, sprucing up everything you see. You get some fresh air and the community gets freshened.

Take care of office tasks.
▶ Return telephone calls.
▶ Reorder supplies:
    — guest or welcome cards
    — applications
    — leases
    — brochures and/or flyers
    — business cards
    — thank you cards

— birthday and anniversary cards

— work orders

▶ Respond to requests and RSVP invitations.

▶ Fill out paperwork.

Handle the paperwork.

▶ Go through the stack on your desk. Rule: Handle paper once.

▶ Handle the one job you are most likely to put off: Do it now.

▶ Avoid loose scraps. If you have any, transfer important information to your notebook or do the task immediately and toss the paper.

Clean out and organize files.

▶ Sort and file.

▶ Toss unneeded files and papers.

Watch Out for Time Wasters

No one is 100 percent efficient. We all enjoy an extra bit of conversation, a quick look at a newspaper, a daydream. Perfection is not the goal; improvement is.

*Wasted time: time spent on
something less important
when it could have been
spent on something
more important.*

There are two major types of time wasters: internal and external. The external time wasters come from outside of you and can be people or things. External time wasters often involve family, customers, suppliers, or co-workers and can include traffic jams, electrical failures, and other factors, some of which are beyond your control. If a time waster is truly uncontrollable, accept it and do the best you can. If it is controllable, take action.

Internal time wasters come from within yourself. These include an inability to say "no" and stick to it, excessive socializing, and incomplete or ineffective communication with clients and co-workers. Internal time wasters are the most difficult to identify and deal with because they tend to be personal.

The first step toward eliminating or reducing time wasters is to identify the time waster and its probable cause or causes. If the problem is you, you may have to be very firm with yourself to improve the situation.

A big time waster is procrastination, the putting off until tomorrow of something that could be done today. Instead of putting it off, do it now. It will be out of the way and you won't have to worry about it or feel guilty from now until you would have done it.

To avoid wasting time:

▶ Focus your attention on the job at hand. Concentrate.
▶ Know the answer, don't guess. If you don't know, find out.
▶ Act, don't react. Be prepared and take action.
▶ Simplify plans, communication, activities. Avoid complication.
▶ Don't hold a meeting if a memo will do the job.
▶ Agenda for every meeting. Distribute it ahead of time and stick to it.
▶ Avoid procrastination. If you can do the task now, do it now.

THE ORGANIZED LEASING CONSULTANT: WORKING SMARTER, NOT HARDER

By Shirley Robertson, RAM®, CPM®, ARM®

Get Organized

The leasing center has to imply "we've been expecting you" from the moment a future resident enters the leasing center. All leasing tools must be out and on hand. If a leasing consultant has to find a welcome card or a leasing application, the office space has not been organized to maintain good time management, not to mention the appearance of good office management. The reception area of the leasing center must always be clutter-free and welcoming. The leasing center is your silent interior salesperson, just as the community's curb appeal is your exterior silent salesperson. The future resident will be sizing up the appearance of the leasing center to ascertain whether or not it appears to be well managed. The leasing center's appearance is the second (if no telephone inquiry has occurred first) criterion the future resident has set to determine whether or not to do business with your apartment community.

Active work areas (desk or tabletops where paperwork is constantly occurring) are necessary in a busy leasing center. Active work areas are hard to keep neat, so it is necessary that the closest desk or reception table to the entrance door be kept neat and clear at all times. It is hard to keep a desk or table from being used as a working space; a leasing consultant can spend valuable work time "taking out" and "putting away" the ongoing work necessary to the leasing function. This is definitely an example of working harder, not smarter. A countertop workspace can be erected in a back corner of the leasing center or along a back wall. This allows the consultant to spread out work projects that can be handled at intervals throughout the day and are out of sight of the future resident.

Adequate storage is often at a premium, and what storage exists is not always used smartly. Reorganizing to maximize storage space begins with all closets. Remove the wooden shelving in the closet and replace it with lightweight, tailored closet stretcher shelving and modules. Keeping an eagle eye on advertised sales will allow you to purchase more pieces to outfit the closet. The storage capacity can be increased three-fold by utilizing the space near the ceiling for items seldom used, while the closet modules allow for storage of odd-shaped items. With additional space now available in the closet(s), it is time to clean out all of the drawers in the office. Items found here can now be stored comfortably in the closet(s), which will allow the stacks of items and papers on tabletops and desktops to be stored in the available drawers. Other items that can make the office space appear cluttered are various pamphlets and brochures for rental furniture and other services. Storage and display racks are available (often free) from the company or can be ordered from a catalog. Keeping all of these items together will give the leasing center a less cluttered appearance. This highly organized and uncluttered work environment will add to the productivity of the leasing team and will also win points with observant future residents.

What Impacted Me Most about this Chapter:

_____
_____
_____
_____
_____
_____
_____
_____
_____
_____

What I Need to Work on:

_____
_____
_____
_____
_____
_____
_____
_____
_____
_____

My Strengths Discovered in this Chapter:

_____
_____
_____
_____
_____
_____
_____
_____
_____
_____

CHAPTER 3

Telephone Inquiries & On-Site Prospect Qualifying

"Handling Telephone Inquiries" -*Sadovsky*

"Telephone Techniques That Work" -*King*

"Initial Qualifying" -*Chasick*

"Make Initial Qualifying Work" -*Nevitt*

HANDLING TELEPHONE INQUIRIES
By Anne Sadovsky, RAM®

Historically, our industry is extremely weak in telephone sales. Many arrivals and leases are lost due to the mishandling of telephone inquiries. The telephone is often treated as an annoyance rather than a traffic- and revenue-producing resource.

Most of us are aware of this situation . . . the phone always rings when you are busy with other things. So let's establish right up front that if you are only good on the phone when it's convenient, you will never be good on the phone! As a matter of fact, the telephone was invented about 25 years after the bathtub, and that was the only 25 years in history that you could take a bath without the phone ringing! So plan to handle telephone inquiries expertly under any circumstances, even if it is interrupting other important business.

Too often, our goal in answering the telephone is to get it to shut up, and the caller bears the brunt of that attitude.

Consider this. It costs a lot to make that telephone ring. Advertising, signage, yellow pages, banners, and business cards are just part of the expense. The actual telephone system plus the salaries of people to answer are a major expense. So when you pick up that ringing instrument, think for a second before you speak. You paid money from your marketing budget to get that phone to ring.

What is the appropriate greeting? Some companies have explicit policies and some leave it up to the individual. It is important to clearly identify the property so that the party knows they have reached the number dialed. Some consultants answer with their name as well, while others hold their name so they can introduce themselves in an effort to secure the name of the caller. An appropriate greeting would be "Good morning, Happy Hills Apartment Homes," or "Thank you for calling Happy Hills Apartment Homes." Be careful about being too "cutesy" or too long with your greeting. For example, "Good afternoon, thank you for calling Happy Hills Apartment Homes, this is Susie, may I help you?" is way too long, and "We're having a great day at Happy Hills Apartment Homes" is too cute for today's sophisticated client.

Always answer by the third ring and with enthusiasm, remembering that your goal in answering is a telephone arrival. The challenge is greatest when you already have a client sitting in front of your desk, on her lunch break, and you are the only one in the office. Simply excuse yourself, answer appropriately, and request a telephone number so you can call them back in a few minutes. Tempt them to give you their number by saying, "I have a dynamite apartment to tell you about, and I can give you the prices at the same time."

In anticipation of telephone inquiries, have everything you need ready. For Fair Housing law purposes, you must document every telephone call just as you do every visit to the property. Have the following ready at your desk:

- ▶ Guest cards or telephone logs at your fingertips. Remember to glance at the clock and note the time on the form.

- ▶ Pencils, sharpened and ready to write. Never have to say "Just a minute, let me go find a pencil."

- ▶ Availability list, including notices to vacate/upcoming vacancies.

- ▶ CURRENT price list/rent schedule.

- ▶ Floor plans, carpet colors, etc., for available apartments.

A typical telephone inquiry may go like this:

RING RING

Consultant: "Good afternoon, Happy Hills Apartment Homes."

Caller: "HOW MUCH ARE YOUR TWO-BEDROOMS?"

Consultant: "I'd be happy to help you with a two-bedroom and give you the prices, my name is Susie . . . and yours?"

Caller: "UH, WELL...MY NAME IS FRED, BUT ALL I WANT IS THE PRICES."

Consultant: (You didn't get rid of the price question, but you got something very valuable...his name!) "Fred, I know the price is very important to you, and my job is to help you find the best apartment in your price range. Is it okay for me to ask you a few questions? And if I don't have the right thing for you, I'll help you find something."

Several things happened in this conversation. You have the client's first name. You were friendly, interested, and willing to be of help. You also, in preparation for asking qualifying questions, gave him a reason FOR HIS BENEFIT for asking and even got his permission to ask! This is a proven technique for handling the price question and getting the client in a friendly conversation.

Once in a while, when trying this technique, you may have a caller who is abrupt, even rude. This person may be demanding, even unpleasant in their response. For example:

Caller: "I DON'T WANT TO GIVE YOU MY NAME, I JUST WANT THE PRICE!"

Consultant: "Sir, I see that the price is very important to you. Our two-bedrooms start at $700 and if you have just a second I'd like to tell you everything you get here for that price and discuss when you need the apartment."

Sometimes your friendly conversational manner puts them at ease and gets them in the mood to talk, and sometimes they'll hang up on you! At least you know that you did everything possible to help the client.

Pre-qualifying on the telephone is both necessary and appropriate as long as you do so in a friendly, helpful manner without interrogating. Notice that you got their name without saying, "What is your name, address, and phone number?" The same method works to gain necessary information to help the client with their housing needs. In an interested, conversational manner, find out the following information:

WHEN the apartment is needed.

WHAT specifically is needed, for example: Do you have any special needs or requirements in your apartment home? Find out desired color scheme, location preferences, etc.

HOW MANY will occupy the apartment. Do they have a PET and, if so, what kind and what size when fully grown.

What is their BUDGET for the monthly rent. Using the word budget implies some flexibility on their part. They might reply, "I don't really have a budget, but would like to pay around $650." Your two-bedroom rents for $700 so you could say, "Fred, it would only be around $1.50 a day more for your new two-bedroom here at Happy Hills. Let's look at your budget and see if we can't come up with that $1.50 a day. Perhaps you could run home for lunch a couple of days a week, and you'll be closer to the office so you'll save on gasoline and wear and tear on your car. Plus, look at the extras you get here for just $1.50 a day more!"

If their needs and desires can be filled now or in the near future, invite them to see the apartment, a model, and your community. Rather than say, "Would you like to see the apartment? Can you come today?" try, "You really need to see this wonderful apartment to appreciate what I've told you about it. When would be the best time for you to come in?" Add an alternate choice invitation. "Is during the week better for you, or the weekend? Saturday or Sunday? Saturday? Great. Can I expect you in the morning or the afternoon?"

After getting a time, commit, confirm, and obligate the client. "Fred, I'm jotting your name on my calendar for Saturday at 3 p.m.. If for any reason you can't make it, please call me because I'll be looking for you at 3 p.m. this Saturday."

Always ask for a number where you can reach them between now and their designated arrival time. You will find it much easier to get their number at the end of the conversation, after they have experienced your friendly, helpful manner, rather than at the beginning.

Again, be sure to document the phone call, including the time. In case you are not available to help them or are out when they arrive, have the documentation of the call readily available to everyone in the office. When you greet them, don't make the mistake of looking at them with a blank stare, as if you've never heard of them before. After spending time with them on the phone, the least you can do is remember their name and greet them warmly when they arrive.

And of course, if they do not show up for their appointment call them back and warmly say, "I'm sorry you weren't able to make it out on Saturday. Let's reschedule now."

Remember, every call counts. If you don't have anything available to meet their needs, offer suggestions like sister communities, locator services, or competitive properties. After all, it is your job to help them find a home.

TELEPHONE TECHNIQUES THAT WORK
by Cynthiann King, RAM®

Leasing professionals are lucky that customers contact them, primarily through telephone leasing calls and on-site visits. Because today's average renter calls and yet only visits three communities, the telephone leasing call is extremely important to a successful leasing sales process. Also, if one calculates the cost of each telephone call by including the marketing expenses, advertising efforts, personnel costs, and utility bills connected with the telephone, the cost of just one telephone call that results in a lease could easily exceed $50. Is it crucial for a leasing professional to be proficient in telephone leasing skills? Absolutely!

Because a leasing professional must build genuine rapport, the examples in this chapter should not be utilized as part or all of a telephone script. Instead, the tone of the call should be individually tailored to the caller, conversational, natural, upbeat, and definitely not "canned."

The most important objectives of the leasing telephone call include: 1) building rapport with the future resident, 2) setting a specific appointment, and 3) acquiring the potential resident's telephone number for follow-up. Building rapport is listed first because a future resident will only keep an appointment if the leasing professional can meet some of the client's most important housing needs while building a relationship that encourages ongoing communication centered around benefits and features of the community or building, property, staff, and services. These three key objectives will be explored further in another section of this article.

The successful leasing telephone experience includes the following components:

1. Preparation
2. Greeting
3. Information gathering
4. Qualifying
5. Benefit demonstration
6. Invitation
7. Closing or setting the specific appointment
8. Directions and confirmation, and
9. Follow-up.

Preparation

Preparation before the leasing call includes gathering the necessary materials as well as developing the proper mindset to best handle the call. Materials include notepaper, pen, welcome guest card, product knowledge packet, occupancy and credit worthiness standards, rental rates, additional charges schedule (deposits, fees), appointment calendar, and a properly working telephone. Since the caller was interested enough in the community to have made the call, the leasing professional should validate that interest by concentrating on the call to the exclusion of surrounding distractions to the highest degree possible. Preparation should also include prior training and practice in the proper techniques for handling leasing calls. Last, but not least, the leasing professional must have an enthusiastic and focused mindset to serve the caller. The leasing telephone call should usually be answered on the second ring to enable both the caller and the leasing professional to be fully ready for the sales conversation.

Greeting

The greeting is the caller's first opportunity to evaluate the community. An effective greeting should be delivered in an upbeat manner and include a welcoming statement, identification of the community or building, identification of the employee answering the call, and a statement of intent. An example of an excellent greeting is: "ABC Apartments is managed by people who care. This is Cynthiann King. I can help you." Studies have shown that if leasing professionals give their own first and last name (as long as the last name is not cumbersome), callers will typically do the same when their name is requested.

Information Gathering

Information gathering includes an exchange of information between the caller and the leasing professional, which enables the leasing professional to gear the conversation toward meeting the caller's needs while trying to develop rapport with the caller. The leasing professional might pose such questions as: "What brings you to the area?" "Why are you moving?" "What is most important to you in your new home?" "What did you like least/best about your most recent housing arrangements?"

Qualifying

The qualifying stage of the telephone conversation may proceed, follow, or coincide with the information-gathering process. This stage involves asking the caller crucial questions to determine the caller's initial eligibility as a potential resident. Qualifying questions usually include: "How many persons will occupy this home?" "Will any pets accompany the occupants?" "How soon would you desire to move in?" "Are any special accommodations needed by any of the potential occupants?" "Will a furnished rental home be required?" It would be great if at this point the leasing professional could also ask such questions as "What is your income?" "Have you ever been evicted?" "How long have you been employed?" It is not advisable, however, to do so over the telephone unless the occupancy guidelines for the community require such information (as in the case of subsidized housing). Many callers become defensive when asked these types of questions, so it is best to ask them during the on-site tour of the community.

Studies have shown that callers will make and keep an appointment to visit a specific community or building if several of their crucial needs are met through this initial discussion with the leasing professional. Rather than listing amenities, the leasing professional should discover a need, determine how important that need is to the caller, and then discuss those features or amenities that would meet the caller's needs. The caller is, after all, not usually interested in everything the community has to offer, but primarily WIIFM, or "What's In It For Me?"

Benefit Demonstration

First, some definitions. A feature is any item that stands alone regardless of a customer's need. A benefit is an item that satisfies a customer's particular need, want, or desire. A need is crucial, a want is important, and a desire is a "nice-to-have" feature or benefit.

Here's an example of a feature statement made by a leasing professional: "All of our one-bedroom apartment homes come with an eat-in dining area." And this is a benefit statement made by a leasing professional: "Since you mentioned that you enjoy cooking and entertaining, you will probably be delighted to know that all of our one-bedroom apartment homes come with an eat-in dining area." To determine if the feature and benefit are crucial needs or merely "nice-to-haves," the leasing professional should follow any benefit descriptive statement with the question, "How does that sound to you?"

Since almost all future residents are experiencing some degree of stress because of a future move, leasing professionals cannot assume that the caller already knows the benefits of the highlighted features discussed over the telephone. The leasing professional should use visual imagery or word pictures to help the caller become more actively involved in "viewing" the community or building and all of its offerings. Here's an example of a visual imagery benefit statement made by a leasing professional: "Since you mentioned that you enjoy cooking and entertaining, picture yourself doing so in our fully equipped, step-saver, eat-in dining area in our one-bedroom apartment home. How does that sound to you?" If you "demonstrate" several important benefits of the caller's identified needs throughout the telephone conversation, the caller will begin to feel a connection or rapport, which usually contributes favorably to the making and keeping of an on-site visit appointment.

Invitation

In the Invitation component of the leasing telephone call, the leasing professional openly invites the qualified caller to visit the community or building. You can say: "I would welcome the opportunity to show an apartment home to you that would best meet your needs," or "I invite you to come by and see our apartment home with the a, b, c features and benefits we've discussed."

Close

The close in a successful leasing telephone call involves the setting up of a specific appointment with the caller. If the caller is qualified and you can meet some of his/her needs, assume that the caller will want to visit the community or building. Instead of asking the caller if they would like to visit, offer alternate dates and times for the appointment. An appointment set for the quarter hour is usually best remembered by the caller. Here's a good closing statement to make: "Caller X, you mentioned that you are looking for an apartment home that is available at x date for x number of occupants and, more importantly to you, has x, y, and z features. Our apartment community or building has all of these and much more, so I would like to invite you to visit us. Would this Monday at 11:15 or Tuesday at 4:45 work better for you?"

Directions and Confirmation

Ask the starting location of the caller, then describe in detail exact directions from the caller's point of origin to the community or building, including visual clues such as number of stoplights, property signage and address. Ask the caller if he/she understood the directions. It is extremely helpful for a leasing professional to drive to the community or building to become familiar with different routes. If there is enough time, you may mail a map with detailed directions to the caller. This is an excellent means of getting the caller's address.

At this point in the conversation, you should try to obligate the caller to the appointment by saying something like, "Your time is valuable and so is mine. Would you please call our community or building at least 24 hours in advance if you need to reschedule our visit?" Then confirm the date and time of the appointment and ask for the caller's telephone numbers at work and home, if at all possible. You cannot follow up with a canceled or "no-show" potential resident without at least one contact telephone number. Of course if the caller is unwilling to release that, you may have to rely on the caller to call back and reschedule the missed appointment. End the call with a thank you and pleasant good-bye statement.

Follow-up

The follow-up stage of the successful leasing telephone call is crucial to the eventual signing of the lease. Many industry professionals believe that a leasing professional should follow up with a potential future resident until one of three things occurs: 1) the caller leases elsewhere, and even then the leasing professional should find out which property the caller selected and why, 2) the caller asks the leasing professional to discontinue any future contact, or 3) the caller dies.

Methods of follow-up may include writing a postcard or letter thanking the caller and including a reminder of the upcoming appointment, mailing the community newsletter, mailing a photograph of an amenity that interests the caller, or inviting the caller to attend an upcoming community event, to name a few. Each can be sent several days apart so that the caller is still connected to the leasing professional until the specific on-site visit is made.

The best advice ever given to me on the subject of the professional leasing telephone call was to whet the appetite of the caller to visit my community or building through both my enthusiasm for my community or building and my personalized presentation to meet the qualified caller's needs. As Henry Ford said, "If you think you can, you can. If you think you can't, you can't. Either way you're right." When it's time to pick up that leasing telephone call on that second ring, do you think you can?

It's up to you. Good Luck!

INITIAL QUALIFYING

By Douglas D. Chasick, RAM®, CPM®

Before you focus on meeting the needs of your prospects, you must first make certain that they meet your resident selection guidelines. Since you also want to establish a rapport with your prospects, the initial qualifying session is the perfect opportunity to establish a comfort level with them, so they are willing to answer your questions without feeling like they are being interrogated.

The main purpose of qualifying is to make certain each prospect meets the criteria established in your written resident selection guidelines. Written resident selection guidelines should be made available to any prospect who requests one. These guidelines should cover minimum income requirements, the maximum number of occupants permitted in each size apartment, what type of credit history is required, length of employment, type of resident history, treatment of bankruptcy, etc. Written resident selection guidelines help ensure consistency and compliance with Fair Housing guidelines. If the prospect does not meet your minimum qualifying standards, there is no reason to give him a tour of your property. A properly conducted qualifying interview can save time for you and your prospects.

Most people visit at least four or five properties each day when searching for an apartment. Unfortunately, the initial qualifying process most prospects encounter consists of being welcomed to the property and being handed a guest card to complete. What's the rush? Why not give the prospect a chance to sit down and relax while you establish a rapport?

If possible, find a relatively private, quiet place to speak with your prospects. Don't sit behind a desk—it acts as a barrier. If you don't have a circular table available, sit on the same side of the desk as your prospect. Not only does it make the prospect more comfortable, but if you're taking notes or completing the guest card, the prospect can see what you're writing. (Yes, some of them really wonder what you're writing down as they speak to you!) Don't sit between a set of two prospects; sit to one side or the other so you can address both people at once.

You should have coffee and soft drinks or water to offer and perhaps some snacks such as cookies. If possible, use glasses and ceramic coffee cups instead of plastic and styrofoam. A nice touch is coasters or cocktail napkins with the property name and/or logo.

When you begin your conversation with the prospect, don't immediately pull out the guest card. You can ask them some of the qualifying questions without taking notes at first—jot down the answers on the card later. Your session should be more of a conversation than an interview.

While each community has its own guest card, most of the questions are the same:

1. When do you need the apartment?
2. What size apartment are you looking for?
3. How many people will live in the apartment?
4. How did you hear about us?
5. What is your price range or budget?
6. Do you have any pets?

While these are important questions, they don't give you enough information to really meet their needs. The following questions will yield valuable information that you can use during your presentation and property tour to focus the prospect on what your property offers:

1. Where do you live now? If you know your competition, and your prospect is from your market area, the answer

to this question yields much more than the name of one of your competitors! It tells you about their current lifestyle, and you probably have a good idea about the pluses and minuses of your competition.

2. Why do you want to move? If you've done a good job establishing a rapport with the prospect, they'll usually open up and tell you why they REALLY want to move— even if it's something they feel foolish talking about, like wanting a parking space closer to their front door, or they don't like the view from their bathroom window. If you've got that parking space, or great bathroom window views, you're able to offer a solution to their problem.

3. What do you dislike about your current apartment and community? Make sure you get specific information about each thing they dislike so you can address these items in your presentation.

4. What is your idea of the perfect apartment? The perfect apartment community? This is a question to have fun with, because it allows people to "build" an apartment in their mind. Of course you won't have everything they want, but once they tell you what their "perfect" apartment would be like, you can work with them to prioritize the really important features, which you will of course point out in your apartments!

During the qualifying interview you should ask "open-ended" questions instead of questions that the prospect can answer with a "yes" or "no." Asking open-ended questions lets the prospect elaborate on their likes and dislikes, and forces them to consider your questions more carefully than if they could agree or disagree with you. Most successful salespeople will tell you that their goal is for the prospect to do 60-70% of the talking, while the salesperson does the other 30-40%.

As you ask questions, be sure to take notes. Studies show that most people forget half of what they hear within a minute of hearing it! Taking notes allows you to refer back to the prospect's likes and dislikes, and to focus your presentation on answering their questions and solving their problems. Remember that most people are interested in "what's in it for me," so make notes about those items you think will be of the most interest and benefit to your prospect.

Since some of your traffic will not meet your minimum qualifying standards, make the best of the situation. If the prospect does not qualify for your property, can they qualify for one of the other properties your company owns or manages? Don't just let the prospect walk out the door—direct them to another property in your portfolio, or to one of your competitors that you feel would accept them. Don't use the word "rejected" when letting a prospect know that they don't meet your requirements—nobody likes to be "rejected." A much more effective technique is to simply state what your requirement is, and then apologize because you won't be able to process their application at the present time. Give them information about the other properties that you feel could meet their needs.

Qualifying over the phone involves the same procedure as a personal visit. The main difference is that most people who call your property will IMMEDIATELY ask the price of your apartments. One way to eliminate price shoppers is to put the price of your apartments in your ad. The most effective way to advertise price is to use a range: "Two-bedroom apartments starting at only $XXX per month" or "One-bedroom apartments ranging from $XXX to $YYY monthly." This allows prospects to prequalify themselves on the price issue!

When answering the phone, follow these simple guidelines:

1. Don't answer the phone on the first ring, and do answer

the phone by the third ring. When the phone rings, stop what you're doing for a moment, and prepare yourself for a sales call. Take out a blank welcome card, grab a pen, put a big smile on your face, and then pick up the phone.

2. Keep your greeting simple and to the point. "Thanks for calling XXX apartments, this is Doug," says everything you want to say. Why say "Can I help you?" or "How can I help you?"—of course you can help them—you're working there! And stay away from the long, cutesy greetings, "Thank you for calling XXX apartments, where the sky is blue, the apartments are huge, the pool is lovely, blah, blah, blah," or "It's a wonderful day at XXX apartments, thank you for calling, how can I help you?" When you answer the phone with your community name, the prospect knows they didn't dial a wrong number. When you follow with your own name, the prospect will usually offer their name.

3. If they don't offer their name, ask for it. The more personalized the phone conversation, the more likely you are to get an appointment.

4. Remember that your goal is to set up an appointment with qualified callers. Don't try to lease an apartment on a phone call, and don't give away so much information about your community that the caller doesn't feel the need to visit you.

5. Speak clearly and slowly. Make certain the caller understands what you're saying.

6. Ask what type of apartment they are looking for, when they need the apartment, how many people will be living in the apartment, how they heard about you, and what their budget is. That's all the information you need right

now. Remember, your goal is to make an appointment, not lease an apartment.

7. Ask for the appointment. Just telling the prospect to stop by when they get a chance doesn't create any commitment on their part to visit you. Ask for the appointment, and then ask for it again. Give them a choice of time or days or both.

8. Frame your answer to the price question with two or three selling points of your community. When you're asked the price of your apartments, don't just say: "$XXX per month," when you could say, "Our huge two-bedroom apartments, with washer and dryer connections and free covered parking start at only $XXX."

MAKE INITIAL QUALIFYING WORK
By Jennifer A. Nevitt, RAM®

Every month your community spends thousands of dollars trying to get the phone to ring. For any number of reasons—the advertising, signage, location, whatever—you receive unqualified calls and leads along with the qualified ones. It is your job to separate the qualified from the unqualified while being both professional and helpful with each caller or drop-in visitor, remembering that every person with whom you come in contact deserves to be treated with dignity and respect.

You must undertake this initial qualifying without violating Fair Housing statutes. It is vital that you understand that initial qualifying has nothing to do with race, creed, gender, or any of the other Fair Housing subjects. You must base your decision on resident screening criteria that are established by each company that offers rental housing to the public. These criteria may include past rental history, employment or verification of income, and credit rating. Expect that different owners may have different criteria.

Initial Qualifying Can Help You Save Valuable Time

A leasing professional's time is extremely valuable, which makes initial qualifying even more important than in the past when the pace of life in general and business in particular were slower. Now, information comes in three times faster than in the early 1980s. Fax, phone, and mobile phones may make communication easier, but they also increase the amount of information received as well as the rate. You probably feel the stress. There is more to do. It can be overwhelming. Effective time management becomes essential to being able to sell.

To be effective in sales, you need information about your client, and that is what initial qualifying is all about. By arming yourself with adequate information, you will know that a client needs a three bedroom apartment on the second floor by the first of next month. Knowing this, you won't waste the client's time or yours by showing a one-bedroom on the first floor that won't be available for three months.

Focus on Specific Questions

The goal of initial qualifying is to identify information that allows you to zero in on viable future residents. You are amassing facts to match the client with the resident criteria of your community and availability while you gather clues about the client's feelings and needs. The facts may include:

- Housing budget
- Presence or absence of pets
- How many persons will live in the apartment
- When the apartment is needed

You are also gathering necessary and useful information, including:

- Name
- Address
- Telephone number at home and at work
- Car phone number
- Fax number
- Media source that led the client to you

While you are gathering facts, there are two easy ways to begin building the necessary relationship with your clients:

- ▶ A welcome card for the client. Take the information yourself; don't ask the client to fill out the card. If you are speaking to a client over the phone, get the basics so that when the client arrives, the card is done.
- ▶ Client's name in conversation. This simple technique is an important and highly effective way to build a connection between you and your clients.

Get Information Without Prying

You know what factual information you need, but how do you get it in a professional manner? If you don't ask the right questions, you waste everybody's time, including your own. Granted that you know what you need to find out, such as how many bedrooms, what floor, etc., how you ask can make or break the sale.

You can't interrogate people. They will resent the overbearing manner and take their business elsewhere. Your manner must be helpful, conversational, and natural.

Look on the initial qualifying process as your opportunity to discover the tools you need to make the sale. While conversing with your clients, you can find out the factual information as well as the hot buttons that will help you to answer their unspoken needs. As you converse with your clients, listen for mention of a job transfer, divorce, promotion, and other events or details that can help you use your product to answer the clients' needs. For example, a client who has just had a promotion can probably afford more and may be looking for an apartment with a special feature or some status. This may be the client who wants the lake view, an extra bedroom and deluxe interior.

Remember, you are looking for facts and feelings that will give you clues to your clients' needs. These are the keys to interpersonal selling.

Build Rapport to Build Trust

At this initial stage of the sales process, concentrate on listening and observing. Work to build rapport with your client. Establishing a level of trust at the outset can help you to overcome any objections that might arise later.

Use What You Discover

Having conversed with your clients in person and possibly by phone as well, you have information at your disposal: facts, such as where they work; deductions based on the facts and on more subtle clues such as body language; and your own gut-level reactions and intuition. Combined, this information gives you clues that can help you adjust your presentation to meet the needs of your clients. For example, what you have discovered can help you plan the tour route, allowing extra time in a specific room or area that gives them what you've found out they want. If you know that gatherings of family and friends are important, make certain your clients spend time in the dining room, point out the best details of the kitchen regarding entertaining, and highlight the spacious dimensions of the living room.

There are two schools of thought about tours and whether to adjust each presentation to suit the audience: There are those who believe that every client should be given the same tour, regardless of stated preferences, and those who believe that each tour should be tailored to its audience.

One Thing at a Time

If you are with clients on the telephone or in person and another line rings, never say "Excuse me, do you mind if I answer this?" Give your clients your undivided attention. Take care of them and nothing else. Why? You can only do one thing at a time well. Concentrate on your clients. Have voice mail, an answering service, or someone else in the office pick up your calls and take messages. (As soon as you can, answer all the messages.)

Verbal Versus Nonverbal Communication

What you say and how you say it work together to send your verbal message. You send nonverbal messages with your posture, the strength and sincerity of your handshake, and by showing hospitality to your clients. Treat them as if they were guests in your own home.

Your posture is especially important. It will set the tone for how you control the entire meeting with your clients. A straight, relaxed posture projects confidence, warmth, and a positive attitude that is appealing to almost everyone.

Be certain that you don't overwhelm your clients. Stay about three feet from them. Any closer, and you risk intruding on their personal space, making them uncomfortable. Any farther away, and you will seem distant and stand-offish. Control your voice, being careful not to be loud, which seems like yelling, or too soft, which seems unsure. Speak calmly and at a normal rate. Talking too fast tells clients that you don't have time for them.

The Importance of Environment

When a client calls you on the telephone, what can the client hear? If the client hears static, employees yelling, a blaring radio, or a leasing professional who sounds rushed and stressed, that client could easily form a negative impression about the community.

In person, environment is just as important. The office area should be clean, uncluttered, and free of smoke or other odors including food, mold, mildew, or excessive air freshener. Windows should sparkle. Lighting should be adequate and well adjusted, neither too dim (looks dirty) nor too bright (which is uncomfortable). An appealing scent, such as amaretto or vanilla, can enhance the atmosphere if used sparingly. Heavy perfume in the air or on the members of the staff can be offensive.

If the immediate environment of the sales office is chaotic, have an appropriate quiet corner or area where you can handle initial qualifying. Likewise, for closing you will need a table, club room, or model apartment where you can take your clients. The quieter, less stressful environment will be conducive to good listening and will increase the probability that your sales efforts will be successful.

What the Client Wants to Know First

Usually, the client is doing his own initial qualifying of your community. The first thing the client asks will probably be "How much?" A good response: "That depends on how soon you're looking to move and the size of apartment, as well as the features you're interested in."

Immediately, make an effort to ask directly two of the three questions you have just posed:

▶ How soon would you like to move?
▶ What size of apartment are you looking for?
▶ What features are you interested in?

You probably will not have the opportunity to ask all three without appearing to be stalling.

Then give the price. Your goal is take control of the conversation. Do not attempt to get every bit of information before giving the price. The client has asked for a price, and with limited information, you must give it.

Basic rules for giving a client a price:

1. *Do not give a price range, give a price.*
Rationale: You walk into a store and see an outfit on a mannequin. You like it. You ask the salesperson, "How much does it cost?" The salesperson begins telling you that the pants are $89, the belt is $27, the shirt is...." What you wanted was the big number, the bottom line. You did not want to be nickel-and-dimed, item by item, and neither does the client who just asked you for the price. Using the information from the two out of three answers you were able to ask, give the price. Keep in mind that it is difficult, if not impossible, to pull a client up to a higher price later. You can always go lower, and if you do, the client will be pleasantly surprised.

What the client wants to know is what amount to write on the check. Do not insult your clients by nickel-and-diming them. Assume initially that all clients are qualified and can afford the apartment.

2. *Know your availabilities.*
If you know that the available three-bedroom apartments include a large number with fireplaces, add that extra to the price when you give it, even though you haven't mentioned the fireplace yet. This gives your client a maximum number and will help you to sell the fireplace.

If there are a number of extras possible—fireplace, washer/dryer, vaulted ceiling—split the difference between the top and bottom of this range and give that as the price. If your clients want everything, the price will be close, and it won't be a big problem to go up that very small amount.

3. *When you give the price, say: "...and that includes water, sewer, trash removal, heat..." and anything else that is included.* Keep in mind that some properties in water conservation states have individual water meters. Having water included could be a big deal to someone coming from a property where water is not included.

Remember that you don't have time to find out everything before the tour, so find out what you most need to know during initial qualifying. Then refine the information as you continue your presentation.

Your Community Is Full?

Even if your community is full, continue to extend the same courtesy, the same effort, and the same care throughout the selling process, beginning with initial qualifying. Then put your viable future residents on the waiting list. That's how you build a waiting list. And that's how you make certain that your property stays full.

Make Use of Information from Initial Qualifying

Think of initial qualifying as the information-gathering stage of the selling process. The information that you gather now can be used throughout the process and afterward.

Marketing. One of the things you will ask is how the client heard about your community. Clearly identify the marketing source. If you find that you are getting a lot of unqualified traffic from a particular source, you can use this information to alter the way you market your property. Likewise, if you are getting highly qualified traffic from a source, you may want to increase your efforts there.

Follow-up. Listen for your clients' interests. This allows you to do something thoughtful for them. For example, you find out that your clients are movie goers. During follow-up, send them two movie tickets to the local theater. Add a note that says something like this: "When you make XYZ Apartments your new home, you'll have time to enjoy a good show. Thanks for letting me show you XYZ." This kind of thoughtfulness will set you and your community apart from the competitors and could give you the edge in a highly competitive market.

Long-term relationships. By using the information that you gathered during initial qualifying, you are strengthening your clients' connection with your community and building an ongoing relationship that can pay off in client satisfaction, referrals, and renewals.

What Impacted Me Most about this Chapter:

_____
_____
_____
_____
_____
_____
_____
_____
_____
_____

What I Need to Work on:

_____
_____
_____
_____
_____
_____
_____
_____
_____

My Strengths Discovered in this Chapter:

_____
_____
_____
_____
_____
_____
_____
_____
_____
_____

CHAPTER 4

Between Qualifying & Closing

"On-Going Qualifying" *-Blake Cline*

"Demonstrations" *-Chasick*

"Demonstrating:
The Art of it All" *-Joy*

"Think Safety" *-Robertson*

ON-GOING QUALIFYING
By Toni Blake Cline

What Should You Know Before You Leave the Office?

Choosing which apartment to take your customer to requires more than just the date they are moving, who will be living in the apartment, and what their budget is. You must also qualify their preferences of style, color, sunlight, and location within your community. Even if the basic qualifying information matches the apartment, they still might not like it!

Many of the top leasing consultants also qualify specific furniture needs by using a checklist of the rooms and asking the customer: "Do you have any specific needs for your new apartment home?" They also ask, "Do you have any specific needs or requirements for your living room/dining room/kitchen/bedrooms? Take notes and you will be able to control the customer's "hot buttons."

You will find that customers are much more interested in a personal presentation that is designed around their specific requirements. People don't want to hear about how large the living room is in B-5 until they know that their navy blue sectional sofa will fit there.

When Should You Ask Sensitive and Non-sensitive Questions?

A sensitive question is one that is defined as a question concerning personal information. A non-sensitive question is one of a non-personal nature.

Examples of a sensitive question: "What color is your sofa?" "Do you have a lot of plants?" "Do you like to cook?"

You should always begin your qualifying with a "getting to know you" time period. Begin by asking a question and then stop talking. Listen to what they tell you and repeat their own opinion back to them. Allow them the space in the conversation to be important and you will find they will fill it up with information vital to successful leasing. During the "getting to know you" time, ask only non-sensitive questions. It is better to leave the sensitive questions until later, when you have earned their trust.

What Is a Leading Question?

A leading question is a non-sensitive question that leads to a sensitive question. Example: "Do you live in this area?" (non-sensitive). "Where do you live?" (sensitive). Leading questions help to effect the transition to personal questions. After all, it's not what you ask, but how you ask it.

Earning Buyers' Confidence and Becoming Friends.

Today, the smart companies are not looking for dynamic salespeople, they are looking for people who are sincere and believable. Earning a customer's confidence is simple, and should be a matter of priority. When you talk to your customer, are you sincere when you say: "May I help you?" How many times have you been greeted by these very words when you know they don't really care if they can help you or not?

When someone is talking to me, I am totally aware of whether they are concentrating on me, or whether they have something else on their mind. Just yesterday I was checking into a hotel and the front desk clerk was so distracted I finally said, "Are you having a bad day?" When I said this it was the first time she had really looked at me and not at the paperwork or her computer screen. "Yes," she said, "and I just got here." We laughed for a moment and she smiled the rest of the time she helped me. Unfortunately, you can't expect your customer to judge your mood and be responsible for cheering you up. It should be the other way around. Whether or not you care is a message you send loud and clear to your customer.

When you are talking to a potential future resident, focus completely on them and push other thoughts to the back of your mind. It's not just a great leasing technique, it's the polite thing to do. Working with the customer's agenda is all a part of the 90's soft sales approach. Remember the golden rule: Do unto others as you would have them do unto you. What would you want someone to do for you if you were looking for an apartment?

How to Change a Looker into a Lessee on the Way to the Apartment.

How many times does the customer come in to look at the apartment and tell you they are just looking? This is simply buyer's resistance. They are not serious about making a decision and they do not want to be sold. If you are going to create a sense of urgency without making them defensive, you must put yourself in a position to benefit them and help them.

The stress related to moving ranks just below the stress caused by a death in the family. If you can help take the headache out of moving, you will find people much more open about making a decision. The best way to do that is to create a useful New Resident Packet. This packet can be started by going through your move-in packet and taking out the things people need before the move-in, such as change of address cards and information about the area. Add information about banks, grocery stores, dry cleaners, and schools.

You can also create a "Here's my new address" card with your community name on it for them to send to their friends.

I recommend that you become "the moving expert." The more information you can share about moving into your community, the more likely a prospect will want to lease from you. Investigate all the information you can that will help someone to move into your community. One of the keys to the effective use of this information is to create a sense of urgency. We have found people are not thinking about moving, they are thinking about looking. If on the way to the apartment you show them the new resident packet and talk to them about the many wonderful services your community offers, you will find you can turn a looker into a lessee.

Questions That Create a Sense of Urgency and Create a Buying Mood:

Discuss customer's search for an apartment.
"How many places have you seen?"
"What did you like so far?"
"How many more places do you plan to visit?"
"When do you plan to decide?"
Notice I did not ask them to decide, I simply asked them to decide when they *plan* to decide. This will get you moving down the right path.
Ask them about the moving process.
"Do you have boxes?"
"Have you located a moving van?"
"Do you plan to change banks?"
"Have you arranged for help with the move?"
Always make sure to inform your future residents that the New Resident Packet has information to help them with these and many others details involved with their move.

What Should You Accomplish on the Way to and from the Apartment?

Most consultants see their job on the way to the apartments as taking the scenic route and taking the customer on a tour. If you look in the dictionary, you will see that the definition of the word "tour" does not at all describe the intentions of a leasing consultant. Webster's says a tour is "a brief trip to or through a place for the purpose of seeing it." We even sometimes say to the customer: "I'll show you an apartment." I have even seen properties with signs that say: "I'm out showing an apartment and will be right back." Is your purpose really to tour (show) the property so they can see it, or are you there to lease the apartment?

I believe you should create a buying mood on the way to the apartment and turn a looker into a lessee with the New Resident Packet. On the way to the apartment, it is YOUR property and amenities; however, on the way back, it is THEIRS! If you make your property presentation on the way back from the apartment, not only is it more personal to them, but you also have the entire amenity package to use as a closing tool.

Understand Customers' Personal Requirements

How often have you had someone come in and ask for a big living room? Why do they ask? They have large living room furniture. Someone else might ask for a large closet in the bedroom because they already own closet space savers. You must take into consideration their personal belongings. I like to ask these questions:

1. "Do you have any specific furniture requirements I need to be aware of, such as entertainment centers, king-size

water beds, or any other oversized or unusual items we need to make sure we have room for?"

This may assist you in helping them select a specific floor plan, level, or location in the community that may be better suited to their needs.

2. "What color themes or combinations are you using to decorate your home?"

This allows you to consider which carpet colors and wallpaper designs will blend better with their decor. The more someone is concerned about these things, the longer they are likely to stay.

People often have distinct feelings about living on a certain floor, near or away from amenities, close to parking, or even close to the office. Take the time initially to find out about any such requirements.

Brag Points

What do they own that they have a great sense of pride in? If they own a prize piece of equipment, such as their grandmother's antique hutch or a beer bottle collection, these items are great for conversation. Everyone's favorite subject is themselves and the things they love.

Qualify the Customer's Decision Process for Finding a New Home

Customers' buying habits have changed. They used to give notice and then go look for an apartment. Today, they look for an apartment and then give notice. The result is a large portion of what I call the "future" future residents. Not only are they looking in advance, but they also are looking at more communities because there is more competition. Discuss with your customers their plan for finding the right apartment. Here is a series of questions that can be used:

"How many days have you been looking for an apartment?"

"How many apartments did you see each day (average)?" If you multiply the days you looked by the number of apartments you saw each day, we know you have looked at ____ apartments.

"How many more days do you plan to look? If you multiply the additional days you plan to look by the average apartments you look at per day and add what you have already looked for, we know you plan to look at ____ apartments."

The answers to these questions will amaze both you and your customer. These questions will most likely make the customer decide how many apartments they actually plan to look at. You are not asking them to decide, only to decide when they plan to decide.

I have found that customers are usually amazed at how many apartments they have looked at. This may help them to seriously consider making a decision today. No matter how long it is before they need the apartment, if they have seen what is available in the market, and your community is the best, then why keep looking?

It's important to let customers believe they are in control of the situation. It is just as important that customers perceive that your efforts will help them to reach their goals. The more separate your agenda appears from theirs, the less cooperation you will get from them. Your role should be that of an advisor. If you can help them put together an effective plan to find the right apartment, you will have done them a tremendous service.

The Future Resident Club

Ask your customers if they would like to become members of your Future Resident Club. This program may help them stop their search and decide today even if you don't have a specific apartment. As a member of the "Future Resident Club," they will be enrolled in a special program designed for people who know this is the community where they would like to live. They need to fill out a future resident application form and pay an enrollment fee (including the application fee and some deposit). Once their application is approved, they will take a preferred status on the waiting list and receive your newsletter and invitations to social activities. Some communities also give future residents access to the amenities in the community. This program will help your customers find an apartment without looking for 90 days at 30 different apartment communities.

Today, you have to be very clever and work within the customers' agenda. If they are looking so far in advance, you should have a way they can make a decision far in advance. As much as 32% of today's traffic in test areas all across the country is looking more than 45 days in advance. The Future Resident Club may be the answer to increasing your closing percentages.

DEMONSTRATIONS
By Douglas D. Chasick, CPM®, RAM®

Are you satisfied with your sales results? Or are you still looking for the secret potion for making powerful presentations, the charm that will allow you to hypnotize every prospect into signing a lease without you lifting a finger? The bad news is that there simply are no magical formulas or potions—there are no shortcuts. The good news is that by following these 12 simple steps, you will definitely increase your selling effectiveness.

1. ATTITUDE IS EVERYTHING: Study after study reveals that "techniques" account for only 20% of the success achieved by professional salespeople (that's us!); 80% of their success is due to their attitude. And, although a positive mental attitude is important, it's not everything; the most successful people have an attitude of achievement. They have clearly defined, achievable written goals, an action plan to achieve their goals, and a commitment to "make it." That's the attitude common to all winners.

2. ESTABLISH A RAPPORT WITH YOUR PROSPECT: Stop rushing into your sales presentation the moment you are sitting face to face with your prospect. Just asking their name and how they heard about your community does not qualify as establishing a rapport. Find out a little about them: Notice how they're dressed, what kind of jewelry they wear, what kind of car they drive. Ask where they work, what they do for a living, what they like to do for fun. Find some "common ground" and use it in customizing your presentation.

3. LISTEN, LISTEN, LISTEN: What most people call listening is really them not talking while they figure out the next brilliant thing they're going to say. The fact that the other person is talking is merely a coincidence. That's not listening. The more your prospect talks, the more engaged they are in the selling process. So talk less, listen more, and increase your sales.

4. BE AWARE OF HOW YOU LOOK AND SOUND TO THE PROSPECT: When was the last time you tape recorded your presentation and listened to the tone and volume of your voice, the speed at which you talk, and the number of distractions that you let escape from your mouth? Do you always say "uh" when you pause, or do you repeat certain words or phrases a lot? When was the last time you videotaped your presentation and watched the way you look while making your presentation? Do you have any gestures that need to be eliminated, like playing with your pen, your jewelry, your clothing, or your glasses? If you don't have access to a video camera, make more sales and buy your own. In the meantime, practice in front of a full-length mirror.

5. DESCRIBE THE BENEFITS OF YOUR COMMUNITY AS THE SOLUTION TO THE PROSPECT'S PROBLEM: What is the prospect's problem? Why did they get up, get dressed and drive to your community today, and walk into your office and ask about an apartment? It might be that the prospect is unhappy with their current living conditions. Probably, but what exactly is their problem? You'll find out if you establish a rapport and listen, listen, listen. We all know that selling features is a waste of time, so we switched to selling benefits. What about selling solutions? If your prospect has a problem with

closet space, maybe your closets are the solution. Or if their current apartment is noisy or dark, you might have the perfect quiet, sunny new home for them. Find out what their problem is and solve it for them.

6. ALWAYS BE CLOSING: Studies show that, on average, you must ask for the order seven times. That means you'll close some on the second try and some on the twelfth. How many times do you ask for the order? If it's not at least seven, you now know why you don't close as many sales as you'd like to.

7. FOLLOW THE S.S.T.T.P. FORMULA FOR EFFECTIVE PRESENTATIONS: That's Short, Sweet and To The Point! The most successful salespeople choose EVERY WORD they use very carefully. Use big, beautiful, descriptive, engaging words and phrases and body language that cause your prospect to visualize their wonderful, new, hassle-free life in their new, gorgeous apartment home. BE enthusiastic, BE excited, go beyond closing and into enrollment. (That's where your prospects lose control and catch your enthusiasm.) If you're a real pro, the amount of time you spend creating and practicing your presentation will far exceed the actual length of your presentation.

8. HAVE SPECIFIC WRITTEN GOALS FOR EACH DAY: At the beginning of each week, make a written commitment of how many presentations you will give and how many leases you will sign. Each day, score yourself and adjust the following day's goals accordingly. If your goals aren't measurable and aren't written down, they're not goals. Yes, I hear your question: "But what if we don't get enough traffic that day for me to meet my presentation

goal?" How about calling your be-backs, old traffic cards, current residents for referrals, your merchant contacts for referrals or the "roommates wanted" section of your newspaper? Get them down to see your property, and get them your waiting list for when their current lease expires.

9. REVIEW AND EVALUATE EVERY PRESENTATION: After each presentation, whether or not you signed a lease, take a few minutes to review your presentation and make written notes about what worked and what didn't work. We're all great at realizing what we should have done, so MAKE NOTES. That way you'll remember to do what you should have done when it counts—during the presentation. Keep a small spiral notebook with you, or start a special section in your organizer. And don't focus only on what didn't work. Although it's important to analyze and correct the areas of your presentation that didn't work, it's equally important to look at what did work, and why it worked. You can then repeat your success—it's the difference between being successful because of yourself and being successful in spite of yourself.

10. YOU ARE THE PRODUCT—ARE *YOU* RENT-READY? Before you sell anything, you've got to sell yourself. Are you a "10," or do you need to call the turnkey company? Are your shoes shined, heels with tips, no runs, clothes clean and pressed, fingernails and hair clean and well groomed? Ladies, how's your makeup and jewelry? Are you dressed for success or decked out for a night on the town? Gentlemen, do you need to reapply the razor around 2:00 p.m.? Of course, there's no smoking or eating in the office, and you always rise to greet your visitors, right?

11. MANAGE YOUR PERSONAL GROWTH: Successful selling involves the effective use of words to paint pictures and establish trust and confidence. If you want to build your muscles, you lift weights; the best way to build your word muscles is to read. Fiction, nonfiction, and magazine articles can all inspire you and help you build your vocabulary. And speaking of nonfiction and magazines, please don't limit yourself strictly to apartment management related publications. Read about marketing and selling in general, and other businesses such as retailing, hospitality, and food service. Read a few books about writing advertising and direct mail copy. Always read.

12. THIS IS FUN, SO ACT LIKE IT! Life is too short to spend eight hours a day being miserable. Selling is a game and it's fun. You get to solve people's housing problems by leasing them an apartment in your community. If that doesn't genuinely turn you on each day, you're in the wrong business. Need a lift in the morning to remind you? Forget the coffee, watch "The Three Stooges" every morning at 6:00 a.m. on WTBS, the Atlanta SuperStation. (Yes, I think they were in the apartment business.)

These 12 steps are proven methods for improving the effectiveness of your presentations. The fact that these are not new, revolutionary techniques doesn't reduce their effectiveness: If you do these things, they will work for you.

Remember how crucial it is during your presentation to ask questions and listen to the answers. You don't need to impress your prospect with the fact that you've memorized 1,001 features or benefits about your community, If you ask the right questions, you only need to include five or 10 benefits in your presentation to write the lease—anymore would be overkill.

SELLING TOOLS

The proper use of tools can create a more professional atmosphere, make your presentations more effective, and your job easier. Two of the most important tools are a product knowledge notebook and a competition notebook.

Product Knowledge Notebook

This is the encyclopedia of your property. It is a reference book and a presentation tool and, as such, should contain only top-quality, original copies of materials. These materials include:

- Site plan
- Floorplans for each unit style
- Map of the immediate neighborhood
- List of all rental rates
- List of all currently available and on-notice apartments
- List of neighborhood services and amenities
- Copies of all lease package forms, including the lease, rules and regulations, addendums, etc.
- Copy of the current comparable shop form
- List and description of all amenities
- Any other information that assists in the sales process

Competition Notebook

This is a tool to use when your prospect tells you they "want to look around." A current competition notebook allows you to assist the prospect by allowing them to look around in the comfort of your office. If you have established a rapport with your prospect, and have effectively determined their needs, you can use the competition notebook to show the prospect which of your competitors will best meet their needs, IN ADDITION TO YOUR PROPERTY, and assist them in their selection process. The competition notebook should contain, for each property:

- Site plan
- Floorplans for each unit style
- List of amenities
- Current rental rates and specials
- Rules and regulations
- Color photographs

DEMONSTRATING...THE ART OF IT ALL!
By Nicki Joy, MIRM®, SHMS®

Where the Money Is

Many years ago, it was said that the great bank robber Willie Sutton was questioned by the police about his unscrupulous escapades. Story has it that the police captain himself was overwhelmed at Willie's boldness, as Willie would take chances robbing establishments with well-publicized and sophisticated security systems. "Why, why do you rob banks, Willie?" asked the captain. "It's quite simple," replied Willie, "I rob banks 'cause that's where the money is."

Whenever I think of that story, I cannot help but think where the money is in our business...in the rental industry, that is. And though there may be conflicting opinions on what brings in the moola, I know that demonstrating your model, the vacancy, and the lifestyle to the prospect with punch, power, and pizazz will surely enhance your chances of bringing in the sale.

The word *demonstration* has several meanings that are applicable to the art of renting apartment homes.

Definition #1: Demonstration means the act, process, or means of making something evident, or proving.

Definition #2: Demonstration means a showing of how something works or is used.

I know, as I am sure you do, that there is a big difference in the final analysis between *showing* and *selling* and that when we talk about demonstrating, we are talking about far more than pointing out or pointing to or simply walking with.

In many cases, the act of demonstrating is underestimated in terms of its importance in making a rental sale. Sometimes the demonstration step in the rental process is "thrown in" as a routine exercise that is done purely because management insists on it. Often it is poorly executed and only serves to waste valuable time and do more damage than good.

I don't know about you, but I find that if I am told a sensible reason to do something, I am much more likely to do it. So here goes. Here is not one reason to demonstrate—but many—and they apply to your demonstration of the lifestyle amenities your community has to offer as well as to the model or the vacancy.

It pays to demonstrate because:

1. A demonstration provides an opportunity for you to build more rapport with the prospect away from the potentially imposing confines of the business or leasing office.

2. A demonstration enables you to see the prospect's reaction and make a judgment as to their interest level.

3. A demonstration generates an opportunity for you to engage in more personalization. "Mr. Smith, I believe this second bedroom would serve very nicely as your office, don't you agree?" or "Mrs. Green, can you just picture Jimmy on those swings and playing in that tot lot with all the friends he'll have here?"

4. A demonstration will make it easier for you to point out the unique features you have in your apartment homes and in your community. Remember, hearing combined with seeing-WOW!

5. A demonstration will give you the chance to build value that will help you, as well as the prospect, justify costs.

But remember two important things here.

   a. The Law of Perception says that a consumer's (in this case your prospect's) decision to buy what you are selling is based on their *perception* of value rather than actual value. So, here is where showmanship, the theatrics of selling, comes into play. Here is where we see that *showing* what you have to show indeed involves more than pointing it out.

b. Value, like beauty, is in the eyes of the beholder. However, all renters must be able to justify the choices they make. The primary way they do that is to relate the cost to the benefits they believe they will get in exchange for the price they must pay. You have a big hand in their value perception!

6. A demonstration provides you with the chance to talk to them and condition them for a positive experience. This conditioning is called predisposition, and it can serve to prime the prospect to see the good.

7. A demonstration enables you to help the prospect mentally move into the apartment home. There is an old saying that before one rents an apartment home, one must move into that apartment home. They have to see themselves living there before they take it. You can encourage them to think in those terms by saying: "Miss Davis, can't you just imagine entertaining in this living room?" or "If you were decorating this bedroom, would you prefer the bed on this wall, or that wall?"

8. A demonstration helps you raise their imagination level. This is especially true if you are demonstrating a vacant or model. You can help them see how space can be used. Also, when showing a vacant (which can be so depressing), your verbiage and picture-painting—two aspects of a powerhouse demonstration—can help turn an uninspiring, empty apartment into a potentially warm and inviting home. "This room is great, notice the view.

Just think. While sitting on the couch, at your dining room table, or at that corner desk, you still get a great view of the sunsets."

9. A demonstration enables you to handle questions and objections when you have time to do it right. Often, questions and objections surface in the prospect's mind after the fact, when it is too late or inappropriate for you to handle them convincingly or adequately. During the demonstration, you have time to learn what is on their mind. If you do not know what they are thinking about, you cannot rent them an apartment.

10. A demonstration gives you a way to create sustained involvement. Yes, it is true, many rental decisions are not made during the first visit. And deposits have to be returned by management to consumers who have had a change of heart. They key issue is that the good feelings, the right feelings that they had when viewing your homes and your community, must be sustained once they leave . . . and remain until they move in (and naturally for resident retention after they move in, too).

Chance Favors the Mind That Is Prepared

I love that axiom, and boy is it true! Yes, the likelihood of things going right for you, demonstration-wise, that is (as well as in life in general), depends on your ability to prepare. Many times, leasing agents who have been in the business awhile say that you prepare as the experience happens to you. Another saying holds true here: "Experience may be the best teacher, but the tuition is so darn high." You do not need experience to finally hit on what steps must be taken to do the job effectively. There are some important preparation rules to follow that will definitely improve your chances to rent, rent, rent!

Step One: Assess everything that you really have to demonstrate. Don't forget that over 50% of the value of living in an apartment community usually lies outside of the "unit" square footage. Therefore, a powerhouse demonstration includes the following:

Lifestyle amenities and features—in other words, you must demonstrate the things that you offer that make for an easy, comfortable, fun, refreshing, convenient lifestyle. Such things as your swimming pool, spa, exercise equipment, bike paths, tennis courts, party room, double-load washers in the laundry room, easy-access mail boxes, quick customer service response forms, great location, proximity to public transportation, routine pest control, easy access to wonderful area stores, lively neighbors, plentiful parking, great school district, community planned events, etc., must all be elaborated on as part of your presentation *if applicable.*

The apartment home itself—in other words, you must demonstrate the liveability of the layout of the apartment home, its versatility, the useable space, and the features included as well as any features that may be available at an additional cost.

Step Two: Gather this information in an organized fashion and then develop a system for logging the information for easy updating. This is critical. I have always suggested using a 3" x 5" or, better yet, a 5" x 8" card catalog to give easy access to the information when needed and a means to update information easily and quickly.

Get a catalog with an alphabetized index system, and begin. First, collect information from other leasing agents, property managers, residents, the interior merchandiser who decorated your model (if there is one), the architect who designed your building (if possible), the chamber of commerce, area merchants, and, if you are in a new lease-up mode, the construction supervisor.

Make a list of questions that they answer that would help you help your prospects. Here are just some examples of questions to ask a few of these people:

Ask the Interior Merchandiser:

▶ Why did you decorate this apartment using this type of furniture?

▶ Can you give me some other ideas where one could place the couch in this living room?

▶ Why did you use vertical blinds here instead of curtains?

▶ This drop-leaf table in the kitchen surely saves space. Where would someone buy a table like that?

▶ Give me an idea of some colors that go with our carpet color selection.

▶ When I bring a prospect through this apartment home, what do you think I should point out to help them to mentally move in here?

Ask the Architect:

▶ Why were the buildings designed with one entryway for six apartments?

▶ How would you describe this type of architecture?

▶ How will the building materials used hold up over time?

▶ What makes this community so aesthetically pleasing from the construction and design standpoint?

▶ Is there anything unique that our building has that others don't?

Ask the Residents:

(Naturally you do this without infringing on their time and when it is convenient and appropriate.)

▶ What do you like best about living here?

▶ When you tell others about us, what do you say?

- What attracted you to our community from the start?
- What makes us different from or better than other apartment communities you have seen in the area?
- What are some of your favorite restaurants in the area?
- What are some of your favorite stores in the area?
- Do you use the libraries in the area, and are they good?
- How is the public transportation?
- Is living here easy? Why?

Ask Your Property Managers and Other Staff Members:

- What makes this community special from your perspective?
- What do we have over the competition, and who is the competition?
- What attracts most people to our community?
- What would people like to have here that we don't have?
- What are our strengths?
- What are our weaknesses?
- Do realtors ever refer people to us?
- Are resident referrals strong?

When you get information of this sort, think in terms of filing it in your catalog. For example, library information would fall under "L." Naturally, you would not be talking about libraries with every prospect who walks through the door, but if you have that information handy (names of local libraries and hours of operation) for the person who *is* interested, you have quickly elevated yourself to the position of community expert—exactly where you want to be! Under "D" in your catalog, you can have a listing of doctors, dentists, and day-care centers in the area. Although you must not recommend one over the other, it is good service to have this list to help residents search for the right doctor or day-care center for them. Under "B" you could have banks, bakeries, Boy Scout troops, and boutiques. Under "S" you could have specialty shops, square feet of the apartment homes, stereo repair shops, shoe stores, and storage facilities.

I hope you get the idea. The plan is to create a file that enables you to have at your fingertips anything anyone would ever want to know about living in your community. You will use this information selectively; however, to have it accessible helps in creating the image that you are indeed a prepared professional and community expert.

After awhile, you will learn a great deal of this information, but having this file handy will help you avoid the possibility of ever having to say, "I don't know." Since things change so quickly, set aside some time every three months to update or make new entries.

Step Three: Make a list of all the features you know about (or have learned about) that your community has going for it. Remember to include features inside the apartment homes as well as outside.

Once you have this list, you must clearly bring to mind an important theory of selling:

People do not buy what it is—they only buy what it does for them.

That's right, and it's been said a million times. Tommy Hopkins, who has trained millions of salespeople, says that every year millions of Americans go to hardware stores all across this country to buy 1/4-inch drills, but no one really wants a 1/4-inch drill—what they want is a 1/4-inch hole!

Now you must take the time to convert these features into benefits for the buyer. Work room by room and then amenity by amenity. Some examples of how to do this follow.

Notice that it pays to think emotionally when converting those features into benefits. Remember that an apartment is rented emotionally. Emotion...Emotion...Emotion. Of course, nothing creates more emotion than a personalized approach to renting. Therefore, when converting the information you have collected above into your verbal presentation, think in terms of saying such things as:

"Miss Johnson, since you said you love to cook, I know you will enjoy preparing dinners in this wonderful, fully equipped kitchen. This microwave will surely come in handy for those spontaneous dinners when you want to defrost a roast quickly."

"Mr. Carr, this hall space has another use that perhaps you may not have considered. It is great space for a mini-office, computer, and desk area. One of our other residents, John Scott, needed an in-home office, like you, and finds this space perfect."

Personalizing the benefits is critical. Move that prospect into the home and put them in the picture. Practice this. Believe it or not, practice does help.

Of course, each prospect is unique. To effectively personalize any demonstration, you must know about your prospects, and I mean *know* about them. That is why when following the renting path, qualifying precedes demonstrating. You cannot, I repeat, cannot provide a proper demonstration unless you know about your prospect. To create the emotion needed to create the renting action you want, you must know what they get emotional about. Probing is critical to good renting. Probing and asking are what selling is all about. Only through effective and thorough inquiry will you be able to learn what it is that your prospects want and need. Only through effective

FEATURE

Kitchen

FEATURE	BENEFIT
Kitchen	
Pass-thru to dining area	Easy serving, can stay in dinner conversation even when working in kitchen, adds light and feeling of space to room, attractive
Microwave	Quick meal preparation, great popcorn, instant hot coffee, guilt remover (can work all day and have a hot meal at night)
No-wax flooring	Fast clean-up, time saver, nice appearance
Living room	
Large picture window	Provides pleasing view, brings outside in, makes room light and bright, creates a feeling of great space
Wall-to-wall carpeting	Creates a feeling of warmth, coziness, softness underfoot, great sound insulator, a big boost to creating a decorated environment
Bedroom	
Long uninterrupted wall	Great space for a king-size bed or two doubles
Large walk-in closet	Great storage, crush-free clothes, neat room, time saver, easy organization

probing, asking, and qualifying will you be ready to turn that apartment into their home. Only through effective probing will you help them feel what living here will be like.

It's Not What You Say, it's How You Say it

The next step in preparing for a great demonstration involves planning even more precisely what you want to say. Most leasing agents know what they want to say, but have trouble figuring out how to say it.

Tips

Here are some of my favorite tips that I have been giving out for years:

▶ Watch what you say. Remember, we never use the words unit, tenant, project, complex, bumped, prepped, etc. We are selling apartment homes, we have neighbors, we are a community or a neighborhood.

▶ Use conceptual language rather than numbers. Avoid saying: "This terrace is 10 by 10 feet" and think in terms of saying: "Can't you imagine sitting out here sipping a cool ice tea and watching the trees swaying." (I know it sounds corny to you, but corny got corny because it worked so well for so darn long. It works!)

▶ Avoid saying "There is Jefferson mall nearby with 126 stores." Instead, say: "Jefferson mall is a hop away and you'll find everything you need under a single roof—talk about easy."

▶ Use words that get the attention of today's renter: you, happy, new, family, love, easy, convenient, comfortable, free, save, proven, fun.

▶ Use words that are interesting: enchanting, enjoyable, exciting, dramatic, inviting, warm, gracious, cozy.

▶ Use their words too. Remember, things get lost in translation, even if using the same language. If they want "roomy," use the word roomy (not spacious or large). If they want a management team that is "dependable," use the word dependable instead of the word "responsive" that you normally use. Yes, this is a listening and a thinking business.

▶ Don't fall into the fast-paced monologue trap. Many salespeople feel that during the demonstration they have to keep talking. Silence is golden and gives prospects a chance to digest and absorb what you have said. Furthermore, it gives them an opportunity to provide you with feedback and input, and that is what it's all about. Remember, they do not necessarily rent the apartment home that is best or right for them, they rent the apartment home they become most involved in.

A Tool Is Only a Tool if it Is Used and Used Properly

During the demonstration portion of your presentation, do not forget to supplement your words with as many pictures or graphics as possible. Remember, hearing is the least effective sense for memory. Use those tools.

Dr. Forbes Ley, a noted educator, stated that today we need tools to enhance any presentation. Why? Well, consider the following reasons:

▶ People today do not rent or buy on unsupported facts or claims.

▶ People need a great deal of emotional, yet some logical, evidence to rent.

▶ People love exhibits and documentation—they are logical. But remember, stories and testimonials can be emotional evidence.

❱ A letter or note from a happy resident says so much more to the prospect than your words ever will.

❱ People tend to spend more time with salespeople who use visual tools to supplement their verbal message.

❱ People who are encouraged to picture or visualize something get more involved because picturing something serves as an experience, and when you experience something, you believe it.

❱ We live in a TV age and, without pictures we, sadly enough, get bored. And we want to avoid that!

By visuals, I mean those lifestyle photos you have (as long as they are current, dusted, and exciting). Or use your community map or topo table, use letters from happy residents, articles on the advantages of renting over buying, and photographs you took of the interiors of some of your residents' homes.

Sensitivity to Key Issues

In every demonstration, show sensitivity to privacy. Also, though you can never guarantee safety, you must be sensitive to it. Talk about neighborhood watch programs, caring neighbors, the family environment, information that management passes out on safety tips for happy apartment living.

And speaking of safety, keep in mind your safety while engaging in a demonstration of an apartment or the grounds. Understand that it is your job to demonstrate, but it is also your job to use common sense.

❱ Wear a contact beeper.

❱ Inform other staff where you will be.

❱ Arrange in advance to have someone else (even a customer service technician) accompany you.

❱ Only show apartments during regular business hours.

▶ If you are in a particularly difficult area, ask for the prospect's drivers license, even if only to copy down and file the name and address.

▶ Go with your gut instincts.

Great Pointers for Great Demonstrations

1. Be proactive, not reactive. Understand that you do not ask them if they want to see the model, the vacant, or the lifestyle amenities. IT IS YOUR JOB TO DEMON-STRATE THOSE THINGS.

   So take the lead. "Mr. and Mrs. Jones, I know your time is valuable. If you will follow me, I will point out some of the things that make our community such a great place to call home." You must take the initiative and lead the way.

2. While you are walking around with them, look at them, not at the rooms, etc. You already know what the rooms look like. Watch their reaction, make eye contact, listen to their comments.

3. Before opening the door to a model or a vacant, inform them that they should follow you. Tell them that you have planned a brief presentation to help them see the features of this apartment home, and that once you are through, you will then be glad to step back and give them all the solitary browsing time they need.

4. Plan your route to the model or vacant. Show them the mail area, laundry room (it'd better be lint-free), the flowers, edged mulch areas, the trees, the pool, all-purpose sport courts.

5. If something is of particular interest to them, point it out first. Consider returning to see it again later.

6. If they want to see the model alone, you must be firm. Policy does not permit that and that is that! If they have to wait a moment for you to finish up with another prospect, remind them that good things are worth waiting for and let them browse through your community photo album while briefly waiting.

7. Yes, cleanliness is next to Godliness. If it ain't clean, you can't show it. Conjuring up a pretty picture in their minds is more effective than having to sell a dirty, messy, or sloppily painted apartment home. Before you show anything, you have to know that it is "showable." In your vacants, it is helpful to have an easel with a printed statement indicating that this particular apartment home was made ready for VIP viewing by (name of person(s)) responsible for clean up and repair. Affixing a big bright bow to the display works well too. Accountability breeds better work.

8. Remember, a model has to look like a model and a vacant has to look clean, smell good, and be "move-in" ready.

9. Lights on! The model should always have the lights on and the lights in the vacant should be turned on immediately upon entering. A lit home looks larger than an unlit home.

10. Highlight brand names, traffic flow, view, convenience features, new features, storage space, versatility, and comfort features.

11. Your job is not to point out rooms. I have often said that if they don't know the difference between the bathroom and the bedroom, you will have problems with these people beyond belief. Your job is to help them envision living here. "Mrs. Jones, can you picture your furnish-

ings in this great living room?" "Mr. Smith, this is that great second bedroom I told you about. It will be perfect for Timmy and that little nook will be great for all his toys." "Johanna (use first names only if they give permission), this bathroom is special for two reasons. First, we have a wonderful window that is perfect for providing great light, and second, our new double sinks will enable you and John both to get to work on time."

12. Be creative. To really get across the concept of large space, one creative agent I knew always conducted her demonstrations with a yardstick. I noted another agent taking Polaroid pictures of her prospects in the model.

13. Tap into as many senses as possible. If there is model music, it had better be the right music for your prospect profile. Offering a piece of candy from the jar in the model or the vacant creates a home-like atmosphere right from the start. Spraying the model, vacant, and, yes, even your office with one of the new scents geared to create positive feelings make good sense. Getting prospects to touch, however, is the key. It is a psychological principle that involvement is enhanced when touching takes place. Yes, they certainly are aware of this principle on the home-buying network. I mean, they practically beg you to try it out. They advise that the return policy is easy—so try it out if you are in doubt. Sure, they know that theory that if you get someone to touch something, chances are they will want to keep it. That's right. So get your prospects to open the cabinets, slide open that terrace door, touch the modern, ventilated closet shelving, and open the drawers.

14. At the pool, help paint the picture of relaxing here or, if they are the type, exercising here. At the club house,

talk about activities that take place here. Discuss again (remember, you already learned this during qualifying) what they like to do in their spare time. While walking around, discuss the ground crew and what they do to keep those flowers fresh and the trees looking so good. I am sure you get the idea by now!

15. At the vacant you must really put your theatrical skills into high gear. Here, you talk about view, neighbors, access to amenities, etc. You must work hard to help that mental move-in process and give them lots and lots of ideas how to use the space. Remind them that an undecorated apartment looks so much smaller than a decorated one. Get their input, ideas, suggestions, and feelings.

16. Always check to see what is on their mind. But a word of warning: Never say, "What do you think about this apartment home?" No, thinking hurts and thinking is logical. Remember, people rent emotionally (even those who think they do it logically). So, instead of asking what they think, consider asking, "How do you feel in this apartment home?" Ah yes, feeling is emotional—get the point?

Service and Showmanship

I have often said that there are two things that rent apartments: service and a sense of showmanship. Service is critical, and it does begin with you! In fact, service is a marketing function, believe it or not. As far as showmanship is concerned, we are all actors and actresses. And actors and actresses can all read the lines of the script when they audition for the part and try to win over the producer and directors. What gets one actor the part over another, however, is simply the ability of one actor to deliver those lines in a more exciting, more meaningful manner.

I do not believe in script selling *per se*. However, if you hear someone say something that you can use during your demonstration, and if you don't write it down and work it into your own "play," you are foolish. After awhile, a personal script of sorts does develop. You tend to use certain words and phrases and even your gestures become routine.

True showmanship in this business means giving what you usually do a new spin from time to time. Use new words, incorporate new material, tell newer stories, get fresher props. To be an effective demonstrator, you must understand that you are putting on a show. Your goal is to get prospects so involved in you and your offering that they just have to live here! Yes, the demonstration is critical to converting prospects to renters. And it is in your hands!

THINK SAFETY
By Shirley Robertson, RAM®, ARM®, CPM®

The leasing and sales occupation carries a certain amount of risk relating to office and personal safety. Three elements must exist for an incident to happen: desire, ability, and opportunity. The leasing consultant has the most control of the latter, by minimizing isolated environments. The practice and pattern of touring the community and previewing available/model apartments should always be undertaken with personal safety in mind.

Community Safety Program

A safety program for the entire on-site management team should be in place, with intermittent refreshers scheduled frequently. The program should consist of several components. One component must address the necessary proactive skills and techniques to be used when alone in the leasing center. Another component should consist of the leasing person being able to identify all help and assistance available from other team members outside of the leasing center, and the equipment needed to ensure a safe workplace. The last component should consist of guidance in assessing the situation and knowing when to call the police. This guidance is best delivered by local law enforcement agencies during a safety team meeting. A separate seminar can also be given on personal self-defense techniques. Always get the facets of a personnel safety program approved by the management company/ owner and a crime prevention professional.

Before Leaving the Leasing Center

Always think in terms of safety and never indicate that you are alone in the leasing center. Be assertive and proactive rather than timid and scared. TRUST YOUR GUT INSTINCTS! Never fail to identify your designation. This can be accomplished by leaving a note on a team member's phone, telling others in the center as you're leaving, or calling the answering service. Give your departure time, the future resident's name, and an estimated time of return. Do this in the presence of the future resident. Notify a maintenance team member to accompany you or to meet you if you feel threatened or unsafe. Pagers and walkie-talkies can be used for this purpose.

Some management companies/owners make it a company policy to ask each future resident to leave a photo I.D. in the leasing center before taking a community tour. If you sense danger before leaving the leasing center, volunteer to reschedule an appointment, notify a team member for assistance, or call the police, whichever you deem the situation requires. Document all of this information on the welcome card/log.

Always bear in mind Fair Housing laws as you exercise various safety techniques. Be sure to use each safety technique across the board regardless of race, sex, and other federal, state, and locally protected classifications. Also, consider that asking for a photo I.D. before taking tours may indirectly imply a safety problem at your community. Think of all the repercussions, but keep personal safety foremost in your mind.

Get in the habit of letting the future resident lead as you follow, rather than the other way around, by allowing them to exit the leasing center first. Continue to gesture them ahead of you during the preview of the available apartment/model.

Community Tour

Refrain from riding in anyone else's car when touring the community and previewing the available apartment/model. Instead, use a golf cart if available or have the future resident follow your car. Using golf carts allows for a great deal of interaction while touring and is highly visible. In small communities, foot tours are often preferable. This is an excellent opportunity to continue to allow the future resident to take the lead.

Available Apartment Model Preview

Leaving the entrance door ajar, throwing the dead bolt lock, or using door stops are preventive measures that discourage isolation and allow for a quicker exit from the apartment home if necessary. Of all of these safety measures, the door stop gives the best advantage. When the apartment home is declared "rent-ready," a door stop is left by the entrance door. When you enter the available apartment/model, slide the door stop under the door while explaining that it is a neat little move-in gift for them. It will hold the door open while moving furniture. Using the door stop prevents the door and their furniture from getting scratched during move-in and is great for inclement weather days while carrying laundry or groceries. Most future residents respond positively to the thoughtfulness. If the future resident had something else in mind, the door stop makes it boldly clear that you will not be in an isolated situation.

Learn the safe habit of gesturing future residents ahead of you when entering the apartment home and when entering rooms. Memorize each floorplan layout so that you can easily place yourself between future residents and the entrance door. Invite future residents to inspect closets, cabinets, and balconies rather then you demonstrating them. This can be accomplished without compromising the quality of a planned tour. As a matter of fact, in apartment previews where the future resident is given the opportunity of a "high touch" experience, more rentals result. It is possible to conduct a successful preview and to practice safety techniques.

Always trust your "gut" feeling of danger. To walk or run from any situation is good advice, but the best advice is not to put yourself in a situation that could harm you. Get all of the education that you can regarding personal safety, follow all company safety policies and guidelines, and act with authority and assertiveness.

Consistency

It warrants stating again that you must implement all safety policies and guidelines uniformly across the board unless you have no other choice. Conduct all tours and previews in compliance with all federal, state, and local Fair Housing laws, and the Americans With Disabilities Law (Title III).

What Impacted Me Most about this Chapter:

_____
_____
_____
_____
_____
_____
_____
_____
_____
_____

What I Need to Work on:

_____
_____
_____
_____
_____
_____
_____
_____
_____
_____

My Strengths Discovered in this Chapter:

_____
_____
_____
_____
_____
_____
_____
_____
_____

CHAPTER 5

The Close-
A Win-Win
for Everyone

"Closing the Sale - A High Touch Invitation to Lease" - *Sadovsky*

"Overcoming Objections" - *Nevitt*

"Closing"- *Cardella*

"Closing Lines That Work" -*All*

CLOSING THE SALE—A HIGH TOUCH INVITATION TO LEASE
By Anne Sadovsky, RAM®

Does this sound remotely familiar? You finish showing the apartment, the client is noncommittal, you don't want to appear pushy, so with a trembling soft voice you say, "Here's my card, we're here every day from nine to six, think it over and let me know."

That Is Not Closing!

To excel in this vital part of the leasing process, you need to review and understand all the steps:
▶ WELCOMING/GREETING/MEETING
▶ GATHERING INFORMATION TO PREQUALIFY
▶ PRESENTING THE PRODUCT/SHOW AND TELL
▶ CLOSING/INVITING THEM TO LEASE
▶ FOLLOW-UP CALLS

The first step is critical in setting the tone for the entire transaction. Always acknowledge the arrival of the client, and greet them warmly. Never ignore them because you are busy. A smile and gesture toward a seating area and refreshment table help keep them waiting.

Qualifying at this point is NOT to find out if they can afford to live there. That attitude is a major turnoff! At this point, expressing sincere interest in their needs and desires helps establish a relationship that will last through the entire visit. Seek permission to ask a few questions and explain why. Try saying, "I want to help you find the perfect apartment home. Is it OK to ask you a few questions so I can find just the right one for you?" Be sure to be friendly, interested, and conversational. DO NOT INTERROGATE! Be thorough so that you can pinpoint special features and benefits that will interest the client. The following information is necessary to prevent wasting everyone's time.

What Specifically Do They Want?

Just knowing that they need a two-bedroom is not enough. Discuss amenities, color scheme, desired location and any special needs or requirements they may have.

When Exactly Do They Plan to Move into Their New Home?

Maybe they need it tomorrow or not for six months. This is important information. Be able to process applications quickly for those who are in immediate need, and keep records of those seeking apartment homes for the future. Follow up with them periodically.

How Many People Will Occupy the Apartment Home?

Remember, asking who will occupy is inappropriate at this point. Based on your written occupancy standards, your interest at this point is simply how many.

Do They Have a Pet?

And if so, what kind and what size when fully grown? Know your property's policies regarding size and type of pet you allow, and what deposits are required. If the pet is too large, or you do not allow pets, BE NICE! Pet lovers are sensitive. Help them find a place that will accommodate their pet requirements.

What Is Their Monthly Budget for Rent?

Assuming that you have put off the price question until now, a polite way to discuss it is by inquiring about their budget. Although many do not actually work with a budget, they probably will reply with what they hoped to pay. If it is less than the market rent on the size apartment desired, break the difference down to a daily amount. For example, they mention a budget of $550 and your two-bedrooms start at $580. That $30 difference is only $1 a day more! Point out all the wonderful amenities and services they will receive at your property for only $1 a day extra!

If you are able to meet their needs, a quality demonstration will help them make a decision. Don't say, "Would you like to see an apartment?" Instead say, "You really need to see the apartment to appreciate all I've told you, so let's go take a look." Know your property well and give a demonstration that will excite the client about living there.

Now the Clincher!

It IS your job to invite them to make a decision, to close the sale, to make closing remarks, to get a deposit! A quick study on how to close should remove all discomfort and reluctance. Remember that you have been thinking of closing all the way through from greeting to here. This helps keep closing from appearing an entirely separate part of what you've been doing. Try the following:

▶ *Begin Your Closing Remarks in the Apartment:* Some people wait until they return to the office. This makes the return tour awkward, and sometimes clients head straight to their car without voicing any objections they may have.

▶ *Summarize:* Say, for example, "Let's see, Fred, you wanted something in an earth tone, with a fireplace, that is available in three weeks, in the $700 price range and you agree that the washer/dryer connections are very important to you, so I think you'll agree that this is pretty much what you're looking for!"

▶ *Create Urgency:* "This is the only (or last) one available that meets your requirements." Or, "You know, another person also wants this particular apartment home, and of course whoever places the deposit first gets it." Both those statements should be true, of course, or you would feel really phony. But do use the truth to your advantage.

▶ *Tell Them They Are Wanted:* A simple, "We'd really love to have you," is sometimes all they need to hear.

▶ *Tell Them What it Takes to Make it Theirs:* "Fred, all I need now is your OK, an application and fee, and a deposit of only $200."

▶ *Know When to Shut Up:* After making your request for a decision, stop talking. A few moments of silence won't kill you, and is not a signal that you should sell harder. Let the client be the next one to talk.

What You Say When They Say:

"Yes"—All you have to say now is, "Great, you made the right decision. Let's go back to the office and spend a few minutes on the paperwork."

"No"—Reply with, "Would you mind sharing with me why you aren't interested in this apartment?" "I want to look around further," or "I want to think it over." Offer to show them a current market study to save them a trip. Ask what specifically they still need to think about, but don't put them on the spot. Try asking, "Are you happy with the floorplan?" "Is the location going to work?" "How about the price?" Getting them to voice their objections gives you an opportunity to overcome them and another chance to close.

If they choose to leave the community without giving you a decision, ask them not to sign a lease anywhere else and to see your apartment at least one more time before deciding. And if you are really good, remind them to compare other places they look at with yours, not just the floorplan or the price, but the way they are treated by the staff! Surveys indicate that the leasing consultant's personality and style has a big impact on the final decision. Suggesting a comparison makes them aware of the importance of a professional staff to serve their needs after taking occupancy. Because a large number of prospective residents do leave the first visit without making a decision, this last step is critical.

Follow-up Phone Calls

As addressed in this chapter on follow-up opportunities, it is critical that you contact the client within 24 hours. Invite them to return, remind them briefly of the special things about the property, and charm their socks off!

The significant difference in a salesperson and an order taker is the ability to close, so remember:

▶ Closing is not sending them out the door with an application! that is the biggest cop-out in use today.

▶ Closing is not handing them your card and asking them to let you know!

▶ Closing is not saying anything and hoping they say they'll take it! It is your job to ask.

Develop the skill of closing the sale, and you'll always be in demand. And you'll stand out in a crowd of mediocre consultants who are simply afraid to ask!

OVERCOMING OBJECTIONS: LEARN TO SEE THEM AS A POSITIVE SIGN
By Jennifer A. Nevitt, RAM®

Having finished the initial qualifying, you show a couple an apartment that you believe is exactly what they want. As you're walking across the living room, they hit you with what you dread most: an objection.

Definition: an objection is an obstacle that stands in the way and prevents a successful closing of the sale.

Most leasing professionals fear objections. But the most successful leasing professionals welcome them. They know that a client who is voicing an objection is a client who is actively considering saying "yes."

An objection tells you that the client is serious.

This does not mean that an objection should be taken lightly. It can kill a sale if not handled properly. Objections must be understood before they can be removed, eliminated, or overcome. The leasing professional must remember to view an objection as a buying signal and act accordingly.

An objection is an opportunity.

The Selling Process Revisited

Almost everybody in the selling business talks about the selling process as Greet, Qualify, Present, Close. These are valid points in the process, but the key word is "process." Selling is a series of steps, with variations possible within each step. If you're going to be involved in the process, you have to be aware that the potential for objections is part of every step.

The opportunity to overcome objections can arise at any point. When it does, most immature, inexperienced, or untrained leasing professionals take the objection personally. It hurts their feelings. They may turn on the client, excusing their own failure to close the sale by making a comment such as: "We just didn't see eye-to-eye."

It is your job as a leasing professional to see eye-to-eye, to build a rapport with your client, to be awake to the many messages your client is sending, verbally and nonverbally.

Your prime responsibility is to be an exceptional listener. You need to be so tuned in to a client's verbal and nonverbal communication that great understanding is built. Because you are so intently and actively attending to their words, their body language, and their moods, you will be able to recognize an objection when it arises. You will be able to see it as an exciting signal: It means the person is thinking about buying.

At that moment, you will have arrived at a critical part of the selling process, and how you handle it will determine the outcome.

See Objections for What They Are

▶ An objection is a positive buying signal. The client with an objection is thinking seriously about buying.
▶ A client without objections is not going to sign. That client is not interested enough to consider what is and isn't pleasing about the apartment.

Five Basic Techniques for Overcoming Objections

1. *Listen and be prepared.*

   A successful leasing agent makes a commitment to give undivided attention to each client. You cannot allow yourself to be distracted by a ringing telephone or by paperwork that is accumulating. You must refuse to allow such pressures to gnaw at you. You must convince yourself that when you are with the client, you are doing your most important work. Do not think of anything else. If you find that it is not enough to believe that each person has value and is worthy of your respect and attention, then think about the money. Keep in mind that each client has the potential to spend a large amount of money each year. It is your job to convince the qualified client to spend it with you.

2. *Convert the objection into a question and answer it.*

   We all tend to be lazy in communication. We also are all too human. It takes extra effort to control your own feelings and keep from jumping from the client's objection to "I really don't like this client." Instead, convert the objection into a question. For example, the client objects to the color of the taupe carpet, even though the carpet is in good shape. You ask: "What color is your furniture?" You find out that the client's furniture is mauve, gray, and lilac.

   You don't always have another color carpet available in an apartment across the hall. But you don't want to lose the sale. Whatever you do, do not make a statement, positive or negative. It will always be wrong. It will get you in trouble. Stick to questions.

   Do not agree with the objection, even if inwardly you think the carpet in question is a hideous shade of green and too tired to use as padding in a truck.

Do not assume that you know what is going on in a client's head. The objection that has been raised may or may not be a clear indication of what is really happening in the client's mind. To get a clearer understanding of the true objection, ask a question. In the case of the objection to the carpet, ask: "What color is your furniture?"

You find out that the client's furniture is mauve, gray, and lilac. You understand that what concerns the client is how that client's belongings will fit into the apartment and its color scheme. Knowing that the client likes everything else about the apartment, you ask what color the client's current carpet is. It is taupe. You realize that while the client had hoped to move from taupe to gray, the client has been managing with taupe. You have an opportunity to close on the sale now.

3. *Close on the objection.*

Here's what you might say to convert your client into a resident: "Well, client. As you can tell, this carpet is in very good condition. Since you have taupe now and your #1 need was to have a view of the lake, and this is the only apartment I have that overlooks the lake, don't you think that this taupe carpeting would work for you?" (Remember: stick to questions.)

To use a sports metaphor, this leaves the ball in the client's court. It takes the responsibility off you and puts it back on the client. The only way to do this is with a question.

The likely response from the client: "Yes, I guess so. Yes. I could live with that. And I do love the view of the lake."

Sale accomplished.

4. *Turn negatives into positives.*

Assume for a moment that the client says "no." At this point, your job is to turn any negatives into positives. You cannot argue with the client.

For example, the client objects to the location of the apartment because it does not have parking immediately adjacent to the front door. The client does not want to get wet running from the car to the door in the event that it rains and an umbrella is not on hand. You ask: "Don't you think that the advantage of not having traffic and parking lot noise and the slamming of car doors at 2 a.m. outweighs the occasional possible inconvenience of walking from your car to the door when it is raining?" It is likely that the client will respond, "I never thought of that."

5. *Objections are buying signals and should be acknowledged courteously.*

There is an apartment in your community that even the most experienced of your colleagues has not been able to lease. You have shown it five times in two weeks. You hate the antique gold appliances. You have decided that it would be easier to ignore the objection the next time it comes up, which undoubtedly will be the next time you show the apartment. You are going to ignore it. You are going to pretend that the objection was never raised.

Don't let yourself fall into this trap no matter how frustrated you are with a particular product, in this case, the apartment with the outdated appliances. Remember that the true leasing professional acknowledges all objections courteously, using the first four techniques.

If you don't, the clients will be appalled at your rudeness and confused because you didn't listen or help them through the process. All that most clients want is a sympathetic listener, someone with experience to lead them through what can be a difficult or unfamiliar process. It is your job to be that someone.

Objections Aren't Always What They Appear to Be

Overcoming objections is a little like playing chess. It's a mind game. You have to get inside the client's head and use what you find there to help the client say "yes."

Leasing an Apartment Is a Lot like Buying a New Car

You really want to buy a new car: a Honda Accord, red, tan interior. You are ready to buy, and you are out looking with money in hand for the down payment. At the fourth or fifth stop, you find a red Accord. You are excited. The sun is shining on its glossy red surface. You jump out of your old car and run over to the new one. Disappointment: it has a black interior, not tan.

Do you climb back into your old car and go away? Unlikely. Even though you have an objection, you were ready to buy. What do you do? Chances are, you start looking at the rest of the package: price, how many miles, the extras. You test drive the car. The longer you are in the car, the more you like it. The fact that the interior is black becomes less of a problem. The objection subsides.

To return to the multifamily housing industry, think about that difficult apartment with the antique gold appliances no one seems to want. How can you make the color of the appliances less important compared with the apartment as a whole?

Keep the clients in the apartment long enough to mentally place their furniture, walk out on the porch, and meet the neighbor across the hall. (That is, let them ride in that new car.) The objection to the appliances should subside. If you can get the clients to take a long enough test drive in a vehicle that is so close to right for them, they will buy. Of course, you have to ask them to buy. But that is another topic.

Strategies for Overcoming Objections

There are five basic strategies that can help you overcome objections:

1. *Make certain that your product is ready.*

    The first and most basic strategy is to make certain that the apartment is ready to be seen. Your product must be immaculate and in a condition that cannot embarrass you or force your clients to look for reasons not to rent.

    After initial qualifying has satisfied you that the clients are right for the apartment, take those clients on the tour. Listen and watch for objections. If they have no objections, they probably don't intend to take an extended test drive. And they don't intend to buy. Immediately look around. Have you missed something? Is it possible that they are so appalled by the condition of the apartment that all they want to do is leave?

    Walk your apartments every day. Make morning inspections, spruce up each apartment, and turn on the lights. Do this yourself so that you will know that the apartments are ready.

2. *Promote a self-confident sales presentation.*

    Know your product. Spend time in each apartment that you will be showing. Make sure the keys work. If a bulb is out, replace it. Know where everything is and what the benefits are of each apartment. Consider the wisdom of merchandising the apartments. (See more on merchandising in Chapter 8.)

3. *Know the objections.*

Identify obvious objections ahead of time. Before the clients mention them, bring them up openly. Acknowledge the objection when clients walk into the apartment. Then show them why it doesn't matter, and get their agreement that, indeed, it doesn't matter.

For example, there was an extremely nice apartment that had a lake view, but only if you walked out to the balcony. From inside, the first thing a client would see upon entering the apartment was not the lake but the unusually bright blue exterior wall of a neighboring building. The apartment stood empty for months, in spite of being shown repeatedly.

Even the experienced leasing professionals on staff were unable to close on that apartment. When they took a client in, they studiously avoided mentioning the all-too-obvious blue building that was the view from the entry. In an attempt to ignore the blue building, they also ignored the lake view, because they would not take the clients out to the balcony. By avoiding the obvious, the leasing professionals sent the unspoken message that something was wrong. When we as leasing professionals do that, clients sense that we are hiding something. Trust is damaged.

Here's how that apartment was sold, in one try, the leasing professional went to the apartment and studied it, assessing its best features, including the lake view from the balcony. She then half-closed the vertical blinds that led to the balcony, thus obscuring the vividness of the blue wall, but not hiding the light or air. When she brought the clients to the apartment, the first thing she asked was when they were at home. Finding that they were almost never home during the day and that they usually closed or half-closed the blinds for privacy in the evening, she walked them onto the balcony, revealing the blue wall. They loved the view of the lake and agreed that the blue wall was of little concern. At night, the blinds would be closed. When they were home during the day, they could easily adjust the blinds to reduce the impact of the blue wall without shutting out the light. The leasing professional closed on the sale, not by ignoring the objection, but by acknowledging and overcoming it.

4. *Concentrate.*

It is important that you keep in mind the desired end result of your efforts: obtaining a deposit. Keep your mind on the business at hand. If you don't, you will miss the hints and overlook the signals that will tell you what you need to know.

Successful selling requires intellectual stamina. It is not for the lazy or those who do best when following an unchanging recipe or step-by-step procedure. The challenge is to perform well consistently, month after month. To do that, you must be mentally prepared. When the client has given you sufficient buying signals and affirmations, ask for the deposit. Watch for the signals. For example:

My couch would look great in this loft.

The living room is huge.

Honey, look at the view.

After two or three strong signals, close, no matter where you are in the process. It's time.

5. *Show understanding, but not sympathy, for your client.*

There is a vast difference between understanding how a client might be feeling and feeling sorry or sad for a client. Understanding is helpful and positive. Feeling sorry or sad means that you have crossed the line marked by professional detachment. To be effective, couple an attentive awareness of the clients' feelings with a firm and understanding professional detachment.

The Life of an Objection

How does an objection evolve in a person's mind?

We human beings spend a large amount of time visualizing, thinking about where we're going to work, play, and live. What will it look like, feel like, smell like? What will the neighbors be like? Where will I park my car? What kind of light is there? How long does it take to get to work?

There are five stages in the life of an objection. In the first stage, anticipation, expectations are high. The product may seem better than it could possibly be. You, as the leasing professional, may have aided this buildup by selling over the phone or by sending pictures in the mail. The clients come through the door expecting something bigger than life. They will be a little disappointed, a little discouraged. No matter how luxurious the apartment, no matter how good the package of amenities is, the apartment won't be quite what they expected.

Because you are dealing with adults, you can anticipate that expectation—and disappointment—will be followed by an emotional adjustment that leads to acceptance. When the clients achieve acceptance, their attitude will be: This is the reality of the situation. At this point, even though the apartment may not be quite what was visualized and expected, it will come close. Usually at this point, you can close.

Making the adjustment that leads to acceptance takes a little time. If you try to close when the clients are at the expectation or adjustment stage, it's too soon. They haven't accepted the situation as fact and reality. They will resent you. They may become suspicious. They will not trust you.

Be patient. Keep listening attentively. Remain calm. Give the clients some space, physically and emotionally. Many leasing professionals find that it helps to take the clients to another area, such as the clubroom. Have coloring books on hand for the children. Offer the clients something to drink. Keep in mind that you cannot close successfully until the client has accepted the reality of the situation.

The Sixth Technique: Feel. Felt. Found.

There is one other technique that can be used when confronted with an objection. You turn to the client and say: "I understand how you feel," or "We've had other clients who have felt the same way," or "I felt the same way."

By saying these things, you reassure the client that his or her feelings have merit. You validate them. The clients will feel that they have been treated with respect. Then, even if they decide not to buy, they will leave feeling good about the property and about you as the leasing professional, which may bring you a sale in the future, either directly or by way of a referral. You will have done your job.

Note: If a client does not buy, make a note of the client's objection(s) on the back of the client card or guest card. If the client visits again, you or your counterpart will be prepared to overcome the objection(s).

Reveal the Hidden Agenda

In most conversations, each person has some issue or agenda that is personally important. If each person's issue does not get discussed or resolved, it remains hidden, and it has the potential to wreck a sale.

Every client, every phone call, includes an agenda. Clients have in mind what they want, but they may not voice it.

Sometimes you're lucky, and they tell you point blank. But usually they don't. They may not even be fully aware of what their own agenda is. If you're not willing to spend the time and energy to listen and observe, you never will know. And that will affect the success of your presentation.

To find the hidden agenda, concentrate. Pay attention to verbal and nonverbal clues. Ask questions as you make conversation. (Remember not to interrogate. Converse.) Make certain that by the end of the conversation you feel comfortable that you've identified the client's hidden agenda and that you know what the client wants.

The Value of Role Playing

To be successful, you not only have to become informed, but you also have to become comfortable and confident about every aspect of your job. One way to increase your comfort and confidence is to role play with your colleagues the techniques for overcoming objections. Then, armed with information and confident about your skills, you will be ready to overcome objections and make the sale.

Common Objections and Suggested Responses

In each case, answer the objection with a question. Then add comments as appropriate.

"I really want a washer and dryer in my apartment."

"Do you have a washer and dryer in your apartment now?"

(Client responds.)

"I understand why you would prefer a washer and dryer in your apartment. However, you will be saving $40 a month on your rent and our laundry facilities will enable you to do all four loads at one time. Don't you feel that the extra savings in addition to the time saved is worth not having a washer and dryer in the apartment?"

"This apartment is too dark."
"Do you work during the day?"
(Client responds.)
"I have found that the majority of people usually work until 5:30. By the time they come home, they tend to close their blinds and window coverings for privacy. I'm sure you enjoy your privacy. (Point out outlets and suggest placement of lamps/lighting.) Do you really feel that this apartment is too dark?"

"I don't like this carpet."
"What color is your furniture?"
(Client responds.)
"I realize that this may not be the color that you had visualized. However, this color is great in that it does not show dirt as easily and resists wear and tear. Don't you feel that it is neutral enough to go with your _____ (color) furniture?"

"I want gas heat."
"Do you have gas heat where you are currently living?"
(Client responds.)
"I think that you will find that electric heat is as affordable and much cleaner than gas. Do you really think this would be that much of a problem? You certainly love the floor plan we offer at XYZ Apartments."

"I want a quiet apartment. Will my neighbors be noisy?"
"Do you have noisy neighbors where you live now?"
(Client responds.)
"I can't guarantee that you will never be bothered by noise, but we enforce our resident handbook regulations, and I can

assure you that we would be responsive to any concerns that you may have. Furthermore, since this apartment has only one wall adjoining another apartment, I feel that the chances are slim that you will have a noise problem. (Mention excellent construction.)"

"I don't like gold appliances."
"What color are the appliances where you are currently living?"
(Client responds.)
"I can understand your concern about the gold appliances. However, I think that you will find that after you decorate the kitchen to your own tastes, they will become less obvious. Since the apartment is vacant, they really stand out, but after you add your personal touch, do you really think that they will be that much of a problem?"

"This bedroom is too small."
"What size bed do you have?"
(Client responds.)
"I think you'll find that a ____-size bed fits against this west/north/south/east wall. How much additional furniture do you have?

Since you have several large bedroom items, you may want to consider putting your dresser against the wall in our huge walk-in closet."

"This apartment is just too expensive."
"How much are you spending now on housing?"
(Client responds.)
"I think that if you shop the area you'll find that we are the best value for the money. We offer _____ (list features and amenities)."

"This is a nice two-bedroom apartment, but I need two full baths."

"Do you have two full baths in your current residence?"

(Client responds.)

"I can understand how you feel. In this hectic world, it is very convenient to have two full baths. However, you will find that you are saving an additional $30 per month by only having one bath. Do you and your husband leave for work at the same time?"

"I'll need to bring my roommate back this weekend to see the apartment."

"How many apartments have you looked at with your roommate?"

(Client responds.)

"I would be glad to show your roommate this apartment. However, I encourage you to leave a $20 deposit so that I may hold it for 24 hours. We have had at least ___ people today who have looked at this particular apartment, and I would hate for you to lose it. If you'd like to use my phone, you could give him/her a call to see if he/she would agree to at least hold this wonderful apartment."

"I would love to take this apartment, but I forgot my checkbook."

"Do you have a few moments that you can take to fill out the application now?"

(Client responds.)

"a. My suggestion is to save you time by filling out the application now, and you can drop off your check this evening on your way home from work."

"b. I would be willing to take $20 to hold the apartment until you can get your checkbook. Is this acceptable to you?"

"I'm just looking. I don't need an apartment until February."

"____ (name), have you already decided that you will be moving?"

(Client responds.)

"I strongly encourage you to get on our waiting list. Our one-bedroom loft floor plan is extremely popular, and I would hate for you not to be able to move in. We usually fill those vacant apartments from our waiting list. Would you like to put down a $50 deposit to get on our waiting list?"

"This is the first apartment I've seen. I want to look around before I decide."

"Do we have everything you're looking for?"

(Client responds.)

"a. I encourage you to leave a $20 hold deposit on this apartment while you shop the competition. We are known for our quality, and I know you'll be back. The deposit ensures that the same apartment will still be available for you."

"b. Saturday is one of our busier days. I encourage you to leave a $20 hold deposit while you look in the area. I can understand how you feel. When making a decision this big, it's important to feel comfortable. I know you'll be back."

CLOSING
Carol Ann Cardella, MIRM®, RAM®, GRI®

So, what's all the fuss and commotion about "closing?" Why does that word cause so much anxiety? And how many people picked up this book just to get some magic words to repeat that would enable them or their employees to write more leases? Why not just skip to this "closing" chapter, snap up the magic words, write a bunch of deals, and be everybody's hero or heroine in your company? Forget all the stuff before and after. Cut to those magic words. All the other chapters are fillers.

Wrong! That's like trying to get to maturity without passing through puberty. Look at all those learning lessons you'd miss: Some were fun, some weren't—and it still isn't over. Your attitudes, behaviors, and relationships are influenced by your experiences. Experience is history and history is made every day. We are, after all, a composite of our experiences. In large measure, experience gives us self-confidence and credibility. And an interesting aspect about experience is that it *shows*.

I'm sorry to inform you, then, that there are no shortcuts to "closing." Now, it's true that "closing" is easier to do for some sales reps than for others. But that has a whole lot to do with mindset. Don't interpret that to mean a "positive mental attitude" because that phrase is overused and misunderstood. You can't wear a positive attitude. It has to permeate your being. The proper mindset has more to do with understanding and accepting yourself as well as understanding the nature of people. Sales reps who have themselves and their relationships in perspective and in tandem with mutual objectives are willing to do whatever it takes to match the message and get the deals. Sales today isn't pitching so much as matching, guiding, directing, counseling, and engineering compromise.

Sales people are no longer pitch people, and customers are no longer victims.

What a great way to get more attention: Write more paper. What a great way to create more of a demand and higher income for yourself: Write more paper. Your reputation precedes as well as follows you. And reputation, along with respect, is earned. Getting noticed by your employers for your ability to generate income will lead to more and better career opportunities. Investors, owners, and property managers need to know they have a sales person on their team who can consistently produce. Your production makes everyone up the line from you be accountable. They all look to you; they're all counting on you.

Develop Who and What You Are

How is it possible then, that not all good sales people are good closers? It's true that some salespeople are naturals at closing and others have to acquire the skill.

We all know some noisy, gutsy, center stage closers. And then there are the domineering, pushy, abrasive closers. So, does that mean you have to be offensive to be a naturally good closer? Not at all. There are many more strong closers possessing a quieter, more temperate personality than there are closers with more obtrusive personalities.

Look, you are who you are. Quit worrying about trying to be somebody you're not and learn to develop your inherent personality characteristics. What works for someone else won't necessarily work for you. You really can't pull off adopting someone else's words or techniques if they go against your grain—your basic belief system or comfort level. The best closers works at their comfort level; they don't try to absorb another's characteristics because their experience has taught them to rely upon their own characteristics.

This chapter is not about how to adopt someone else's behavior or words so that you can be more successful. It's about developing you and your relationship with yourself and your relationships with others, primarily prospects.

The world is full of strong closers who don't even know they are. Maybe you're one of those people. If you're paying attention to this chapter, it's reasonable to assume you're seeking, searching, and exploring. Then, too, you could be a disgruntled, resistant reader who was told to read this chapter for a sales meeting and be prepared to discuss it. You see, none of us can have illusions about the way things are or the way people respond, or why they do what they do. Assuming anything is not only naive but it also circumvents reality and results. That's really what closing is all about—*reality*.

Reality seekers need to separate fact from fiction, dreams from possibilities related to timeframes, and need to be able to process logic or the sequence of actions that will lead to reaction.

The good closer seeks an answer, a resolution, a conclusion, even if you don't come out ahead. The good closer doesn't take "no" as a personal rejection or affront, but instead as a decision that needs to be put in the past to make room for the future. And the future begins now. But the difference between a "closer" and a "noncloser" is that the closer takes it as far as possible in as short a timeframe as possible. The noncloser takes a circuitous route, postpones the final reaction, delays or complicates the process of decision making, ever hopeful that the potential deal will occur. Then they have the nerve to say they're "thinking positively." That's not thinking positively, that's living in la-la-land, totally clueless about the events that need to take place to produce certain timely reactions.

The Numbers Game

Another fact about good closers is that, regardless of their personality type, they understand they have to play the numbers game. I've never met either a noisy or quiet closer who didn't grasp the numbers concept: They're going to sell to a certain percentage of people they encounter. When good closers become great closers they achieve higher percentages of closings. Their reward for getting better and better is more sales and fewer time wasters, greater income, and more focused production—all with less energy expended.

Good closers know they have to go through a certain number of prospects before they will write up a deal. Yet they look at every prospect as a potential deal. I say "deal" in place of "lease" because each party must feel like a winner. There can be no losers in a good transaction. The best closers understand that a customer must choose to buy (lease) and really cannot be "sold" something they don't want in a commodity like housing. The good salesperson is a master at presentation and developing rapport. But the good closer takes it one step further: The closer is a master at sniffing out reality, staying focused on the objective, channeling the decision making process to enable a favorable conclusion for all parties.

Good salespeople who are not yet good closers have simply stopped short of success; they don't take the encounter as far as they might have or as far as it could go.

Either they assumed too much, or personal baggage and fear got in the way of fruition. We stop short of success when we impede the process and sequence of decision making. We reap success when we facilitate the process and the sequence of decision making, and see it through to a timely resolution.

"Sales" is the art of timely introductions and the ability to listen, disseminate, and take or present actions that focus on the customer's issues. "Closing" is the art of timely eliminations, channeling decisions, considerations, and timeframes to achieve the ultimate go or no go decision in favor of your offering. A good closer can't win them all and doesn't expect to. But a good closer tries to sell something specific to every qualified prospect within a given timeframe. Whichever way the prospect's decision falls, the closer moves on to the next decision waiting to happen and doesn't look back. There are no losses because you can't lose what you don't have. And there are no regrets because you can't regret giving 100% and doing all that you can do to accomplish your objectives. Regrets can only occur when you're looking backwards instead of forwards, and when you know you were remiss. You're not going to write everybody you encounter but that doesn't mean you shouldn't try.

Get Specific

During my 25+ years in sales management and marketing, I have seen the primary reason why salespeople don't close more deals reinforced time and time again. The salesperson fails to be specific enough and fails to take the situation as far as it can go at the time of the encounter. This is true of sales reps leasing apartments or selling single homes, condos, or retirement housing.

By "specific," I mean that the sales rep aspiring to be a good closer cannot simply show a model, the community, or building amenities, be pleasant and chatty, and then ask the prospect if they want to take an application with them. It isn't even specific enough for the sales rep to demonstrate the model and one apartment, tell them about the current specials being offered, and then ask the prospect if they want to put in their application. The latter is better than the former approach—it just isn't enough.

Now, I know that someone somewhere told you that you should only show one or two vacants so as not to confuse customers, but you need to use your head if you're going to be a closer. First, you need to select the right product to show based on the customer's present situation, wants, and needs. It needs to be the right floorplan, the right location, the right level in the building, the right whatever. Before you leave that plan ask the prospect how she or he feels about it. *"What don't you like about this plan?" "What do you like about this plan?" "What concerns do you have about living here?"* Then, really listen to the prospect's answers and try to resolve the issues he/she has, one at a time. The solution may be another floorplan, another floor in the building, a different view, or something within that particular apartment that can be remedied.

If you sense that a person is not really enthralled with what you have shown them, ask, *"How does this apartment compare with what you had in mind?" "What would you change if you could?"* Be warm and human and friendly, not artificially cheerful, but genuinely approachable with the truth. The customer will hold back true feelings if they feel you will only try to dissuade them. If you don't establish a relationship built on trust, then that customer won't allow you to lead, guide, or direct them to another potential solution. Sometimes there aren't any solutions to whatever objections they have about your offering, but you do need to draw them out so you will cease wasting your time and theirs.

If you sense the customer really likes what you've shown, ask this simple question: *"You seem to like this apartment, do you really?"* Listen to their response and ask them what they like most about it so that you can reaffirm that to them again in the immediate or distant future depending on their situation and timing. Often customers leave a property, they forget specifics, and all the products they saw melt into one confused image. You and the customer each need reference points to reinforce what it is that they do and do not like while they're inside the apartment.

It's your role to help the prospect eliminate those considerations that do not meet his/her needs and to easily recall those that do. It's you who must help the prospect make many mini-decisions during this process of introductions and eliminations. Each little decision needs to occur at the point where it's time to move on. Don't go from apartment to apartment or model to model or building to building without eliminating or arriving at a definite conclusion about each product you show.

What you want to avoid is pumping out oodles of information and showing a variety of apartments or too few, and then expecting someone to make a decision at the end of it all. The prospect will be unable to digest it all and make a decision on the spot. You also don't want to fall into the trap of saying or assuming they should or will go home and think about the situation. Before a prospect leaves, both of you should have a clear understanding of how they feel about your community or building, which apartment plan would be the best for them, which location would be their first choice, and which would be their second choice.

You can't be a good closer and
avoid truth or reality

During your encounter with the prospect, you should also learn where else they have looked and where else they will be looking? Ask, *"How do we compare to _____?"* Then, of course, you will know your competition so well that you will be in a good position to reinforce those good points about your offering that you know are better than the good points about the competitor. Emphasize the positive and allow it to compensate for the negative without having to say so aloud. This doesn't mean you should ignore any real issues of concern over something your competitor has that you don't, but be factual and relate your knowledge to your prospect's needs and lifestyle. Always reinforce whatever it is about your offering that your prospect prefers over the other one. Don't get into an "us versus them" match.

It should be clear by now that you can't be a good closer if you avoid the truth and pretend that the customer's real issues, needs, and concerns don't exist. The sales rep who is not afraid to explore the truth and to air the issues will leave an indelible impression on the prospect. In the end, the prospect often makes compromises because of their rapport with the sales rep. The rep came across as interested, honest, and genuine, and most of all demonstrated leadership qualities in helping to channel needs and wants into reality. Life is full of compromises.

Compromises come in the form of mini-decisions and mini-concessions. When people surrender their ideals or preferences willingly, albeit reluctantly, they do so because something of equal or greater value is taking its place. It's the salesperson's role to make certain that each step constitutes a gain and not a loss for the prospect, even though the prospect may need to make some adjustments in his/her way of thinking or imagined lifestyle.

The "Process" to Bring about Decisions

Now, because I've asked *you* to be specific, I need to be more specific. You see, I can't leave it to chance or assume you know what I mean or that you get my message. The following pages offer an outline to help ensure that you can arrive at your destination. Of course, *we* would have to buy into the same destination in order to achieve mutual success, wouldn't we? That's not unlike the relationship you must share with your customers.

If you follow the process, you'll be where you want to be—at the top of your field, in demand, and feeling good about yourself, your future, and the role you play in the lives of others.

Closing does not consist of borrowed or invented phrases that will lead to the ultimate magic moment. Closing consists of a series of logical actions that will lead the prospect to a conclusion, even if that conclusion is to decide against your offering for reasons that you and the prospect have together fully explored.

Since the "process" has been introduced as a solution to increasing your closing percentage, I want to share my list of actions and the sequence they should be in if you want to achieve the stated objective. The purpose of following the sequence is that each action occurs in a logical pattern that the prospect is able to digest as it is introduced. If you present information out of sequence to its reference point, confusion occurs. Confusion leads to mixed messages and an inability on the prospect's part to recall the truly relevant facts and impressions that would lead to a mutually favorable decision.

1. Greet prospects warmly; seat them immediately while exchanging names, at which time you also learn their marital status and who's who.

2. On your prospect card, write in their names, address with zip code, how they were referred, and their phone

number. Never ask the prospects to fill in their own cards or to check off boxes. Do it for them so you have real information on which to build an honest communication.

Also ask and record the answers as they share them with you:

a. *How large an apartment do they need?* You might also ask what about the apartment is important to them. (Which level, number of baths, color of carpet if you offer choices).

b. *How many people will be occupying the apartment?* Listen and learn while you write their response. This is a good time to inquire about their pets and share your policy.

c. *How soon do they need an apartment?* Ask if their lease is up or home is sold. It's also a good time to listen to their urgency and reasons for wanting to make a change. A new nesting place is always traumatic.

d. *Is there a price they want to stay within?* You might share your price range for that particular apartment type that would meet their needs. Or, if you have a variety of floorplans and prices you might want to give them the current range available. Write down the price they said they'd like to pay. You might ask what they're paying now. You learn a lot that way. Don't forget to add or subtract the cost of utilities. Of course a washer-dryer connection or equipment inside the apartment is also a financial consideration if they've been using coin-ops where they presently live. That could make a difference of $35 to $50 per month plus convenience.

Acquiring this information should take no more than five minutes but it's an extremely valuable five minutes that will enable you to show them something truly relevant to their needs instead of taking pot shots and guessing at their needs. This is the first step to closing—getting off to a good start.

3. Demonstrate the appropriate model or models based on their price and size requirements. Get their reaction to the space and floorplan so you know what to show next. By now you should know where they work and what they do. You should also know how they feel about the product so far. You should expect to have a good exchange. After all, this is not a National Park Service guided tour you're giving. Or is it?

4. Before you leave any vacant, find out why they did or did not like it. That's how you determine which apartments to show next. Do that until you find one that they like. Along the way, learn all you can about their needs and interests so you can talk to them about how those points relate to your community and their potential neighbors.

5. Tour laundries and building or community amenities, including recreation. This is a good time to learn what's important to your prospects related to hobbies, personal interests, etc.

By now you and the prospects know which apartment is preferred and why, and which would be their second choice. You and they should each know what issues and concerns they have that could affect their decision to live there. They should know a lot about your builder or your management company and what to expect regarding management policies and procedures. They should know what it would take to lease if they are inclined to do so. You should know where else they looked and how your offering compares. You should know where else they still plan to look and why in the event they say they have a few places to check out before deciding.

6. Return to the rental office to either write up the application and lease or to put brochure information together for them to take. Never give out brochures first and never leave brochures around for them to take. If they feel they have all they need, why do they need you? Give them the information that is specific to the apartment of their choice, that way they know what they will be comparing to when they look elsewhere. Ask them one more time what is standing in their way of taking their first choice off the market today? Remind them of your special, if there is one. Ask them by when do they plan to make a decision. Ask them what they liked the best and the least about your property and their preferred apartment. Even though you've phrased this question differently and asked it a couple times already, it's surprising to learn how the answers vary, and every variation gives you another insight into their decision-making process.

7. Record all the points you've learned on the prospect's card; fill it up with relevant information. You can never have too much so long as it's insightful and applicable.

8. Write a warm note the same day, while the exchange is still fresh in your mind and while you are still on the same emotional wave length as you were when they encountered you. Our moods change from day to day and it's important for them to get your note in the same tone and mood as they recall you. Let's hope it was one of your better days.

9. Deposit their card in your filing system to continue the follow-up process.

10. Telephone the prospects within 24 hours if they're pretty warm, or three days at the latest if they're pretty cool. Maintain their card as you continue your communication with them. Call them back and invite them to your next social event. In any event, work them until they make a decision. And if your offering isn't their decision, ask them if, for you future reference, they'd share the reasons why. Share your information with your supervisors.

We've come full circle, you and I. I've generalized, philosophized, idealized, and been specific. Let there be no room for you to wonder if you're doing what you need to do or should do to be a good closer. The one thing I haven't and can't do is to make you do it. The best I can do is what I asked you to do: Be a facilitator. Lead your prospects, channel and guide them into a series of mini-decisions and mini-commitments. And don't be afraid of the results, provided you've done all you can to get them there, in the same respect I believe I've done all I can to get you there.

Now, don't you think that as a critical person in the decision-making process you owe it to yourself and your customers to bring all the issues, confusion, and indecision to some sort of closure and solution? It's good to be a catalyst and a part of the solution.

*You are empowered
to make the difference.
The choice is yours.*

"My Two Favorite Closes"
By Cynthiann King, RAM®

Me: "Ms. Future Resident, I would like to take this apartment home off of the availability list today for you. Would you like to take the apartment?"
Future Resident: "No, I don't think so."
Me: With a look of shock or disappointment, "OH?!?" And then I am silent.

What typically happens next is that most Future Residents will either tell me their true hidden objection(s) or talk themselves into the decision right then and there.

Another favorite closing technique:

Me: "Well, Ms. Future Resident, would you like a hot cup of chocolate or an iced cold glass of lemonade while you complete our application?"

"My Two Favorite Closes"
By Tami Siewruk

THE "WHERE DID I GO WRONG?" CLOSE—This close is used when all else fails and the future resident is getting ready to walk out the door. The professional asks "Where did I go wrong? Was there something I did or said that upset you?" This will give the future resident a chance to voice any objections he or she may have. Keep in mind that since you've been very helpful, the future resident will not want you to think you made a mistake.

THE 24-HOUR HOLD CLOSE—This is simply holding an apartment for 24 hours or less with some form of deposit ($25 or more). This close creates a commitment and will give the leasing professional the opportunity to close again if the future resident waffles or decides to lease elsewhere.

Note: Do not destroy checks or charge card slips. Make it a requirement that the future resident return to the community. If you don't, the 24-hour hold is pointless.

"My Two Favorite Closes"
By Douglas D. Chasick, CPM®, RAM®

Close #1: Comparable Properties Notebook: "I still want to visit some other communities before making a decision."

This close requires a complete and updated product knowledge notebook for each of your competitors. The notebook contains a "chapter" for each property, with photographs of the amenities, buildings, grounds, entrance sign and any other photographs that you think are appropriate, even if they don't reflect the other property in its best light.

Each chapter also contains all information about the apartments, including measurements of rooms, windows, floorplans, current prices, specials, and information about the amenities, parking, management company, etc.

By the time your prospect tells you they want to look around, you will already have a petty good idea of what they are looking for. (You DID do an effective need determination, didn't you?) Try the following:

"I can understand that you'd like to see some other communities before you make your decision, and perhaps I can save you some time. Based on what we've talked about, I think that you'll find what you're looking for at (name two or three competitors). Rather than spending a lot of time driving around today, why not look through our Comparable Properties Notebook? We've got pictures, floorplans, and current pricing information on all the properties I just mentioned, and if you like what you see, you're welcome to use our phone to call them and get additional information and make an appointment to see their apartments. Let's sit down for a moment and see what they've got."

This close shows you're just as interested in the prospect finding their perfect home as you are in selling them one of your apartments—and goes a long way toward reinforcing that you care about people, not just their money!

Close #2: Negative Inference: "I'm not ready to make a commitment today."

One of the biggest problems we face when closing is to create a sense of urgency without appearing desperate. By using negative inference, you can create urgency in the prospect's mind by showing them that they will still have their problems if they don't lease your apartment TODAY. What problems? The problems that caused them to get in their car and visit your property, the problems that you uncovered during your need determination—the problems they have with their current apartment and community!

For example, if their main problem is a lack of parking at their current community, and you can offer parking right outside the door of the new apartment, you would say: "I can appreciate you're not feeling ready to make a decision today, but, unless I misunderstood you, this apartment will completely solve your parking problem. I just hate to see you leave and go back to driving around, in your own parking lot, looking for a parking space everyday. Why not leave a small deposit to tie this apartment up until you're ready?" You can use this technique with each problem you've uncovered. The point is to make sure your prospect is aware that you can solve their problems, and that if they don't take action today, they will still have their problems when they leave.

"My Two Favorite Closes"
by Anne Sadovsky, RAM®

The Summary Close—Understanding that today's apartment clientele is more mature and sophisticated, the "too cute" closes of yesteryear are ineffective. Many apartment renters have had sales training themselves and immediately recognize canned closing techniques. The summary close works when done with sincerity.

For example: "Fred, I've enjoyed showing you our community today, and I'd like to take a second to make sure that I've done my job. You wanted something in an earth tone, upstairs with a good view, in the $600 range, and you agreed that the fireplace for only $25 more is a really good deal, so it looks like we've got the right apartment home for you. It is the only one I have available like this, so let's get the paperwork taken care of, and this will be your new home!"

The Sincere Counselor Close—Most people are very hungry for, and persuaded by, a genuine care and concern for themselves, and their needs. Choosing an apartment home is a very emotional decision for many people. Here's the gentle approach:

"Fred, I know that this is a very big decision, one that you will live with for a good while. I just want to say again that this is a great place to live. We have a caring, well trained staff, outstanding maintenance service, and neighbors who have met our qualifications. The most important thing is that we'd really love to have you. And all we need to hold it for you is an application, a deposit, and your name on the dotted line, and then I'll get back to you tomorrow. So all I need now is a yes from you, OK?"

As you can tell, this only works if you really mean it. It must be natural and sincere. Some worry that after saying, "We'd really love to have you," that the application will prove them unqualified. Don't worry, you didn't sign anything. All future transactions are pending approval. It's also important how you "deny them occupancy" or turn them down. Always leave them with their pride, be kind, and say something like: "Gee, we'd really love to have you but we can't lease you an apartment now. In checking your application, we found a couple of problems, but when you get them straightened out, come back to see us."

"My Two Favorite Closes"
By Jennifer A. Nevitt, RAM®

Where Did I Go Wrong?

Scenario: An immaculate, perfectly appointed leasing center, full of natural light. The clients come through the door and you greet them professionally, offer refreshments, answer questions, manage initial qualifying without appearing to pry. You're patient, kind, interested. You make certain that their children or guests are well taken care of, spoken to, given balloons or whatever is most appropriate. You show the clients an apartment that is clean, well designed, and in excellent condition. It is what they have indicated they need and want. The tour goes well, and you successfully use all of the techniques you know about overcoming objections. It's time to close. You say, "We've toured the apartment and the beautifully landscaped grounds, and you don't have any other questions. Would you like to put down a deposit today?" And they unexpectedly say, "No." If you are a strong, self-confident leasing professional, you will be surprised and stunned and you will show it. Then you will say with sincerity, "You know, Client Names, I feel that I've shown you an apartment home that fits your needs well. Was it something that I did wrong?" Immediately the clients says, "Oh, no Jennifer. You've been charming and gracious and accommodating," or something like that. Then, because they don't want you to feel bad, they have to tell you the truth, and the truth is an opportunity. They will say, "To tell you the truth, it really bothers us that _____." Now that the true objection is no longer hidden, you can deal with it. And dealing with it should lead to a deposit.

The 24-Hour Hold

The clients have looked around. You've shown them an apartment that suits them. But today's consumers are so sophisticated that they want to comparison shop. They say, "This is lovely, but I still want to look around." Immediately, you are reassuring. "You know, Client Name, I understand how you feel. There are a lot of apartment communities in the area." (Do not slam the competition.) Then you say, "I would hate for you to lose out on _____ (Give the specific address) because it seems to fit what you're looking for so perfectly. And I can't promise that it will still be here tomorrow. Why don't you leave me a totally refundable, nominal deposit, say $50, and I'll hold _____ for you until 10 tomorrow morning." (If you are showing the apartment before noon, say: "I'll hold _____ for you until 6 tonight.") Then you say to them, "I know that you'll be back. But this way, you'll have the reassurance, the comfort of knowing that this apartment will be waiting for you. I'll see you _____ (today by 6/tomorrow by 10)."

CLOSING LINES THAT WORK
By Brenda McClain, RAM®, CPM®

1. I have just one (brown carpet, poolside, upstairs, etc.) apartment left. Will you be deciding today?
2. Do you like the first or the second apartment best?
3. You've made a smart choice. That (color, location, floorplan) is excellent.
4. Will you be paying by check or money order?
5. I find this floorplan the easiest to work with, don't you agree?
6. Before someone else gets it, would you like to put a hold on this one?
7. We can guarantee the rental rate for six or 12 months.
8. Would you like me to see if we have that size unit (poolside, closer to parking, in a quieter area)?
9. Now that you've seen both, do you think the one/one den, or the two/one den would better suit your lifestyle?
10. This floorplan is a bit more expensive, but all the residents love the little extras it has. Don't you?
11. With rents going up so fast, would you be willing to sign a longer lease to protect yourself?
12. Don't you agree that this apartment has most of the things you wanted in your new home?
13. With rising electric bills, our energy-saving (air conditioner, fireplace, heater, appliances, etc.) will save you money. Do you like that?
14. Would you like to reserve it today to take advantage of our special offer?
15. It's not exactly what you are looking for, but it's the only one we have. Why not look at it, okay?
16. They aren't building apartments like this anymore. It may be the only one available in the area.

17. Would you be signing up for our (free tennis lessons, beer party, van pool, etc.)?

18. I believe I can get you the larger apartment for the same price. Do you want me to check with the manager?

19. The company rumors say rents are going up on the first. Will you be deciding today?

20. If you sign today, I'll guarantee that price for (six, 12) months.

21. Is this what you were looking for?

22. Do you want us to set up daily newspaper delivery for you?

23. Do you prefer the apartment with or without (dishwasher, fireplace, assigned parking, cathedral ceiling)?

24. Can you afford ($10, $20, $30) more a month? (State the difference between the two prices, not the total amounts.)

25. If you apply today, I can waive the pet deposit.

26. You can get settled into your new home before the holidays. Why wait?

27. I can hold this for you today while you think it over, but this floorplan goes fast. I don't want you to miss out on the home you really want.

28. The larger apartment is actually a better deal. The rent per square foot is less than the smaller apartment.

29. Someone with good taste should have this apartment. I'll make you a special deal on it.

30. We're only offering this special price (this week, to new residents, on this floorplan).

31. If you lease today, I can include (washer/dryer, ceiling fan, extra parking space, etc.) at no additional cost.

32. If you have any problems in the apartment, see me and I'll make sure they get taken care of.

33. Will you be needing an extra (TV jack, ice tray, broiler pan) when you move in?

34. I don't have any one-bedrooms available right now, but I have a lovely two-bedroom for only $15 more a month.

35. Have you selected which color (appliance, carpet) you would like in your apartment?

36. This is the same floorplan that (judge, football star, or any well-known person) lives in.

37. Would you be interested in our Early Payment Discount Plan?

38. Which apartment will your (husband, wife, girlfriend, boyfriend, mother) prefer?

39. You're making the right decision. This is the best apartment available in the area.

40. If you want to save (time, money, effort, etc.), this is the apartment for you.

41. How soon would you want to move in?

42. Do you plan to lease an apartment today?

43. Do you think this apartment has most of what you are looking for?

44. (While filling out the Guest Card) Will you be the only one living in the apartment?

45. I don't want to sell you anything. I want to try to help you find the right new home for you.

46. How do you know if you're getting the best service?

47. If you change your mind and come back today, I'll refund your deposit.

48. Would you prefer a six- or 12-month lease?

49. We make sure that you will never be embarrassed when bringing your friends here to visit.

50. If we make you happy here, will you recommend us to your friends?

51. Are you convinced that this apartment is right for you?

52. Will you be using a moving company or doing it yourself?

53. Would you want to move in this Saturday or the next?
54. You can start with the smaller unit and then transfer to the larger, if you need the space.
55. If I show you the right apartment, can you sign a lease today?
56. Will you be needing the keys to move in Friday night or Saturday morning?
57. If I offer you a really special price, can you put a deposit on it today?
58. I can reserve this apartment if you give the okay.
59. I don't think you'll find a nicer apartment than this one. Are you ready to move in this week?

What Impacted Me Most about this Chapter:

_____
_____
_____
_____
_____
_____
_____
_____
_____
_____

What I Need to Work on:

_____
_____
_____
_____
_____
_____
_____
_____
_____

My Strengths Discovered in this Chapter:

_____
_____
_____
_____
_____
_____
_____
_____
_____
_____

CHAPTER 6

Follow-up & Watch Your Closing Ratio Soar

"Phenomenal Follow-up in Professional Leasing" -*King*

"Telephone Follow-up and Other Opportunities" -*Sadovsky*

PHENOMENAL FOLLOW-UP IN PROFESSIONAL LEASING
By Cynthiann King, RAM®

The leasing process would be destined to doom if it did not include the crucial component of *follow-up*. This step of the process is needed to keep future and current residents connected to the apartment home, community, services, and staff members.

Residents usually respond favorably when follow-up is delivered with appropriate timeliness, sincerity, and an overall concern for compatible needs resolution. Several prominent national property management companies have so affirmatively recognized the importance of professional follow-up that these firms have incorporated their commitment to follow-up in their company mission statements. These statements contain such wording as "responsive," "service-focused," "timely," and "win-win," to name a few. If national companies are so attuned to the importance of follow-up on such a grand scale, how much more important it is that the individual leasing professional be as well!

Have you noticed that when a real connection is made with a future or current resident through rapport, relationship building, and service that this connecting resident prefers to deal with "their "connecting leasing professional whenever a need arises? Usually this happens because a leasing professional has exhibited professional concern in dealing with that particular resident.

Residents' requests range from additional move-in information to a maintenance service need. Since leasing professionals have been trusted and empowered by residents, follow-up techniques must reflect both the residents' concerns and the leasing professional's commitment in responding to those requests.

Opportunities for follow-up with a future resident may occur in the following: the actual close, application process, coordination of moving day efforts, lease documents' signing process, dealing with potential buyer's remorse, handling of special accommodations, return site visits, responding to additional inquiries, and more. These are all opportunities to show the resident that their concerns are valid and that the leasing professional is committed to serve.

The successful leasing professional responds as soon as possible to the resident by: 1) Listening carefully to the request; 2) Writing notes related to the request; 3) Acknowledging the request; 4) Restating and confirming the elements of the request back to the resident ; 5) Researching potential win win resolution options; 6) Seeking supervisory approval when necessary; 7) Communicating the options to the resident, preferably both orally and in writing; and 8) Resolving the request.

The leasing professional should "own" the request all the way through completion even if other staff members will perform the actual resolution. In other words if a resident's request would involve the referral to any other team member, the leasing professional to whom the resident first requested service should check back with that Resident to verify that options have been discussed and steps have been scheduled and/or already taken to resolve the request.

In the leasing process, the leasing professional will find that most future residents are in trauma because of the upheaval of an impending move. Frequently, the stress of moving creates an almost over sensitivity on the part of the moving resident. Therefore it is even more important that all follow-up be done not only with timeliness, but with patience as well.

Most leasing experts state that the leasing professional should continue to follow up with a potential resident until one

of the following occurs: 1) the potential resident leases elsewhere (for marketing purposes, find out where!), 2) the
potential resident asks the leasing professional to stop further
communication with them, or 3) the potential resident dies! In
other words, it is a key responsibility of the leasing professional
to continue communicating with a potential resident in the
hopes of turning the potential resident into an actual resident.

Additionally, follow-up with a potential resident should
occur immediately following the initial telephone conversation, on-site visit, and whenever at least 24 hours exist between
the scheduling of an on-site visit appointment and the actual
appointment. Follow-up at these occasions could be in the
form of telephone calls and handwritten, personalized notes.

Some other interesting types of follow-up techniques that
keep both the future and current resident connected to the
rapport established initially with "their" leasing professional
include: personalized handwritten notes congratulating the
resident on occasions such as promotions, engagements, retirement, travel opportunities, and personal successes; anniversary
cards celebrating an anniversary of residency at the apartment
community; a letter from one of the other team members
emphasizing the team's commitment to service; a note from the
leasing professional's supervisor welcoming the future resident to the community and/or inquiring as to the resident's
comfort there; a personalized invitation to an upcoming
community event; a "free pass for one day" to future residents
to try out the community's amenities for one day prior to
moving (get a signed waiver of liability from the user); a city
map with places of interest to the specific resident highlighted;
a welcoming card from a designated neighbor; a "thinking of
you" card signed by the entire on-site team at intervals
throughout the resident's stay; a telephone call by a maintenance service team member to the resident after every

completed or scheduled service request;a "warm call" visit in which the leasing professional drops by the resident's apartment home to continue to build rapport with the resident; coloring books or postcards mailed to younger residents; an invitation to an open house to meet the manager and other team members; and a videotape about the community sent to the future resident to share with friends and families.

In every follow-up action there is an excellent opportunity to continue building the rapport that encourages and maintains faith in the leasing professional. Usually when a leasing professional takes the extra time to provide high-quality follow-up and exhibit a true commitment to service, both the resident and the leasing professional experience success. Dr. William Menniger states, "The six essential qualities that are the keys to success are sincerity, personal integrity, humility, courtesy, wisdom, charity." Each of these qualities can be aptly portrayed by the successful individual who exhibits and delivers professional follow-up.

TELEPHONE FOLLOW-UP AND OTHER OPPORTUNITIES
By Anne Sadovsky, RAM®

Given the number of choices in the marketplace, today's customer often fails to make a decision during the initial contact. This applies to all major purchases, not just an apartment home. As many as 70 percent of prospective renters do not lease on their first visit to the property. They rarely say no, and more often say they want to look around or think it over. This gives you the opportunity to make follow-up calls to invite the client back to the property for a second visit.

Follow-up is one of the most neglected opportunities available to apartment leasing professionals. When polled, leasing consultants often reply that they are not comfortable calling people at home or at the office. Perhaps it will help remove some of your hesitation to call if you examine how you got their number in the first place.

Do Not Ask for the Number During Initial Qualifying

Let's assume that the client agreed to let you ask some questions and you start to fill out the guest card. Get their name by introducing yourself and then pausing. Most will respond with at least their first name. Begin to discuss their needs, features that are important to them, when they need the apartment, their pet, and budget requirements. Proceed through the presentation of the product, appropriate closing requests, and invitations to return to the office for more information. ONLY when the client sees your interest, sincerity, and friendliness do you ask for their number. By now you are a friend, and they are much more likely to give their number and receive your follow-up call than if you'd asked as they walked in the door. Try saying, "I'd love to check back with you and keep in touch while you're in the market for an apartment home. Can I get a number where I can reach you during the day?"

Make your follow-up calls within 24 hours. Mailing a thank you note should not take the place of a call, although it is a nice gesture in addition to the call or for the distant future occupancy. Notes may also be used when you have nothing available that meets their needs due to high occupancy.

When making follow-up calls, follow this procedure:

Identify Yourself Clearly

Do not say, "This is the person who showed you an apartment yesterday." They may have looked at 10 with 10 different consultants!

Be Brief

Say, "I won't keep you but a second."

Let Them Know They Are Important to You

Say, "I was just thinking about you," or "I was just talking to the manager about you. Have you decided where you are going to live?"

Invite Them Back Using Alternate Choices

Say, "You really need to see the apartment again because it's such a big decision. When would be the best for you, today or tomorrow?"

Ask for a Commitment

Say, "I'll be looking for you at 10 o'clock tomorrow morning. If for any reason you're running late, please call me because I'll be expecting you."

Always Mention Something They Liked

Of course, if the client refused to give you a number, or asked you not to call, DON'T CALL.

Overcoming follow-up call reluctance will improve your self-confidence, your capture rate, and your bottom line, so give it a try and see how easy and profitable it is!

Don't miss out on other follow-up opportunities. For example:

Prospect from Your "Prospect"

This is a twofold plan. After the client leases, call to congratulate them on their decision (after they have been approved) and ask if they have any friends who may be considering a move. Remind them of the opportunity to choose their own neighbor. Or if they do not lease from you, still call and ask for referrals. Try saying, "We're sorry we didn't have what you were looking for, but perhaps you have a friend or co-worker who might be interested in living here." Ask for leads, telephone numbers, and ask if it's OK to use their name.

Keep in Touch with Clients Who Didn't Lease

Get their new address by offering to keep in touch to invite them to social activities at your property. Place them on your newsletter mailing list and keep them in your tickler file so you can drop them a note and a floorplan about six weeks before their lease is up. Consider them a possible resident until they tell you to drop dead or you read their name in the obituary column.

What Impacted Me Most about this Chapter:

_____
_____
_____
_____
_____
_____
_____
_____

What I Need to Work on:

_____
_____
_____
_____
_____
_____
_____
_____

My Strengths Discovered in this Chapter:

_____
_____
_____
_____
_____
_____
_____
_____

CHAPTER 7

Selling within the Law

"Leasing & Fair Housing"
-Sadovsky

"Affirmative Leasing
Techniques and
Fair Housing Compliance"
-Robertson

"About "the Law":
Rumor vs. Fact" *-Daniels*

LEASING AND FAIR HOUSING
By Anne Sadovsky, RAM®

Many multifamily leasing professionals don't find Fair Housing completely fair. It's not that they want to discriminate, but their possible liability and the manner in which the laws are implemented make them edgy. Some operate out of fear to the point that they are ineffective in leasing. This information is provided on the premise that knowledge and an understanding of the laws and why they were written will aid professional leasing consultants in doing their job with assurance and without fear.

Today's Fair Housing Laws are closely tied to the Civil Rights Act and the Americans with Disabilities Act (ADA). The first civil rights law was passed in 1866 and was the original legislation of the Thirteenth Amendment (outlawing slavery, prohibiting all racial discrimination in the purchase, sale or rental of real estate and personal property). This law was resurrected in 1968 and again in 1987.

The current protected classes under Fair Housing legislation and the dates passed are:

▶ 1964 Race, Color, National Origin, Religion
▶ 1974 Gender
▶ 1988/1989 Familial Status, Handicapped

The groups that attained protected status were able to do so because they proved that they had been discriminated against.

Basic definitions of each class are as follows:

▶ Race is defined as ethnic background.
▶ Color not only indicates the color of the skin but also the shade of the color.

❱ National Origin implies the country from which one originated.

❱ Religion protects the right of Americans to practice their faith and beliefs.

❱ Gender provides protection and equal opportunity and rights for both men and women.

❱ Familial Status is defined as a person or persons under 18 years of age living in the household with parent(s), parental designee, or legal guardian. Also protected is any person who is pregnant at any age and anyone in the process of obtaining legal custody of a person under 18. Exemptions are housing for persons 62 years of age or older living in designated elderly housing in 100% of the apartment homes. Also exempted is housing for people 55 years of age or older occupying 80% of the apartments in the community.

❱ Handicapped includes both physical and mental impairments that substantially limit one or more major life activities such as walking, seeing, hearing, breathing, and caring for oneself. Also protected are those with a record of or regarded as having such impairment and persons residing with the renter.

Specifically not included for protection are current illegal drug users, transvestites, and pyromaniacs (people who deliberately set fires). Specifically included for protection are recovered or recovering addicts and people with AIDS.

You are not required to make housing available to an individual who presents a direct threat to the health and safety of other residents. A handicapped resident can reasonably modify an apartment to make it accessible at their own expense. Reasonable restoration of the apartment can also be required. In most states and in most apartment communities, a guide animal is not considered a pet as directed by the Fair Housing laws. Therefore, a pet deposit and or pet lease is not required.

IMPORTANT FACTS TO KNOW
AND UNDERSTAND

▶ In other areas of law you are innocent until proven guilty. However, in Fair Housing it appears you are guilty until you prove yourself innocent. The burden of proof of innocence falls on you, your property, and the owner.
▶ Your clientele has been educated by the media, the Department of Housing and Urban Development (HUD), and others that it is profitable to sue housing providers. It is said that as many as 40 percent of the complaints filed since 1988 have been bogus.
▶ There are people out there trying to trip you up and it is perfectly legal. There are plenty of people out there posing as prospective residents whose job it is to see if they can get you to violate the Fair Housing laws.
▶ HUD has been awarded millions of dollars by the federal government to test and shop properties for noncompliance with Fair Housing laws.
▶ An individual has up to one year to file a complaint and up to two years to file an actual Fair Housing lawsuit. Therefore, proper documentation and recordkeeping for a minimum of two years is necessary.
▶ Both individuals and HUD can bring complaints and lawsuits against real estate providers.
▶ Fair Housing laws apply to all areas of real estate, including multifamily, single family, condominiums, lenders, title companies, insurance companies, land zoned for residential, advertising, etc.

- It is mandatory that your office display a Fair Housing poster for public view.
- Consistent treatment of all prospective renters, applicants, and residents is the intent of Fair Housing laws.
- It is imperative that all policies and procedures be properly documented and implemented consistently.
- The law allows owners to set reasonable occupancy standards. While a two-persons-per-bedroom standard is typical in the industry, there may be situations where such a standard would be considered discriminatory, especially when a family is involved. Regardless of the occupancy standard you set, do not limit the number of children and do not set age limits on children. Also, do not distinguish between one and two parent households. If you accept two adults with four children, you must also accept six adults.
- Many of the complaints filed occur during the application process and other qualifying techniques. You must be consistent in implementing all criteria for occupancy.
- Be consistent in documenting times of events, i.e., telephone inquiries, visits to the property, move-out notices, notification of non-notice vacated apartments (skips).
- It is advisable when serving refreshments to post a sign that says, "Refreshments are for everyone, please serve yourself."
- It is illegal to steer. For example, you may not segregate families from adults, the elderly from children, or segregate by race or other protected classes.
- Fines have increased through the years to over $2 million. HUD is as concerned with familial status as it is with race.

As you can see, these laws have been in place and pretty clearly defined for many years. Yet as a leasing consultant, you will continue to see and hear discriminatory behavior, remarks, and questions. You may be asked, "How many blacks, children, Jews, etc., live here?" An appropriate answer is, "Our company policy coincides with federal law. We lease to everyone who qualifies, including all protected classes. I will be happy to help you with an apartment, but I cannot answer your question."

Fair Housing is a complex issue, constantly changing and being defined. It is your responsibility to know the laws and to comply with them.

In circumstances of inconsistency in treatment of others, i.e., shaking hands with some but not others, you must document a nondiscriminatory reason.

States and cities cannot take away any rights guaranteed by federal law, but they can increase the stringency of federal laws. Many states, counties, and cities have added additional "protected classes" against whom it is illegal to discriminate. Several states and cities offer protection against discrimination on the basis of one's sexual preference, i.e., homosexuality. Therefore, you must know the city and state laws and guidelines as well as federal ones.

A professional housing provider/management company should have in place a written policy regarding Fair Housing; a Fair Housing officer who can answer questions and get additional information for employees; written occupancy standards; and criteria for leasing. It is important to note that the housing provider has ultimate responsibility for fair housing compliance by employees, contractors, vendors, etc. An owner can not delegate responsibility for Fair Housing compliance. Fair Housing training should be provided regularly for all employees, including service technicians, porters, and housekeepers.

On a personal note, treat others as you would like to be treated and avoid judging others on discriminatory factors. The application for residency is truly the only legal tool available for choosing apartment renters.

Keeping these facts in mind, continuing your education in fair housing, and being consistent in policies and the treatment of others should help you avoid any accusations of discrimination.

AFFIRMATIVE LEASING TECHNIQUES AND FAIR HOUSING COMPLIANCE
By Shirley Robertson, RAM®, ARM®, CPM®

It is important that leasing consultants and leasing managers have accurate knowledge of all federal, state, and local Fair Housing laws, as well as the Americans With Disabilities Act (ADA) and Section 504 of the Rehabilitation Act for those employed at government-assisted apartment communities. Often it is not stressed that state and local protected classifications are just as powerful and demand as much compliance as the federal ones. Fair housing is not only the law, and good business, but is also the right thing to do.

Basic Fair Housing Laws

It is not your **INTENT** but the **EFFECT** of what you say or do that can get you into Fair Housing problems. The best Fair Housing pledge on which to base all leasing activities is one that will ensure that the same information is given via phone or in person to all persons that telephone or visit your community. Always provide similar treatment in similar leasing and customer situations.

Fair Housing Training for New Employees

An on-site Fair Housing orientation should occur in addition to your company/owner's new employee orientation. Some property management companies feel so strongly that additional training should take place that the leasing consultants are not permitted to answer the phone or give out rental information to future residents until this additional training has occurred. All on-site management team members should receive Fair Housing training and sign a Fair Housing compliance statement. This reinforces the seriousness of being in compliance with all Fair Housing laws, regardless of job function. Once is not enough. Annual Fair Housing refresher courses are a must to keep abreast of changes in interpretation and lawsuit decisions.

Your Current Leasing Team

It is imperative to introduce and discuss Fair Housing issues and incidents in weekly leasing team meetings. The first contact the future resident has with your community and company is through a member of the leasing team. Unlawful, opinionated, biased, or prejudiced statements or actions not only insult and embarrass the future resident, but also will leave a negative impression about the community and the owners, not to mention possible complaints filed with local Fair Housing agencies and testers.

The leasing team cannot afford to have a really "bad day" as far as judgment is concerned. Because of personal liability, you never want a physically or mentally exhausting workday to keep you from treating everyone with dignity, integrity, and nonjudgmental behavior. In these times of boundless litigation, it is best to avoid coming into work if you cannot be your professional best.

Leasing Activities

Leasing policies must be developed with "intent vs. effect" in mind. Policies and guidelines must be objective, clearly written, and consistently enforced. Be sure to document dates and topics of changes in leasing policies and guidelines. Also, keep a file of these changes and the revised form(s).

In small apartment communities, a non-office team member, such as a maintenance person, is often asked to "sit in" while the leasing manager is away. If you allow nonoffice employees or part-time employees to deal with the public, either by phone or in person, it is just as important to train these employees in Fair Housing compliance as it is to train the leasing staff. These team members should not be left to use their best judgment as to how to communicate correctly. Remember, part-timers are often the least informed and least trained and often handle the busiest days of the week. Many courts will assess liability against an owner for misstatements made by untrained team members. It is beneficial to have all of the leasing team members tested, or at least shopped, by a reputable testing or shopping company. It is a cost that you can no longer afford not to absorb.

Two of the most discriminating practices causing the majority of filed complaints are refusing to rent or misrepresenting the availability of an apartment, and applying more burdensome leasing criteria to some future residents than to others. Sometimes, the only method to ensure that this is not happening in your community, especially on a "bad day," is to have everyone routinely shopped or tested.

Record keeping and documentation will be your best defense in a court of law. Retain welcome cards/logs for a minimum of three years. Attach this card/log to the declined application along with all telephone discussions, notes or letters from the applicant, as well as management's notification that the application has been declined. If the application is approved, all of the above items are to be transferred to the resident's permanent file. They should never be discarded because the application was approved. Although scraps of paper and stick-ons do pass the legal test of "documentation," the chances of these items being lost or misplaced are greater than if an office tracking form is used for all tasks and communications that take place with the applicant.

Leasing team members never outgrow the need to refer to a leasing list, no matter how many years of sales experience they have. Once consultants have graduated from the basic skills taught to lease, tour, and preview available apartment/models, they may often feel that they no longer need to carry a reminder folder or need to attach a small bulleted list to their telephone. To prove that the same information is being given to each future resident, a completed leasing checklist should be attached to every welcome card/log to show that certain information was discussed or was given to the future resident during the community visit.

It is imperative that leasing consultants know the difference between qualifying a caller and screening a caller via the telephone. Inquirers often accept the need for leasing consultants to ask qualifying questions, but when sensitive screening questions are asked, callers can be insulted and respond negatively. Screening answers the question: "Does the future resident have the income, acceptable landlord/tenant history, and acceptable credit history required to rent at your community?" Qualifying answers the question: "Does your apartment community fit the requirements of the future resident?"— including the date needed, size needed, pets or the desired rental amount. Screening questions should be handled during face-to-face meetings with the future resident rather than on the phone because you must be able to see the physical response to such questions so that amends can be made if you have insulted or embarrassed someone. You are not able to determine this when communicating via the phone until the complaint has been filed. Management companies/owners require that the leasing team capture a certain amount of marketing and traffic information. The intent in obtaining this information is innocent, but without being able to measure the inquirer's response, you may cause numerous Fair Housing tests to be conducted on you and your team.

Always invite rental inquirers to visit your community for a tour or to receive a community brochure. Also, volunteer to mail a community brochure if an appointment to visit your community was not the result of the communication.

Community Visit

It is always advisable to have an office chat with each future resident visiting the community. There are two benefits of conducting this activity. First, the chat allows the consultant to find "the" best apartment home by matching the future resident's requirements with the availability list. Second, it provides a written record as to why future residents are shown certain apartments versus others. This documentation is most helpful if you have to defend why the same apartment homes are not shown to everyone.

During the office chat, sensitive screening questions are often asked or are worked into the conversation. Refrain from asking for such information as income, marital status, and the number of children. This information is beyond the necessary qualifying questions that must be asked at this time. You do not need to know such information at this time and it has no bearing on previewing an apartment/model home. There is a need to know the total number of occupants who will be residing in the apartment home, but not the number of children. If the future resident becomes an applicant, he/she will provide this information on the application after deciding to rent. When you ask for this information before the decision to rent has been made, you are engaging in subtle unlawful discrimination. The future resident often responds as if this is none of your business, and it isn't!

One of the most uncomfortable situations for a leasing consultant is to be asked to respond to a racially motivated inquiry. You may not answer questions or respond to special requests if they are based on an unlawful discriminatory intent toward a protected class. Instead, all leasing team members should give the same response. Here are two of the most favorable responses: "We have a variety of residents here at XYZ Community," or "XYZ Community is an equal housing opportunity community. Everyone who applies has the right to reside here upon meeting our qualifications without regard to race, color, religion, national origin, sex, familial status, and mental or physical handicap."

Because you may not have daily inquiries from disabled future residents, always keep on hand the Fair Housing law and ADA regulations pertaining to handicapped applicants and residents. It is wise to have the correct guidelines to refer to rather than to try to remember the information from your most recent Fair Housing refresher training. Never refer a physically disabled future resident to a partially or fully accessible sister or competitor community **before you have sold your community first.** The disabled future resident must have the opportunity to declare your apartment home unsuitable to him/her before you volunteer additional locations. If you fail to do this, you may indirectly appear to be steering the disabled future resident.

Available Apartment/Model Preview

There are two schools of thought as to how to offer specials or incentives to create an urgency to rent. The first method is to advertise and display any and all specials up front for everyone who calls or visits your community. The second method is to offer the special or incentive only when the future resident is not ready to rent at this time and still "wants to look around." This incentive or special is used as a closing tool only. Of the two methods (although both are legal if consistently applied), the first method is the safest. If you use the second method, you must offer it across the board to *everyone* "still wanting to think it over." Given its obvious problems in terms of subjectivity, this method is being used less often.

It is extremely important that the entire leasing team know the legal definition of "available." An apartment home is technically available from the time the notice to vacate is received until the apartment home is occupied again. Saying that a particular apartment home is not available because there is an approved application and security deposit on it is not legally correct. It is better to respond: "We have a two-bedroom apartment home with a pending application," or "We have a two-bedroom apartment home that has an approved application and security deposit on it. Should the application not be approved or the current applicant change his mind, would you like to fill out an application and be placed on our waiting list?" Giving this response shows that you are sincerely interested in offering an apartment home to the inquirer, and not pushing them away.

Wrapping Up/Rental Applications

Discouraging future residents from leasing is unlawful. You should give future residents choices whenever possible but you should refrain from making any choices for them. You can summarize the attributes of each choice, but any additional help can be construed as steering. Some cities and counties have a protected classification, SOURCE OF INCOME. It details what is to be considered legal income and states that an applicant cannot be denied an apartment home based solely on the source of that income. This is a new area for Fair Housing complaints.

Source of income and your community's occupancy standards can be the two most frequently challenged procedures/policies for management companies/owners. To minimize the chances of suspicion, have your leasing policies and procedures approved by legal counsel.

Community brochures should be offered freely to everyone who visits or requests one by phone. Refusing to offer a brochure regardless of whether you think the future resident may qualify can have serious consequences. Always include your rental criteria sheet and what to bring with them on their return visit to rent. This shows your intent to give the same information to everyone; including it in the brochure helps to ensure that it is received just in case something was overlooked or omitted during the community visit.

Re-marketing (Resident Retention)

It is a lot cheaper to retain a current resident than to acquire a new one. Today's future residents are far more knowledgeable and savvy about civil rights laws, landlord/tenant laws, and the ADA. It makes sense that if the applicant knows exactly how the leasing team may or may not treat them when applying for an apartment home, they will also know exactly how the management team may or may not treat them while they reside in your community. They also have very clear ideas about the extent and quality of service they are due according to their rental lease.

Residents communicate among themselves and often compare residency notes. They expect similar treatment in similar situations and they expect consistency in the enforcement of community policies. When they feel that they have been taken advantage of or have not received all that is due them, they begin to inquire. Legal counsel, experienced in

Fair Housing issues, should have a hand in developing community policies and in reviewing them on a regular basis, especially policies solely for children. Policies for children only are appropriate if they are expressly designed for the safety of the child. Otherwise, community policies should be for all residents and guests regardless of age. All resident communications (written, oral, or actions) must be courteous and of the highest quality and customer service. The treatment residents receive must match the quality and enthusiasm that they were given when they applied for their apartment home. It is the way in which residents are treated, not the actual words used, that can cause a resident to file an unlawful discrimination complaint.

All on-site team members should be trained to give technical opinions rather than personal opinions when communicating with residents. If you are asked questions outside of your area of expertise, it is best to refer the question to the leasing center or the resident services office. It is even better to offer to escort a stranger to the proper person for the correct answer. It is not unusual for a tester to explore the community and to talk to on-site team members regarding the availability of apartments for rent before visiting the leasing center. It will not be beneficial if the tester is given different answers at the leasing center. Using this "name, rank, and serial number and I'll be glad to escort you to the leasing center" is a useful technique when dealing with strangers. You should not use it when dealing with customer service or emergencies.

Last, much care and thought must be given when offering residents incentives to renew their leases. All decisions should be based on fact (length of residency, original condition of the apartment when moved in, the current rental amount, the resident's report card) rather than on subjective criteria. Remember that residents do compare notes. Being able to back up incentive decisions with documented criteria helps to reduce any chances of suspicion. Remember that a good deed gets "repeated" (the resident will tell three people) three times. A bad deed is repeated eleven times by residents.

Don't increase your personal risk and that of your management company/owner by being ignorant of the laws as they apply to housing.

FAIR HOUSING IS NOT ONLY THE LAW AND THE RIGHT THING TO DO, BUT ALSO IS THE ONLY WAY TO DO BUSINESS TODAY.

A Fair Housing Testing Agency*
Gives Leasing Tip:

▶ Greet everyone and offer seating.

▶ Provide community literature, a brochure, and rental information.

▶ Introduce yourself by name and title.

▶ Ask the future resident's name and address consistently.

▶ Offer your business card.

▶ Request orally or in written form, information about the future resident's housing needs, number of occupants, etc.

▶ Indicate to the future resident your apartment availabilities. Qualifying criteria should be posted in the leasing center in a conspicuous place.

▶ Offer a rental application to all applicants. Also provide assistance in completing and/or providing necessary data verification. Indicate that this information will be processed by the local credit bureau and any other verification company used.

▶ Offer up front any restrictive policies (pets, additional occupants without approval, etc.).

▶ Provide in writing all monies required such as the rental amount, rental application fee, security deposit, other fees or deposits, etc.

▶ Don't make the applicant "drag" information from you—provide it freely.

▶ Offer to show the future resident an available apartment home or a sample of one to become vacant.

▶ Have a clear and concise waiting list.

▶ Invite all future residents to call again by phone or visit.

▶ VOLUNTEER NO DEMOGRAPHIC, RACIAL, ETHNIC, RELIGIOUS, OR OPINIONATED INFORMATION.

* Source: Fair Housing Council of Greater Washington D.C.

ABOUT "THE LAW": RUMOR VS. FACT Q&A ABOUT FAIR HOUSING
By Rhonda Daniels

Question 1

In light of potential discrimination practices, does a leasing professional have to provide a consistent handshake and the same refreshments or no refreshments to every person who walks into the leasing center?

Response:

It is best to treat everyone the same. Even simple gestures such as offering refreshments could be seen as favoring one person if the gesture is not offered to everyone. We advise each office to develop written practices to be followed by everyone.

Question 2

In modifying an apartment for a disabled person, who, according to the Americans with Disabilities Act, pays to restore the apartment to its original condition—the resident or the disabled person?

Response:

The Americans With Disabilities Act has nothing to do with apartment modifications for disabled persons. The Fair Housing Act is the law that pertains to this issue. Under the Fair Housing Act, a disabled resident may make modifications to the unit at his or her own expense. It is against the law for an owner or manager to refuse to allow "reasonable" modifications of the premises. The tenant or resident is supposed to pay to restore the premises to the original condition when he or she leaves, but only if it is reasonable to do so. For example, a person who widened a doorway would not have to change the doorway back to its original size since a wider doorway benefits all future residents of the building.

Question 3

Based on the Americans with Disabilities Act, please elaborate on an owner's responsibility to accept seeing-eye dogs, even in a community that does not accept pets.

Response:

The Americans with Disabilities Act does not cover this issue, or other issues pertaining to multifamily dwellings. Under the Fair Housing Act, it is illegal for an owner to refuse to make a reasonable accommodation for a disabled person. Thus, it is generally illegal to refuse a person's request to have a seeing-eye dog if the person is in need of such an aid. The community that bars pets would have to modify its rules in such a situation. Furthermore, pet deposits should not be charged for seeing-eye dogs or any other animal required because of a resident's disability. Many courts consider them medical equipment. To determine if a dog is really a seeing eye dog, you may contact your state Health Department or state office Service for the Blind. All guide dogs are supposed to be registered with the state.

Question 4

If an owner chooses to request photo IDs from clients who wish to tour the community, what are the ramifications if the leasing staff is inconsistent in requesting this document prior to showing apartments?

Response:

The key to Fair Housing compliance is to treat all prospective residents the same. This means that if you ask one person for a photo ID, you must ask everyone for it. If you don't, you open yourself to charges of discrimination under the Fair Housing laws. Your community might also want to consider requesting a photo identification at the time the application is taken. Many people have access to other people's credit cards, and unfortunately, will sometimes rent an apartment in another person's name.

Question 5

If a woman is pregnant, how does this affect the occupancy standard for the apartment she may choose?

Response:

Under the Fair Housing Act, a pregnant woman is protected from discrimination just like any other family with children under 18. A pregnant woman would be considered to be two persons for purposes of renting a dwelling unit.

Question 6

Is it legal for an owner to require drug testing as part of the resident application screening process?

Response:

There is no legal basis to require drug testing as part of the resident application screening process.

Question 7

What is the minimum age a person must be in order to sign a lease document? Are there exceptions? For example, when a minor is pregnant and seeks housing?

Response:

The age of majority is governed by state law. In most states, a person has to be 18 years old to enter into a contract. If a minor can prove that he or she is "emancipated," which means that he or she is living independently from his or her parents and receives no financial support from them, then it is possible for that minor to enter a valid contract.

Question 8

According to the Americans with Disabilities Act, what obligations does an owner have to provide Telecommunications Device for the Deaf (TDD) access for prospective residents and existing residents?

Response:

The Americans with Disabilities Act (ADA) requires operators of public accommodations to provide TDDs when customers, clients, patients, or participants are permitted to make outgoing calls on more than an incidental convenience basis. For example, TDDs must be made available on request to hospital patients or to hotel guests where in-room phone service is provided. There is nothing in the ADA to suggest that owners of apartments have to provide TDDs to prospective tenants or residents.

Question 9

Is it true that units cannot be held off the market or "reserved" for anyone without having money on it (to avoid being accused of discrimination in event someone else wants that unit)?

(*Note:* We take a maximum 24-hour "hold" provided we have a $25 minimum to hold it off the market during that timeframe. Then the customer has to come in and fill out an application and lease, plus put down the balance of the deposit.)

Response:

The best way to "hold" a unit is to request a deposit. Even a small deposit such as $25 will do. This prevents anyone from asserting that units are held for certain people in violation of the Fair Housing Act. To avoid any appearance of steering, however, you might want to consider requiring a full deposit.

Question 10

Does "consumer law" require a customer to have a copy of whatever binding document they are asked to sign at the time they sign it? That would imply that a customer who fills out an application and/or lease, plus addendums for transfer, pets, or roommates, must leave the office with a copy of those documents even though management has not approved the applicant.

Response:

There is no particular federal law that requires a customer to be given a copy of a document before the customer has been approved for occupancy. It is common courtesy and, perhaps, good public relations that suggest that someone be given a copy of a document. You can always ask the person to sign the documents at the time of application and let them know they will be given a copy upon acceptance. It is important to note that there may be a state law that requires customers to be give a copy. Be sure to check with a local attorney before developing your policy.

Question 11

Is it true that once management approves an applicant, the applicant must receive the newly signed/approved application (with or without lease) in a timely manner? And that if the signed copies are not returned to the applicant, there's no official binding agreement until received?

Response:

It is not true that there is no binding agreement unless the applicant receives a copy of the signed application with or without lease. Your application should indicate how acceptance of the application will be communicated. For instance, you could include a statement on the application that once accepted, he/she agrees to abide by the terms of the lease agreement and commence payment of rent on a particular day. There can be a binding agreement once the person has been notified that he/she has been accepted, and indicates that he/she will move in.

Question 12

It's common practice for some management companies to take an application from a prospect and not prepare a lease at the same time. When the "applicant" then shows up for move-in, the management company presents the lease and some other addendums requiring an immediate signature at the time of move-in/key pick-up. Of course, with this practice there are a number of expected lessees who don't show up or move in as expected. Some other management companies prepare a lease with addendums at the time the applicant completes the application. The applicant then signs the lease, which is not binding on management until management signs same after approving the application. Please give us your legal opinion.

Response:

To minimize confusion over whether the applicant intends to assume occupancy and be bound by the terms of the lease, it is better to adopt a policy that requires signing the lease prior to the date of move-in. Lease signing could occur when the application is filled out, with the understanding and a written statement indicating that the lease is not binding on either party until the application has been approved by management.

Question 13

When some companies take an application they also require a copy of the driver's license for proof of identity and citizenship status. Other companies do not require any proof of identity or of potential alien status. Many leasing agents are also permitted to offer any and all interested prospects an application to take home and fill in. Of course, they have no control over this process. Please comment.

Response:

Verification of identity or citizenship status can be done at any time. The applicant is free to fill out an application anywhere and return it to the office later. You can ask for verification of identity after the application is turned in.

Question 14

Some on-site leasing personnel may hand out a key permitting someone to self-inspect. And that key may be a master key. Can you comment about potential liability to the owner and management company?

Response:

Never give out a key to a prospective resident, particularly a master key. This poses a potential liability issue for owners and managers as well as potential security problems. The prospective resident could have the key copied and then return later to take the appliances or even commit other crimes. It is better to have an authorized person escort a potential applicant to a unit or to leave the unit unlocked during certain specific business hours.

Question 15

Is it true that you cannot use white-out on a legal document? What about blue pens?

Response:

White-out should not be used on a legal document. It is better to strike through words or material to be deleted or changed with a pen, and then initial the changes. Copies of the document will reflect that changes were made and initialed. If white-out is used, and there are carbon copies under the original, the copies will not reflect the changes that were made.

Question 16

When an applicant signs the application and the lease, should each copy have an original signature or can they be carbon signatures?

Response:

A document only needs to be signed once to be legally binding. Persons generally sign the original, and carbon copies are valid without another original signature on that copy.

Question 17

Do signatures have to be witnessed? What about witnessing after the signatures are made and not in the presence of those who signed?

Response:

Unless required by state law, there is no reason to require a witness to a signature for a lease. However, if there is some particular witness requirement in your jurisdiction, the witness should be there at the time the original document is signed so that the witness can attest that the person actually signed the document.

Question 18

Is there a consumer law that allows people to change their minds 3 days or 10 days after they sign their lease?

Response:

There is no federal law that allows persons to change their minds and cancel a lease within a certain time period. Only in the event of a home solicitation sale is there a federally mandated cooling off period. There may be particular state laws to this effect, but it is unlikely since most consumer laws that pertain to cancellation of contracts for consumers pertain to products and services such as health club memberships, not real property transactions where there is less of a chance that the consumer was misled as to what was being sold or leased.

Question 19

If a leasing agent tells a customer something that is misleading or untrue, is the company bound by what the employee quoted?

Example: Wrong price quote on an apartment, wrong deposit quote, an expired rental concession give-away.

Response:

The company may be bound by erroneous information given out by a leasing agent if that leasing agent is acting within the scope of his/her position. Many states follow the law of agency, that is, a principal may be bound by what an agent says. The federal courts have followed this policy for some time and they are doing so now as it relates to fair housing situations. The answer is that only well-trained employees should be dealing with the public. Never let a maintenance person answer the phone. You are better off leaving the answering machine on than having untrained individuals deal with the public by phone or in person.

Question 20

If a management office is left open and not monitored, and some private resident information is taken, what is the potential liability? Who gets penalized?

Response:

It is possible that someone could sue the management company under a negligence theory if someone found out, for example, that the resident was handicapped, divorced, had a small salary, etc. Previously, in order to prevail on such a claim, the resident would have to show actual damages resulting from having this information made public. Recent federal case law, however, provides that lawsuits can be brought and damages assessed even without a showing of traumatic damage by the damaged party. All records should be kept under lock and key at all times.

Question 21

If someone asks for the address or phone number of a resident and an office worker/leasing agent gives out that information without the prior knowledge and consent of the resident, what are the potential consequences?

Response:

This presents a serious issue. Resident addresses and phone numbers should not be given out without authorization of the resident. If the resident's home is burglarized or some other crime is committed on the premises, and it can be shown that but for the information about the address or phone number provided by management, the crime would not have taken place, the management company could be liable for damages.

Question 22

If someone shows up and claims to be a relative or has some reasonable or legitimate sounding need to be let into a resident's apartment, and the employee lets that person in or gives that person a key, what are the consequences? What if it's a police detective or some other government agency?

Response:

No one should be allowed in a unit without the permission of the resident. If management allows a relative or someone else into the unit without written permission of the resident, the management company is at risk for damages resulting from such an unauthorized intrusion. Police detectives or other government agencies have to show a search warrant signed by a judge before you can let them in.

Question 23

What if a leasing agent shared a little piece of information from the lessee's application or resident file with someone requesting information?

Response:

Unauthorized use of information provided by a resident, including giving out information to another person, is not legal. A resident could bring an action in negligence or invasion of privacy against the management company, but would have to show that the released information did some actual damage to him or her.

What Impacted Me Most about this Chapter:

_____
_____
_____
_____
_____
_____
_____
_____
_____

What I Need to Work on:

_____
_____
_____
_____
_____
_____
_____
_____
_____

My Strengths Discovered in this Chapter:

_____
_____
_____
_____
_____
_____
_____
_____
_____
_____

CHAPTER 8

Merchandising:
Your Silent Partner

"Merchandising:
The Art of Packaging Boxes" -*Nevitt*

"When You're Asked to Help
Set Up a Model" -*Green*

"Setting up and Maintaining a
Model Apartment Home" - *Chasick*

MERCHANDISING:
THE ART OF PACKAGING BOXES
By Jennifer A. Nevitt, RAM®

Merchandising is to multifamily what packaging is to product retailing. It is the difference between plain and powerful in terms of selling.

For example, take paper plates. You can choose to buy the generic brand, and the quality and appeal of the packaging will probably fall somewhere between dismal and basic: white plastic or paper plates wrapped in clear, plain plastic. On the wrapping, you might get one color ink that has the necessary product information: quantity, dimensions, etc. Your other option is to go to your local card store or look a little further in the same section of a superstore that stocks the plainly packaged plates. For the price of 100 generics, you can buy 12 anything-but-plain plates that are packaged in bright colors with themes that may include licensed characters, sports, flowers, colors, holidays, or imaginative designs. Which plates are more appealing, the plain ones or the decorated and carefully packed ones?

Themes are popular for paper plates. Think for a moment about how many times and in how many variations across all product lines you have seen characters or settings from the most recent Disney movie or re-release. Themes sell. With luck, the theme may continue to sell for 10 years or longer. Some themes—along with most Disney characters—have an indefinitely long life: holidays of almost any description, birthdays, sailing, picnics, colors in various combinations, patriotism, etc.

Now, back to apartments. The truth of the matter is, an apartment is an apartment is an apartment. It is a box with four walls, floor, and ceiling. It has windows: some strictly utilitarian, some with a view, but still just windows. It has a bathroom—one or more—and a kitchen. An apartment is a plain package; it is a box until you merchandise it.

> *Definition: Merchandising is the art of taking a basic commodity and accentuating it or creating an environment by using a theme that gets an emotional reaction from the target audience.*

Merchandising can set your product—apartments—and your community apart from the competition. Even in a difficult market, you can create that vital difference between your product and anyone else's. Merchandising allows you to create the feeling of a home, a residence, a specific and memorable place. Merchandising removes your product from the realm of plain boxes and makes your product special. At its best, merchandising can give you the Unique Selling Proposition (USP) that is vital to compete and win.

Why Do You Need a USP?

The Unique Selling Proposition is what separates your product from everyone else's in the same category, whether you're selling paper plates, clothing, soft drinks, luxury automobiles, or apartments. Your customers must perceive that you are offering something extra, something special, and, most important of all, something they cannot get anywhere else. The USP allows you to set yourself and your product apart. After visiting your community and touring your merchandised apartment, the next place your clients see can only look plain.

In the highly competitive marketplace of multifamily housing, merchandising can give you a USP for the apartments you show, beyond the attributes of the community at large. Best of all, merchandising can be surprisingly inexpensive and easy to do.

Low Cost, High Benefits

The recommended amount to budget per apartment for merchandising is between $25 and $50. To get the most out of this investment, choose and follow a theme. Then, apply the budgeted amount to creative thought and carefully planned purchasing for maximum impact.

There are property management companies that refer to the application of merchandising as "mini-models." However, in most instances, the budget for a mini-model exceeds $50. Merchandising is a more modest, extremely cost-effective way to market apartments in a multifamily community.

Popular author Alexandra Stoddard preaches the gospel of beauty in everyday elements. She urges her readers to indulge in small luxuries, to make the effort to live well even without large budgets. People respond to the details that make them feel that they will be comfortable, happy, and well cared for if they choose your community.

Another benefit of merchandising: By getting clients involved in the apartment, you help them to visualize themselves living there, and that can make the difference between "maybe" and "sold."

When considering the cost, remember the income you will gain when the apartment is occupied. Consider also the way the resident feels, the loyalty you will be building from the beginning, and how that can set up a renewal a year from now. Merchandising can help you make the sale, now and it has long-term benefits as well.

Cleanliness Comes First

No amount of money spent on merchandising will hide dirt or disrepair. It is critical that your product—the box—be clean and well maintained before you begin to add the merchandising that will transform it into something more than a box. The glass on the windows must be so clean that sunlight fills the room, because light sells. Do everything you can to maximize the good features of the apartment, such as abundant light, roomy closets, and a good floorplan. Don't let dirt or overlooked litter or bugs distract your clients from the apartment they are touring.

Techniques

Here are six steps to help you merchandise an apartment:
1. *Establish a theme to aid you in creating excitement.*
      Make the theme simple and straightforward. Direct it at your target audience. You will merchandise a one-bedroom apartment differently from a three bedroom townhome located near a community center. By keeping your target audience in mind, you will be able to sort out the ideas that work, and those that don't.

2. *Include the six basics.*
      These six basics are critical. Keep in mind the state of mind and physical condition of a person on move-in day, and merchandise accordingly. Minimum basic requirements:

- ▶ Paper towels in place in kitchen
- ▶ Toilet paper in each bathroom
- ▶ Box of tissues
- ▶ Hand pump soap at the sinks
- ▶ Six-pack of soft drinks in refrigerator
- ▶ Some sort of salt or sweet snack in the kitchen

3. *Include logo items as the budget allows.*

Annually, when overall advertising budgets are prepared, set aside a budget for novelty items that include the property's logo and phone number. Some of the most versatile possibilities can be used to merchandise the apartment as well as the community and can be used as giveaways at special events:

▶ Water bottles

▶ Ink pens

▶ Key chains

▶ Refrigerator magnets with emergency numbers

4. *Choose items that will help your target audience to feel at home.*

Merchandising is not just putting items in an apartment. Consider the difference between placing unadorned toilet paper, paper towels, soft drinks, and a big bag of pretzels in an apartment versus using colored paper, ribbons, signs, and containers such as baskets to display them. The former is boring, sterile, and unlivable. The latter is merchandising, and merchandising has impact. Use it to add color to a neutral kitchen, emphasize a strength, and draw attention away from a weakness. Bring warmth, atmosphere, and welcome to the apartments you show.

Here are some ideas for items to include, as your budget allows. Remember to consider the needs and preferences of your target audience when choosing the merchandising items:

▶ Guest towels

▶ Candles and candlesticks

▶ Satin hangers in closet

▶ Paper fan to create depth in fireplace or on shelf

▶ Tray

- Moving Book in the kitchen; coupons from local merchants; free food certificates
- Mugs, spoons, and drink mix; cocoa, fruit-flavor soft drinks, coffee, tea
- Popcorn
- Shower curtain and/or liner in a neutral color (tie with a colorful bow)
- Placemats
- Miniatures and travel-size toiletries
- In washer/dryer area: detergent and softener in a laundry basket

5. *Use creativity as an important element in your merchandising.*

Wrap and decorate each item and the apartment itself. Get creative. Think about how you can add interest, color, and pizzazz to the items you are using to merchandise an apartment.

Some ideas:

- *Wrap items in transparent or wrapping paper.* For instance, tie toilet paper in colored tissue (one or more colors) and tie with bright curly or metallic ribbons. Add colored transparent wrap to a basket filled with individual snacks in the kitchen.
- *Use ribbon.* It's inexpensive, colorful, festive, and effective. Use varying lengths of metallic blue and silver ribbon to tie up a shower head and suggest water. Wrap bright ribbon around the clothes bar in a closet or around doorknobs. Highlight a balcony rail—and the great view from it—with a large single bow or a wrapping of multiple ribbons.
- *Use balloons.* Blue and white balloons or multiple shades of blue balloons in a bathtub suggest a relaxing bubble bath. Add a bouquet of balloons in

the colors you have chosen. This helps to fill a dull or empty space or to highlight an interesting feature.

▶ *Roll, wrap, cut, and arrange tissue paper.* Use it to add color in a fireplace where gold and red paper can suggest the warmth of a crackling fire. Wrap other items in paper to add color and interest.

▶ *Add Easter grass for a festive feeling.* Put some in champagne glasses tied with ribbon by the fireplace or on the kitchen counter with a note of congratulations or celebration: "Congratulations! You've found the right place to call home." Another possibility in the glasses: colored marbles.

6. *Add sales messages throughout the apartment.*

Marketer Tami L. Siewruk suggests writing sales messages on pieces of paper or poster board. These can be in the shape of clouds, such as the shapes that hold the thoughts of comic strip characters, or can be written on fold over cards or framed in inexpensive frames. These messages act as a silent salesperson, pointing out features and benefits and reinforcing the sales message. Examples:

▶ Frame a small sign that says: "We picture you living here."

▶ In or on the closet: "Isn't this closet huge? There are three more in this apartment."

▶ "Welcome Home"

▶ "The fun is here."

▶ Place a cardboard cutout of a dog or cat on a counter with a sign that says, "Your pet is welcome here."

▶ Dangle three or four colorful paper fish from strings in the shower, bathtub or sink: "Get hooked on our lifestyle." This works especially well with a lifestyle theme that includes fishing or a lake.

❭ In the kitchen, frame your community's Quality Guarantee Card or similar policy or vision statement. Place it on the counter or table where it will be noticed.

❭ Place long matches by the fireplace. The first one could be out of the package and tied with a ribbon. The attached note says "Welcome home." This allows you to point out a feature—the fireplace—and it helps the clients imagine themselves at home in the apartment.

Remember, as you adapt these ideas to the theme you've chosen, always keep in mind your target audience.

Budgeting Your Merchandising Efforts

When you begin your merchandising efforts, you will establish a budget per apartment. As you buy or order items, take the per-unit price off the allotment of funds for each apartment. Be aware that you may be buying in very large quantities when you buy paper goods, and that the unit price may be small. Don't overlook it. Just take it off the allotted amount.

To make your funds go as far as possible, consider buying in bulk with other apartment communities that are part of your owner's group, even if those properties are in another city. This requires a bit more coordination and effort, but you will be able to stretch a small budget even further.

Take advantage of free items from local retailers and services. Many restaurants, dry cleaners, and other establishments are happy to give you discount coupons to give to your clients. Fan out a selection of these on the kitchen counter, add a dry cleaning discount coupon to hangers with cleaning bags in place in the closet, or prop a selection of restaurant coupons in a glass or basket.

All or None

If you choose to take advantage of merchandising, use it with every vacant apartment. Fair housing rules dictate that your selling efforts be consistent. This requires a commitment. You will need to plan your merchandising, order in bulk and/or shop for items, and then do the merchandising in each apartment.

Applications Beyond Conventional Housing

The concepts presented here under the banner of merchandising are not limited to conventional housing. Put them to work in assisted housing, especially in the 236 Program. Keep track of market conditions and let them dictate the degree and nature of the merchandising you do.

Merchandising Gives You the Edge

Merchandising is a marketing advantage that any property owner can use to turn a box into a more appealing apartment home. Your goal is to help your clients picture themselves in the apartment. Especially if they don't sign the day they tour the apartment, you want them to remember what they saw. If they have toured several communities, you want to make certain there is some reason for them to remember yours. Merchandising can be that reason. Let your clients know that you want them to be comfortable and happy in the community. Make the effort, and it will pay off in more sales.

Themes

Here are some basic and not-so-basic themes that you can adapt to fit your community. Keep in mind that almost anything can make a good theme, if you follow through with it. Don't mix themes, or you risk confusing your clients and diluting the impact of your merchandising. Consistency is important.

▶ *Italian:*
Fill a basket with ravioli or pasta, tomato sauce, two wine glasses, checked napkins. Decorate with the colors of the Italian flag: red, white, green. Use ribbons, tissue paper, streamers. A poster of Italy. Serpentine streamers like the ones tossed at departing travelers en route to Europe via boat. A travel magazine featuring Italy and/or a cookbook of Italian specialties.

▶ *You're always #1 at XYZ:*
This lends itself to a sports theme. This is especially easy to merchandise using printed items from a card store. Use bright colors and consider decorating with one or more trophies, printed or real. Use the number 1 throughout.

▶ *Mexican:*
Decorate with piñatas and hats, sunny primary colors, ribbons, Easter grass. Add a travel poster of Mexico.

▶ *Fourth of July or Independence Day:*
Red, white and blue all the way. Flags. Metallic ribbon to simulate fireworks. Play off the word independence: "Declare your independence from yard care and maintenance."

▶ *Holidays:*
Every holiday has its colors and objects. Choose a favorite holiday and then follow that idea. Greeting cards make colorful decorations and would be ideal as a follow-up card to send after the visit.

▶ *Countries:*
Almost any country lends itself to specific colors, festivals, activities, foods, and refreshments. Let yourself think imaginatively to get the most out of a country-related theme.

Travel agencies often have travel posters that you can obtain for little or nothing.

▶ *Seasons, especially summer:*

While all four seasons make excellent themes for merchandising an apartment, summer seems to be the easiest to do and is highly effective, probably because people associate summer with vacations, relaxation, and being happy. Consider filling a picnic basket with plates, cups, napkins, and snacks. Include plastic cutlery. Line the basket with a checked tablecloth, or put the cloth on the floor and set the scene for a picnic.

▶ *A day at the beach:*

Use silver (or white) and blue as your colors throughout. Tie metallic ribbon streamers to faucets and showerheads. Add a bouquet of multihued blue balloons to the living room and/or fill the bathtub with them. Use blow-up swim rings, beach balls, shovels, pails, and sand toys. Put a bottle of sunscreen and a beach towel in the bathroom. Pack appropriate snacks and drinks into a lightweight cooler. Hang a poster of the ocean. Put a sign on a blow-up shark: "Find safe harbor here at XYZ."

▶ *Romance:*

Bring on the bottle of something bubbly, two glasses tied with ribbon, matches for the fireplace, candy kisses or hearts in a bowl on the counter or on a bureau in the bedroom.

▶ *Lifestyle themes:*

A few of the possibilities include sports (golf, tennis, swimming, etc.); major events such as the World Series, Super Bowl, and the NCAA championship; country living; sailing; health and fitness.

For health and fitness, merchandise with bottled water in the refrigerator, a life-size cutout of a well-known fitness celebrity such as Arnold Schwarzenegger, sweatbands, healthy snacks. Add signs: "Work out in our fitness center," "We fit your lifestyle," "Ready to move in? We'll work it out."

▶ *Archaeology:*
This can be especially effective when you're merchandising a large apartment and expect that your audience will include families. However, don't think that children are the only ones with a sense of humor and playfulness. Use dinosaurs and dinosaur footprints. Leave signs that play off archaeological digs, dinosaurs, exploration. For example, on the front door: "Great find: three bedrooms, two baths in excellent condition." Put dinosaur jelly candies in a bowl or basket. Use an inexpensive pith-type helmet as a decoration. Tie the neutral-color shower curtain with ribbons and a plastic dinosaur. Use a magnifying glass over your business card on the counter. If your budget allows, include a videotape of *Jurassic Park.*

Sources for Ideas

Toy stores, even if you're aiming at adults. For example, if sailing is your theme, you should be able to find boats and related items at a toy store.

▶ Pier One Imports
▶ Large supply vendors. Buy toilet paper, paper towels, soap in bulk. (See vendor list.)
▶ Dollar Store, Dollar Tree
▶ Big Lots
▶ Target
▶ K-Mart
▶ Sam's Club
▶ Hills Department Store
▶ Woolworth's
▶ Party warehouse stores

WHEN YOU'RE ASKED TO HELP SET UP A MODEL
By Kay Green, MIRM®

What's the value in setting up a model?

There are many reasons; some achieve more generalized benefits than others. For example:

▶ A model shows how the space can be best utilized by the individual who will be living there. It needs to look live-able enough that the prospect can envision himself living there in comfort.

▶ A model helps establish memory points that the prospect can recall later. This is accomplished through skillful use of color as well as a style suitable to the market profile. Themes can also be conveyed, and they can leave a strong impression for easy recall.

▶ The model can also help you relate to the lifestyle of a prospect that may vary from your personal experience. Your age, background, personality, and tastes may be different from those of the consumers who are likely to live in a particular floorplan or community.

▶ The model is an opportunity to help your prospects separate your community and floorplans from others they are considering. You want yours to be the most memorable experience. How well you merchandise your space determines the degree of positive or negative impact you have on your prospects' recall.

In a highly competitive marketplace where several communities are trying to attract the same renter with similar product and rental rates, what can I do to position my community above the others?

When many factors such as square footage, prices, and amenities are really pretty comparable, how you merchandise what you have may be your only real edge over other offerings.

Cleanliness, neatness, well-manicured grounds, and buildings in good repair leave a composite good impression. It doesn't matter how well you merchandise or what color you paint, if the basics aren't in good condition, nothing else will mask the obvious. The salesperson must be the person who looks at the product and total offerings from the eyes of the consumer. This will also assist in resident retention. Residents and prospects see your community as their home and want to make the best possible impression on their friends and relatives. And they expect you to do that for them.

Once you feel confident that the basics are in excellent condition, it may be time to periodically bring in a designer who is more than a local "decorator" to review your image. A true "designer" will help you plan how you need to come across to attract the market profile that meets your investment's objectives.

If your property is planning to paint exteriors or renovate hallways or apartment interiors, it's best to call in a professional to discover what's hot and what's not, without succumbing to trends that will not wear the test of time. The same is true of sign colors, brochure artwork, new landscaping focal points, or however else you may be asking your company to create change and awaken a sleepy property or call attention to your offering over another. You aren't likely to achieve a professional impression without the input of professionals in their respective fields.

What is the most cost-effective way to merchandise my model?

Get a furniture leasing company involved to display their furnishings for free. But be aware that they expect referrals in exchange for their no-fee monthly investment in your property.

Sometimes, "free" is not realistic or advisable. You may elect to pay a monthly fee to get the furnishings you want in order to appeal to your consumers and/or because your company prefers not to be in the furniture leasing referral business. Many properties just are not the right ones to expect referrals in exchange.

Make arrangements with a window treatment company to furnish attractive, appropriate treatments in exchange for referrals. Maybe your prospects are tired of mini-blinds? You probably don't want to have window treatments that close off the natural light. Drawn draperies and shears tend to shrink your interior space.

Invest in lamps and lifestyle-oriented accessories that can be reused and adapted to other plans when the need arises in the future. For example, use children's lamps and oversized stuffed animals to dramatize space, a handsome library desk lamp to suggest a "den" or "at-home office," fireplace equipment if you offer fireplaces, memorable area rugs if you have wood floors, or lots of current hardback books to place around. Sports accessories are underused: If you have a decent public golf course nearby, golf clubs and training tapes or golf posters may highlight that neighborhood advantage. The same is true for tennis or water sports. If you can't think of anything close by to advertise through accessories, how about starting a community softball team or soccer team and placing memorabilia around with activity photos of residents at play?

What are some potential problems if we elect to have a furniture rental company install a model "for free?" What can I do to ensure a positive and rewarding experience?

A furniture company may display too much furniture in an attempt to clean out their warehouse.

The leasing reps who install your model may have tastes very different from the tastes of the consumers you are trying to attract.

The furniture leasing companies tend to furnish and accessorize in colors and textures that are too feminine, and they tend to be very trendy.

Here are some rules for proper merchandising:

▶ All furniture, colors, and accessories should be appropriate for the intended target markets and for the feeling you are trying to convey. A good understanding of color theory would be helpful.

▶ Furniture should be the proper scale, no overcrowding, no sparse looks. A fully dressed model should look completed and ready for company as well as ready to be lived in.

▶ Furniture should be properly arranged to demonstrate the function of the room. Prospects should be able to imagine their furniture placement because of how they view your space. Prospects do not generally have all apartment-scaled furniture sizes.

▶ The furniture style should be the same, or similar, throughout the model. If you vary the furniture styles in the rooms, the prospect will come away confused and disoriented. The space won't flow because the theme and style will become a distraction. It can be attractive, but it is not easy to recall and is not especially memorable.

▶ Colors should be consistent throughout the model. Again, this continuity of color helps promote the prospect's recall and minimizes confusion when seeing too many models. Conflict can be overwhelming and creates indecision.

Establish an overall scheme of two to three colors for all fabrics and accessories. Attempting to use fabrics and accessories from your 10-year-old model to save money is counterproductive to your objective. Sometimes you can use what's on hand, but don't limit yourself.

The colors you use should not be those of your personal preference but should relate to the target market's personality profile.

▶ Accessories should demonstrate space and lifestyle while achieving a lived-in look. "Lived-in" should not translate to clutter and lots of little stuff sitting about that you snitched from your "maybe someday I'll use it" junk drawer. Little items leave a little impression. Remember that you're not just trying to use up space. The space use must be relevant to the objective.

▶ Models must be properly maintained. At the top of the list is that the apartment should be in top-notch repair condition. There should not even be one squeak in the subflooring or hardwood, or burnt-out bulbs, or a speck of dust (not even on the silk plant leaves), or a dead leaf on a live plant. If your plants or indoor trees are not doing well, take them out of the model and revive them. This is not the place to nurse them back. Traffic patterns should be shampooed, seams repaired, windows washed, screens in good, clean condition. Commodes must be spotless, flushed, with covers down, and no blue water. And please, no room deodorizers. Open the windows and air the place out regularly. Remove the source of the odor.

If I have more than one floorplan available, how do I choose one plan to merchandise over the others?

If you need to choose only one model, choose either the floorplan that you have the most of or the one that would be the most difficult for your renters to picture furnished. Sometimes, that plan is the one where you typically experience the greatest market resistance and one that your company may have reduced or offered specials on to get them rented in the past. That tough-to-rent plan might be just the right choice for a model, provided you have enough of them to justify the model investment.

You might want to select the best location from a renter's point of view, or your model can show off your community's best feature. You do want the model to be accessible to your leasing office and to your amenities, but it doesn't need to be the best location on the property.

Which floorplan you select may have a lot to do with the age of the prospects who would be likely candidates to rent that plan. Selecting a floorplan that is typically hard to rent may prove to be a smart move if you show that floorplan to whatever advantage it has to offer. Models, after all, are all about "enhancement."

Remember that the model area is not confined to the space between the front door and the exterior walls. The model begins with the curb appeal, how the windows show from the approach, how clean the windows are, how attractive the little balcony or patio slab can be, even off season. What you see from each of the windows and how clean and well-tended the area is are also important.

What are the rules concerning window treatments in models?

Cover no more than 20 percent of the window itself. Frame the views, soften the effect. The color and style of the treatments should complement the furnishings. Trying to conceal a less than desirable view with shears or other treatments only calls attention to the fact that you are "covering up" something. An undesirable view or location to one person may be totally inoffensive to another.

Miniblinds are being overdone. Just because your competition may provide miniblinds does not mean you are obliged to do the same. Why put miniblinds up when you have a desirable view? Not every window in every apartment throughout an entire community needs miniblinds. Use them where they're helpful and necessary to the prospect.

How do I find a professional interior merchandiser?

Shop competitive properties, ask your peers in the industry, or call your local Home Builders Association (HBA) office and see who has a really good reputation among area builders. What you probably want to avoid is a "home decorator." You really need a space merchandiser, which is a good reason why you should consult your local HBA to discover "designers" who truly understand how to deliver what you need.

It is also helpful, as well as fun, to attend seminars on merchandising. If you don't have those opportunities through your local apartment association or multifamily council, try contacting your HBA once again to see if they have any national designers coming to town to put on a program for their homebuilders. You can pick up plenty of tips and you really don't need to restrict your sphere of influence to apartments only. New homes are full of good design ideas.

What should I expect from a merchandising firm that is asked to bid?

Color boards including fabrics, furniture layouts, and catalog sheets depicting the styles, as well as sketches of window treatments. A contract including price, terms, delivery schedule, and inventory should also be included.

What are vignetted models?

Vignettes are partially furnished models that usually include window treatments, wall art, and plants. You may also want to accessorize the kitchen and baths. Include an artistic display of the floorplan with furniture drawn to scale.

What are some inexpensive ways to dress up walls in a model or vignette?

Accent color paint and wall mural graphics if you allow renters to paint walls. Other ideas include interesting fabric stretched on art frames, shelf scones, inexpensive mirrors or photo poster enlargements. Make sure the art is appropriate for the target renter.

What do I need to know about potential renters to merchandise the model properly?

You need to know their age, family makeup (including ages of children), income, and lifestyle (hobbies, sports, interests, etc.).

In terms of merchandising, what are the considerations in designing the leasing center and clubhouse facilities for a rental community?

Function, durability, and market appeal are the main considerations. A leasing office should be planned so that it complements the leasing process and includes the necessary tools to inform the prospective lessor who the developer is, what product is available, and what the advantages of the community are. The clubhouse should serve the lifestyle needs of the users—entertaining, exercising, group meetings, etc. Both types of facilities should be furnished to be durable, so that age, and wear and tear are not apparent. A clubhouse can be a great tool in the leasing process. Properly designed, a clubhouse can get potential renters emotionally involved and excited about entertaining (and maybe impressing) their friends.

If I choose to hire a merchandiser, how much can I expect to pay?

Depending on the price range of the product, target market, and geographic area; $15-$25 per square foot.

If I choose to involve a professional merchandiser in a new community, when do I contact the firm?

As soon as possible. If appropriate, the merchandiser should look at the community floorplans with the architect, to provide furniture layouts and suggestions of how the units could be improved for better function or emotional appeal. A merchandiser can also help you choose finishes that are the most appropriate for your target market.

Model Maintenance Checklist

A properly merchandised model home is one of your sales team's most powerful selling tools. But, like any tool, it performs best when carefully—and consistently—maintained.

This checklist is designed to help monitor the myriad details that make the difference between showplace and shabby. It is geared for use during daily walk-throughs. Space has been allotted for notes, so the checklist can also function as a work guide for maintenance crews. You are welcome to photocopy the checklist for ongoing use.

We recommend that a full inventory of furnishings and accessories be taken weekly, even if nothing appears to be missing. It's easy to overlook items we see every day. Ask your merchandiser for a sketch of furniture and accessory placements for use in a weekly review. Small, self-sticking paper dots beneath accessories are helpful placement cues, too.

Your merchandiser should also conduct a pre-opening walk-through with both sales and cleaning personnel to explain the merchandising rationale, suggest traffic patterns, and give cleaning and care instructions.

For convenient use, the checklist is divided into eight categories: pre-opening, overall model, kitchen/dining, bedrooms, baths, exteriors and patio, plus a final section where you can add items that are potential trouble spots in your particular model(s).

PRE GRAND OPENING	NOTES
Merchandiser walk-through with sales staff.	
Merchandiser walk-through with cleaning crew.	
Full inventory check (repeat weekly).	
Tap valves turned off under sinks?	
All move-in damage repaired?	
Toilet seats secured shut?	
Garage, closets free of paint cans, wallpaper samples, packing materials, etc.?	
Maximum wattage lightbulbs throughout (at least 100-watt)?	
Tags, covers removed from furniture/accessories/lampshades?	
DAILY CHECKLIST	**NOTES**
OVERALL:	
Carpets—dirty? Stained? Worn in high-traffic areas? Ravelled at edges?	
Tiled surfaces—grout stained? Tile chipped? Cracked?	
Wood flooring—unpolished? Stained?	
Intercom or radio—music/message too loud or too soft? Wrong station?	
Wallpaper—seams separating? Soiled? Torn? Corners worn?	
Painted walls—marked? Fingerprints?	

Cobwebs in corners? Beading showing through at corners?	
Light fixtures/lamps—dusty? Wattage not maximum? Not all turned on?	
Area rugs—not lying flat/straight?	
Furniture cushions/pillows—improper position? Chair/couch cushions crooked?	
Glass tops—dirty? Streaked? Finger prints?	
Candy dishes—empty? Used wrappers/trash in them?	
Windows—dirty? Spotted? Cobwebs? Dusty sills?	
Paintings/pictures—dusty? Crooked?	
Furniture/accessories—dusty? Damaged/ nicked? Improperly placed? (Use merchandiser's placement sketch as a guide.)	
Mirrors—dirty? Streaked? Fingerprints?	
Plants—dead leaves? Waterspots under pots?	
Doors/jambs—fingerprints? Loose knobs?	
Drapes—improper position? Dusty? Hooks missing from rods? Cords showing?	
Louvers—broken bottom chains? Not partly open for light and view?	
Valences/blinds—dusty	
Electrical cords—not hidden?	

KITCHEN/DINING:	NOTES
Waterspots on sinks, stovetops?	
Appliance warranties, manuals left sitting out?	
Task lighting not turned on? Small appliances out of place? Fingerprints?	
Table settings disturbed? Incomplete? Countertops dirty?	
Appliances not plugged in?	
Garbage under sink? In drawers? In cupboards?	
Range drip pans soiled? Crooked?	
Pleasant aroma missing? (Sprays, potpourri)	
BEDROOMS:	**NOTES**
Bedspread rumpled? Soiled? Not meeting floor properly?	
Pillows out of place?	
Skirted table covers crooked? Not meeting floor properly?	
Closet accessories improperly positioned?	
Bureau drawers open? Dirty?	
Toys/games disorderly? Damaged?	
Silk flower arrangements dusty?	

BATHS:	NOTES
Towels crooked? Soiled? Guest soaps missing? Used?	
Glass shower enclosures spotted/streaked?	
Tile chipped? Grout/caulk missing?	
Vanity tops, sinks dirty? Spotted?	
Garbage beneath sink? In drawers?	
Pleasant aroma missing? (Perfumed spray, scented candles, potpourri)	
EXTERIORS:	**NOTES**
Name plate soiled? Damaged? Missing?	
Doormat dirty? Missing?	
Fingerprints, cobwebs on front door?	
Front doorknob dirty? Loose?	
Door not operating smoothly?	
Doorstep/front porch unswept?	
Debris in outside potted plants?	
Cigarette butts/garbage on sidewalk or lawn?	
Lawn/landscaping ill-kempt?	
Exterior paint trim peeling, faded?	

PATIO:	NOTES
Mildew, stains, fading on cushions, furniture?	
Furniture dirty? Wet?	
Cobwebs in corners?	
Stains or spots on concrete or tile?	
Screen enclosures torn? Dirty?	
Floor unswept?	
Pool/jacuzzi not full? Dirty? Tile dirty?	
Outdoor accessories missing? Dirty?	
OTHER:	**NOTES**

SETTING UP AND MAINTAINING A MODEL APARTMENT HOME
By Douglas D. Chasick, CPM®, RAM®

When set up and used properly, the model is one of the most important selling tools available to you. Many factors contribute to the effective model, including your target prospect profile, the location and decor of the model, and how the model is used.

The most effective models are specifically targeted to appeal to the prospects who typically lease at your property. A current resident profile is essential in determining who your market is.

The resident profile is created by reviewing each lease and compiling the following information: marital status, age, income level, profession, geographic workplace location, number of children, and how they learned of your property. By examining this information, you will be able to create a profile representing your "typical" resident.

Research shows that different styles of models are required to appeal to different profiles based on age, sex, and marital status. If your primary prospect is a single male, the use of darker, heavier furniture and accessories is typically recommended, while women and married men prefer brighter colors and accessories.

When purchasing furniture and accessories, use items that are within or only slightly above the purchasing power of your typical prospect. A model decorated with expensive furniture can scare off prospects who might fear that they won't be able to afford to decorate with the furniture they see. It might also raise the concern that their neighbors' apartments will be nicer than their own. Once the model style is decided and the furniture and accessories are in place, the issues of sound and smell should be addressed. Soft music playing in the background enhances the atmosphere, as will the smell of cinnamon or an apple pie baking in the oven.

The model must be kept spotlessly clean at all times. The model should be dusted and vacuumed each day, and any maintenance items should be considered an emergency! Each morning, the model should be inspected prior to being shown. Carry a "spiff kit" containing a dust mop, paper towels, glass cleaner, and extra light bulbs. Turn on all the lights (use 100-watt light bulbs in all table and floor fixtures) and adjust the temperature to a comfortable level. Open all window blinds or shades, and flush all toilets to prevent water rings from forming. Maintain a supply of blank lease applications and any other leasing forms used to close a deal. Always carry a blank work order, and turn in any service requests immediately.

Any items shown in your model but not included in your standard apartment should be identified with a small tent sign. "Optional Decorator Item" printed on the card works much better than "Not Included" or "Available for Additional Cost."

What Impacted Me Most about this Chapter:

_____
_____
_____
_____
_____
_____
_____
_____
_____
_____

What I Need to Work on:

_____
_____
_____
_____
_____
_____
_____
_____
_____
_____

My Strengths Discovered in this Chapter:

_____
_____
_____
_____
_____
_____
_____
_____
_____
_____

CHAPTER 9

Don't Wait for Traffic to Come to You - *Go Get 'Em!*

"When You're Asked for Your Input on Advertising"-*Levitan*

"The Leasing Professional's Guide to Understanding Advertising"-Siewruk

"Planning and Implementing Promotional Activities and Events"-*Nevitt*

"Superior Promotional Activities & Events" -*Siewruk*

"Prospecting for Traffic"-*Sadovsky*

"Outreach Programs to Business, Industry and Other Organizations"-*Siewruk*

WHEN YOU'RE ASKED FOR YOUR INPUT ON ADVERTISING (AND EVEN WHEN YOU'RE NOT)

by Daniel R. Levitan, RAM®, MIRM®, SHMS®

Usually the leasing agent is not actively involved with the creation or placement of advertising for the community. Instead, that function is often fulfilled by the manager, owner, or an outside advertising agency while the leasing agent concentrates on his or her prime function of showing and leasing apartments. Because the successful performance of the agent's prime function is directly related to and dependent on the results that the advertising produces, perhaps it is time to change that practice.

Advertising can be defined as the paid placement of a commercial message. And there are several choices or media that we can use such as print (newspaper—display or classified, magazine), electronic (radio, television, computer billboard), outdoor (billboards and off-site displays), direct mail, and direct distribution (flyers).

Advertise to Generate Traffic

The sole reason to advertise for rental apartments is to generate qualified traffic to you, not to rent an apartment. And while that traffic may first be in the form of a phone call from the prospect, the final goal is to get that prospect out to your community where you have the opportunity to personally sell your benefits and thereby sign up a new resident. The ads create the traffic but you must make the sale.

In addition to advertising, many communities utilize other vehicles to generate increased awareness and interest.

Publicity is the creation and placement of a news story, typically in the local paper or on radio or T.V., and generally provides third-party credibility because it is not paid for. However, there may still be costs involved in creating a special event worthy of news coverage or in retaining a professional public relations consultant to write the story and assist with placement.

Promotion is the creation of an event or special program that produces awareness, interest, or traffic and often is developed in conjunction with and supported by advertising and/or publicity. Whether designed to generate new prospect traffic, or to support resident retention programs, promotional activities can involve different groups of people in your community's special lifestyle.

Merchandising is the presentation of your product in its most favorable condition, thereby creating an appropriate atmosphere in which to make the sale. Elements may include furnished model apartments, on-site signage and graphics, the leasing office and displays, rental brochures, even special career apparel.

Together with the initial and ongoing research, advertising, publicity, promotion, and merchandising combine to create *marketing*, the program by which we inform the market of our existence and the benefits we offer.

The rental apartment business is unique within the housing industry. If we were building a community of 200 single-family homes, we would expect to have to obtain 200 sales. We would then take our profit and move onto another development. But with a community of 200 rental apartments, we are in a permanent sales posture and are marketing for the entire life of the community. Every resident who has a job transfer, every resident who buys a home or moves to another rental complex, and every resident who retires to Arizona or Florida must be replaced, preferably immediately. With resident turnover averaging 20 percent to 50 percent annually around the country, we must not only "sell" 200 residents initially, but also 40-100 new residents each year thereafter, forever.

What You Need to Know to Advertise Effectively

I suggested earlier that the leasing agent should be actively involved in advertising the community, as well as in publicity, promotion, and merchandising. The rationale for this recommendation is very simple. There is no individual within the organization who is better qualified to determine the effectiveness of the marketing efforts or to provide the valid input required to properly direct those efforts.

The leasing agent's first responsibility is to be thoroughly informed and knowledgeable in all aspects of the community, the market, the prospects, and the residents. But that is the same knowledge you use every day to lease apartments. Specific knowledge needed to direct the advertising includes:

1. A profile of your existing residents including age, household size and composition, activity interests, type and location of employment, income and previous residence type and location.

2. A profile of your current prospect traffic including the same information as on your residents, as available.

3. The source, by media, of your traffic and your leases (which often may not be the same).

4. The community's historical and your current conversion ratio of traffic into leases and where your prospects are going if they don't lease from you (as verified by exit surveys).

5. The competitive position of your community within the market relative to residence sizes, design, features, amenities and price/value (and the determination of your "unique selling proposition").

Planning Your Marketing Strategy

In planning a marketing strategy, there are several questions you must answer. Is the prospect traffic generated truly qualified and in sufficient numbers to satisfy your leasing goals? Does the traffic follow your existing resident profile, or has a newer potential market segment developed? Is the traffic spread adequately throughout the week so that you have the time to make proper presentations?

Calculating the required traffic volume is easy—it is the number of residences to be leased multiplied by your sales conversion ratio. If you are converting one out of five visitors into a new resident, and have an average of five new vacancies each month, you need 25 new qualified visitors each month or an average of six per week. However, as vacancies usually become available on the first of each month, and hopefully you are preleasing before the actual vacancy, you will try to increase your traffic during the early part of each month to ensure no loss of occupancy and income. Moreover, an effort should be made to channel traffic to you mid-week when you have the time to work one-on-one with visitors.

Even when you are fortunate enough to have a waiting list for available apartments, the waiting list must be constantly updated and replenished.

Understanding your current resident profile should be relatively simple because the information should be readily available from the lease applications. Profiling your prospect traffic is more difficult and cannot be accomplished by merely having each visitor complete a survey card, since the information received will be incomplete and unreliable. Instead, you must obtain the information from the prospect as part of your warm-up and qualifying during the sales presentation. By the way, offering something special to new residents (which does not have to be expensive) and requiring them to bring the ad with them to qualify is an excellent way of verifying the source of traffic and the effectiveness of your advertising.

Keeping current on your community's competitive position requires that you commit time each week to shop the market. Maintain a file on each of the competitive projects, including their brochure, copies of their ads, an analysis sheet of apartment sizes, features, and current prices, and their current occupancy/availability. Join your local multifamily council and get to personally know your counterparts at other developments so that a phone call will give you updated information (and they know that you will reciprocate).

Know Who You Are and What You Need

Knowing who you are and what you need will give you the tools to create an effective marketing program. And with that as a basis, you are ready to provide your guidance. But remember that there is no single formula for success—every community and every market is unique and distinct. The only general guideline is that after initial rent-up, a typical rental apartment community in a decent metro market will budget approximately 2 percent of gross income annually for marketing, but that number can escalate substantially in a soft or highly competitive market.

If you are fortunate enough to be located with frontage on a heavily trafficked main road, or are visible from a nearby expressway, and market demand is strong, your total advertising program may consist of nothing more than on-site signage. And it is impossible to overstate the importance of attractive, appropriate on-site signs for any community. Signage must provide the name of the community, include a positioning statement such as "a luxury rental community" or "the largest apartments in Atlanta," and the phone number of the leasing office, at a minimum. Also appropriate, on the sign and/or as banners on the building, would be an availability message such as "now leasing." Additionally, it is essential to provide on-site directional signage to "walk" the visitor from the community entry to the leasing office, where a visible sign provides your office hours.

Most advertising for rental apartments is limited to print placement, generally a half-page display ad in the local apartment magazine, frequent small-space classified ads mid-week and weekends in the main local newspaper, and possibly a display ad in the Saturday or Sunday rental section. The rationale behind this practice is that the majority of prospects are self-motivated (they are actively looking for an apartment) and they know where to locate the advertisements. Other print media to be considered would depend upon the specifics of your marketplace and your target resident profile.

"AIDA"

The goal in creating an ad is based on the principle "AIDA"—

▶ get Attention,
▶ create Interest,
▶ generate Desire,
▶ produce Action.

To get the prospect's attention, you must stand out from the competition, a difficult task in small-space classified ads. Some will try to accomplish this goal by promoting "specials" such as rental discounts or freebies. Invariably, such an approach creates problems as the competition quickly offers a better deal and a price war soon develops. And, having been offered a deal in your ad, the prospect knows you are in a weak position and will try to negotiate something better or use your competition's offer as a bargaining tool. When you advertise the special you also have no other incentive to offer as a closing tool once you have sold the visitor on the community, the lifestyle, and the residences.

Experience has shown us that ads should be limited to providing a verbal and graphic portrait of an attractive residential environment. Whet the prospect's appetite so they must come out and see what you have. While you want to provide enough information so that the prospect can self-qualify (number of bedrooms, base price or price range, restrictions, and amenities), too much information can be a distraction. Unless you have the largest apartments, providing the apartment size (square footage) can be counterproductive because the number may seem small until the prospect can see how comfortable and efficiently designed the residences really are. When you provide too much information in the ad, the prospect tends to make the buying decision from the ad and never comes out to see what you really have.

The adage that "a picture is worth a thousand words" is especially true in print advertising, but a bad picture does far more harm than good. Professional, well-lit photography will show apartments as spacious and can highlight their special features. Dark, dreary photos fail to generate any interest whatsoever. Amenity and lifestyle photography is also effective, especially when portraying attractive target-profile prospects enjoying the community's facilities and activities. But remember that Equal Opportunity regulations must be followed and lifestyle photos must be appropriately racially/ethnically balanced. And pictures of either unused or overcrowded facilities seldom create the image you wish to portray.

Electronic media (radio and television) are reasonably expensive both to produce and place; therefore, they are not often used for advertising rental apartments except under special circumstances. The broad reach of radio and T.V., however, have often been useful in generating the large volume of traffic needed for initial lease-up, especially in conjunction with special promotions. As the audience for electronic media is not self-motivated, as with print, the message must be repeated several times to reach the target market. Frequency of placement is an important consideration, as is station selection. Fortunately, radio and television stations will usually provide you with specific demographic profiles of their audience and the station's market share so you can match that group to your target market. With the arrival of the information age, we are also beginning to see an active transformation toward computer-based advertising.

When your community does not front upon or have a "window" on a major road, consideration should be given to securing a billboard on a nearby high-traffic artery. This medium is especially valuable for initial rent-up campaigns. A "fixed" location for your board is usually preferable to a rotating site, because the billboard can also act as a convenient directional guide. Because people are driving by at high speeds, copy should be limited to the community name, a seven-word selling or positioning message, and directions. A graphic will increase readership while further establishing your lifestyle theme. In major metropolitan areas with strong transferee markets, many complexes utilize displays in airports and shopping malls as alternatives or supplements to billboards.

Direct mail is a cost-effective method of reaching a prospect, especially one who may not actively be seeking a new residence. If you utilize prospect mailings (sent to area renters), be certain that your list is current. You will substantially increase your response if you follow up the mailing with a phone call, personally inviting the prospect out to visit. One useful campaign to consider is a regular series of mailings to major area employers, offering your services to assist them with their relocation and/or corporate housing needs.

Marketing Through Publicity, Promotion, and Merchandising

In addition to advertising, most successful communities include elements of publicity, promotion, and merchandising as part of their ongoing marketing efforts. Your community newsletter and calendar can help to promote your lifestyle image and are also an important part of the materials given to a prospective resident. Resident parties, perhaps on a cooperative basis, sports teams, and clubs all create a desirable atmosphere in which to live and provide an attractive ongoing opportunity for a prospect to participate in and "try on" your community. Making certain that your amenities are utilized during periods of high prospect traffic provides instant credibility and passive testimonials from your residents.

If you have furnished model apartments, consider adding seasonal and holiday themes to give them an added attractiveness. Becoming visibly active in your industry association and getting to know the local real estate editor or writer of the lifestyle or business section will help you to become a quotable source for mention in future stories. Other special merchandising elements include sprucing up the community signage to include a sales message (such as 14-mile-per-hour speed limits with a notation, "Please drive carefully, we love our children") and using seasonal flower displays at the community entry, clubhouse, and office. Consider extending your leasing office hours to make it convenient for prospects to stop in before or after work. Your consideration of their needs provides the basis for a "caring community" presentation and story.

Working within your budget and knowing your prospect profile and your conversion ratios will enable you to help evaluate and direct the marketing program. What is the volume of prospect traffic? Is it qualified? Which media are working (and which aren't)? What can be done to increase traffic numbers and quality? Is there a potential market that you're not currently reaching? How are you doing compared with your competition?

Keep in mind these two general concepts. Ads are not like wine or cheese. They don't improve with age. If your ad does not work within the first two weeks, there is no reason to assume that it will miraculously start working the next week. Don't wait, change the ad. The cost of a new ad is far less than the cost of holding vacant apartments.

Alternatively, as there is a new rental market every three to four weeks, a good ad that produces quality traffic can continue to run almost forever. Just because you are tired of the same ad doesn't mean that the market is. Don't waste money needlessly.

Finally, allocate 5 percent to 10 percent of your marketing budget for "exploration and experimentation." Keep trying something new. You just might be pleasantly surprised.

THE LEASING PROFESSIONAL'S GUIDE TO UNDERSTANDING ADVERTISING
By Tami Siewruk

Marketing is generally defined as the business activities involved in moving a product from the producer to the consumer, including advertising. As this relates to our industry of apartment management, the product is an apartment community. The consumer is the future resident or resident.

In spite of old clichés, no product sells itself. No matter how attractive or essential a product is to the consumer, you can count on having to employ varying degrees of enticement, education, and even a little friendly coercion. In short, you'll have to advertise.

There are many ways a leasing professional can advertise an apartment community, but certain decisions have to be made before beginning any significant leasing campaign to guide your efforts toward the desired result. Developing a marketing plan provides you with a strategy for leasing vacants and notices while retaining current residents. Additionally, a well-conceived marketing plan serves to make best use of often limited marketing budgets.

No community should be without an established marketing plan, but it is especially recommended that one be developed for any community whose occupancy is below 96%, or availability is greater than 6%. Availability is defined as the number of apartments that are vacant and/or on notice to vacate, but have not yet been leased.

The following process will take you step by step through the development of an effective marketing plan. Each of the major items included in the development of the plan will be discussed in detail in later chapters. Be completely honest in answering all questions that involve the current state of your community. Be creative and innovative in developing new advertising ideas and marketing techniques.

Step One—Define Your Objective

My current occupancy is _____%. My current availability is _____%. Today is (date)_____.

My goal is to achieve _____% occupancy and _____% availability by (date) _____. My current available marketing budget is $_____, which I now dedicate to achieving this goal.

Step Two—Develop a Plan to Reach Your Objective
Prepare the Product

1. Common Areas: What needs to be achieved? What can be accomplished within budget?_____
   _____
   _____
   _____
   _____

   Cost: $____ Assigned to:____ To be completed by:__/__/__ Completed:__/__/__

2. Rent-Ready Apartments: Are you going to add tent cards? Move-in gifts? What are your target apartments? Is the rent-ready mix appropriate? _____
   _____
   _____
   _____
   _____

   Cost: $____ Assigned to:____ To be completed by:__/__/__ Completed:__/__/__

3. Pricing: Apartments must be priced correctly. What are your recommendations? What value can you add? Are concessions being given? _____

_____
_____
_____
_____

Cost: $____ Assigned to:____ To be completed by:__/__/__ Completed:__/__/__

4. Furnished Model: Is it working? Targeted toward your market? Is it memorable?_____

_____
_____
_____

Cost: $____ Assigned to:____ To be completed by:__/__/__ Completed:__/__/__

5. Mini-Models: Thought clouds? Merchandised?_____

_____
_____
_____
_____

Cost: $____ Assigned to:____ To be completed by:__/__/__ Completed:__/__/__

6. Additional Services: What are you offering? Can you add more? Are you using them as a leasing tool? Do you have a brochure or flyer?_____

_____
_____
_____

Cost: $____ Assigned to:____ To be completed by:__/__/__ Completed:__/__/__

Traffic Generation

1. SIGNAGE: When was the last color change?

   a. Directionals

   b. Bootleg—trucks, sandwich boards

   c. Entrance signs—clean, well-lighted

   d. On-site directionals

   e. Amenities signs

   f. Bus bench signs

   g. Billboards

   h. Flags

   i. Banners

   j. Roof statements

   Cost: $____ Assigned to:____ To be completed by:__/__/__ Completed:__/__/__

2. ADVERTISING: What are you using now? Is it effective? Why? What is the cost per traffic? What is the cost per rental? What are your competitors using, and what strengths are they projecting?

   a. Newspaper—freebies and city

   b. Apartment publications

   c. Entrance signs

   d. Radio

   e. Television

   f. Area magazines

   g. Flyers

   h. Mall kiosk

   i. Cinema billboards

   j. Corporate newsletters

   k. Direct mail

   l. Restaurant placemats

   m. Local events

   n. Publicity

   Cost: $____ Assigned to:____ To be completed by:__/__/__ Completed:__/__/__

3. MARKETING CALLS: Must repeat constantly to be effective. Is a marketing call log being kept? Are results being recorded? What new techniques can be used to make them memorable?

   a. Churches

   b. Chamber of commerce

   c. Schools and universities

   d. Implement a merchant referral program

   e. Hospitals

f. Corporate rental

g. Cross-marketing

Cost: $____ Assigned to:____ To be completed by:__/__/__ Completed:__/__/__

4. RESIDENT REFERRAL PROGRAM: Good public relations create positive word-of-mouth marketing. Why create word-of-mouth marketing?

One additional lease per month @ $500 x 12 months = $6,000 additional income from just one additional rental. With 12 additional new leases per year, that's $6,000.00 x 12 leases = $72,000 in additional income. Capitalize at 10% = $720,000 in added value to the community. (Note: Capitalization (or to capitalize) is one of the approaches used by an appraiser to determine the value of a community. In the example, 10% represents the current interest rate.)

a. Flyers   d. Newsletter spotlight

b. Signs   e. Parties

c. Posters   f. Business cards

Cost: $____ Assigned to:____ To be completed by:__/__/__ Completed:__/__/__

Evaluating the Competition
Who Are Your Competitors?

Before you can begin to market or advertise your apartment community, you must first thoroughly understand the competition. Remember that you are not just trying to draw the future resident toward your community, but away from someone else's. Knowing your competitors' strengths and weaknesses gives you a definite strategic advantage.

You will know your competitors, and be well on the way to meeting their challenge, once you have completed the following cursory evaluation:

1. My number one competitor is_____
   Its single greatest weakness is_____
   Its three greatest strengths are_____
   _____
   _____
   _____
   _____
   _____

   Its advertising and marketing strategy is_____
   _____
   _____
   _____
   _____

   Its largest resident profile is_____
   _____
   _____
   _____
   _____

2. My second most challenging competitor is_____
   Its single greatest weakness is_____
   Its three greatest strengths are_____
   Its advertising and marketing strategy is_____
   Its largest resident profile is_____

3. My third most challenging competitor is_____
   Its single greatest weakness is_____
   Its three greatest strengths are_____
   Its advertising and marketing strategy is_____
   Its largest resident profile is_____

4. The most common complaint or objection to my community is_____

What Is a Comparable Survey, and What Does it Contain?

The use of any market survey enables the owner, supervisor, and manager to study the market conditions pertinent to the community and to examine the supply and demand for various types of communities and apartment home styles. The information that such surveys provide is invaluable in developing a profile of the residents that each community attracts, setting rental rates, and determining the best means of reaching future residents. Results also highlight market strengths and weaknesses, and identify opportunities and threats to successful marketing. This assists management in setting realistic objectives and priorities.

The first step involves defining the community's market area. Do not include communities from outside your market area, as this will distort the survey's findings. A comprehensive comparable survey will include a comparison of similar communities in the area, including such factors as the property's accessibility to shopping areas, educational institutions, entertainment, and transportation.

A periodic update of the comparable survey is necessary, and should include notes on any additions or changes at the competing communities and any new trends in the market. It is imperative that detailed and accurate information be obtained and that subsequent changes recommended for your community be prioritized and acted on accordingly.

A well conducted comparable survey is an excellent marketing tool. An effective marketing plan must take into account what the competition has to offer and include a strategy for setting yourself apart from everyone else. Additionally, the information provided by your survey will offer a good indication of the current market condition, and can often be used as an effective leasing tool. The most accurate information is obtained by visiting and shopping the competition in person, to include first hand inspection of:

1. Amenities
2. Size of apartment homes
3. Styles of apartment homes, rental ranges, and interior condition
4. Location
5. Resident profile
6. Types of services provided

Before beginning your survey, note that not every apartment community in your area can be considered competition. Competition can be defined as any apartment community that challenges the maximum leasing potential of your community in any way. Remember that your goal is to thoroughly evaluate your competitors so that strong features and weak points may be identified. The competition should never be underestimated.

Comparable surveys should be completed for all communities that are considered in competition with yours, and should be updated periodically to allow for continual monitoring of market trends.

Following are two forms that will assist you in gathering the necessary information to conduct comparable surveys of your competition.

Comparable survey #1 records specific details about each individual community, and should be completed and periodically updated for every competing community.

Comparable survey #2 is used to summarize the overall marketplace for each individual apartment home style, and should be completed and periodically updated for each apartment home style in the subject community.

As it is often difficult to accurately compare rental values among apartment communities because of differences in size and square footage, both forms allow for comparison of rental value per square foot. Rental value per square foot is calculated by dividing the monthly rental value by the total number of square feet in the apartment. (Example: $535 rental value ÷ 832 square feet = $.643 per sq. ft.)

COMPARABLE SURVEY #1

Community name_____

# of units_____

Year built_____

Address_____

Type of construction_____

Phone number (_____) _____

Management co._____

Energy-efficient   _____

Construction   _____

Parking/apt. (circle)

    Covered/open

    Reserved

    Garages

        Detached

        Attached/direct access

Kitchen (circle)

    Gas/electric

    Resident pays

Microwave   _____

Washer/dryer   _____

    Connections

Laundries   _____

Balcony/patio   _____

Screened porches   _____

Sun rooms   _____

Fireplaces	_____	Storage	_____
Gas logs	_____	Basement	_____
Skylights	_____	Unit	_____
Ceiling fans	_____	Separate building	_____
Vaulted ceilings	_____	$_____	
9-foot ceilings	_____	Pets OK	_____
Roman tubs	_____	Pet rent:	$_____
Wallpaper	_____	Lease terms	_____
Where:	_____	Bond financed:	_____

Type of carpet/ceramic
tile used: _____

Colors: _____

Deposit amounts:

Pools (#)	_____	Security	$_____
Tennis courts (#)	_____	Cleaning	$_____
Clubhouse	_____	Pet	$_____
Planned activities	_____	Application fee	$_____
Exercise room	_____	Pet fee	$_____
Racquetball (#)	_____		

Special services offered
_____

Basketball	_____
Volleyball	_____

Explain:_____
_____

Picnic areas (#)	_____
Jogging trail	_____

What is the current leasing
incentive or concession?___
_____
_____

Jacuzzi	_____
Sauna	_____

What media sources are used?

Cable TV	_____
Satellite dish	_____

_____

Security (circle)
   Controlled access entry
   Individual alarms

Other_____

Model	_____
Window Coverings	_____
Mini-Blinds	_____

Other _____

Type:_____

Record of Rents

Apt. Type	Size Sq. Ft.	Date:____ $_____ $S.F.____	Date:____ $_____ $S.F.____	Date:____ $_____ $S.F.____	Date:____ $_____ $S.F.____	Date:____ $_____ $S.F.____	Date:____ $_____ $S.F.____

COMPARABLE SURVEY #2

Community name: _____

# of units: _____

Year built: _____

Address: _____

Type of construction: _____

Phone number: (_____) _____

Management co.: _____

Apartment home style: _____

Rent/rent per sq. ft. (*electric included, **gas included)

Apartment Community Name	Phone #	Deposit	Sq. Ft.	Date	Date

Demographics and Current Resident Profiles

What Are Demographics?

Demographics is defined as the study of general information regarding the population of a given area, including population growth and trends, economic studies on the community, growth projections, and any other pertinent information that may have an impact on a marketing strategy.

Why Demographics Are Important

It is important to your marketing efforts that you establish as much information as possible about your community's location. Don't overlook specific information about people in your community, including their average age, race, sex, income, education, and marital status. All of the details that help make an individual who he or she is are pertinent to their choice of a home community.

How to Obtain and Utilize Demographic Information

For information regarding the demographics of your area, you should begin by contacting your local Chamber of Commerce, newspaper, and county offices responsible for human resources development. These organizations should be able to provide you with information regarding size, location, and number of employees of local companies; population trends; economic trends; and other related information that will assist you in creating an effective marketing strategy.

Once you have collected the demographic information for your marketplace, you will need to complete an analysis of this information. You will be particularly interested in determining the current supply and demand for housing in your area. This supply and demand in a marketplace changes over a period of time, so you should consider updating this information periodically.

Completing a Resident Profile

Who are they anyway? They are young and old. They are retired and they work. They drive cars and trucks, and have boats. They are single, divorced, married, and living together. They are your residents, and they can tell you a lot about where, how, and when you should market to others just like them.

Forming a profile of your current residents will help you to target your marketing program most effectively. The resident profile should, at the very least, include the apartment number and type of apartment, number of occupants, length of occupancy, the residents' occupation and employer, income, age, sex, and marital status. Usually, this information can be taken from the rental application, but gathering information from formal and informal resident interviews can also be useful.

Your resident profile will be used in conjunction with the market survey to identify the preferences of your residents, which will help you better target your ideal market. You can also base profile information on the apartment style, which can help target marketing efforts for apartment styles with high availabilities.

It is possible to complete your profile within a short period of time. Follow these simple steps. The effort required to compile this information will be rewarding and extremely worthwhile.

1. Pull out all your current residents' files.
2. Using the sample form below, record key information for each resident.

Resident Profile

Apt. #	Type	Marital Status or Rmmt	Children No/Yes Ages	Age of Resident	Income	# Cars	Length of Occup.	How Long on Job	# of Adult Males	# of Adult Females

3. Based on the profiles that you've completed, determine your community's overall resident profile, using percentages to complete the form on the following page

Resident Profile

Property: _____ Date: ___/ ___/ ___ Page: _of: __

Sex: M____ F____

Marital Status:	Length of Occup.:
Single _____	< 1 Yr. _____
Married _____	1-2 Yrs. _____
Divorced _____	2-5 Yrs. _____
Roommates _____	5 Yrs. or more _____

Children:

No   _____

Yes   _____

Avg. age   _____

Age:

18-25   _____

26-35   _____

36-45   _____

46-55   _____

56 and over _____

Income:

< $15,000   _____

$15-25,000   _____

$25-30,000   _____

$30-35,000   _____

$35-40,000   _____

>$40,000   _____

Autos Owned:

0   _____

1   _____

2 or more   _____

Occupation:

Administrator/executive

Banking   _____

Child Care   _____

City/State/County/Fed. Govt. Office ___

Clerk/Typist/Mailroom   _____

Craftsman/Tradesman   _____

Disable   _____

Education   _____

Enlisted Person-Armed Services   _____

Farming/Agriculture   _____

General Medical Personnel   _____

Graduate Student   _____

Housewife   _____

Industrial Worker   _____

Insurance   _____

Law Enforcement   _____

Manufacturing   _____

Ministry   _____

Nurses/Hospital   _____

Officer-Armed Services   _____

Retail   _____

Sales   _____

Secretarial   _____

Self-Employed   _____

Supervisor   _____

Technical (Computer)   _____

Undergraduate Student _____

Unemployed   _____

Other   _____

How Long in Present Job:

< 1 Yr.   _____

1-2 Yrs.   _____

2-5 Yrs.   _____

5 Yrs. or more   _____

Using Resident Profile Information

Are you surprised by your resident profile? Surprised or not, now you know who you are really marketing to. Make use of it in determining the type of marketing, resident activities, and community upgrades that you employ, and you and your community will be more successful!

Creating a Pin Map

A pin map is one of the most valuable marketing tools to have at your disposal, and it is relatively simple to create and maintain.

Begin with a map of your local area. Make sure that it extends at least 10 miles from your community in all directions. With your community at the center, use a compass to draw three radiating circles around your community. The first circle will enclose a three mile radius, the second will enclose a five mile radius, and the third will enclose a 10 mile radius.

You'll need map pins (or push pins) in three distinctly different colors (I recommend blue, white, and red). Place pins of the same color at all of your residents' previous addresses. Use a second color to mark their places of employment. Use the third color to show where recent losses have moved. High concentrations of each color on the finished map will show where most of your residents are coming from, where they work, and maybe even point out a strong competitor. Target your marketing efforts toward these areas for maximum results.

There are two basic reasons why an apartment community would want to advertise: 1) to reduce current availability; and 2) to ensure against any future availability. It is important to consider that each time the telephone rings or a future resident walks into the leasing center, some number of advertising dollars have been spent. All advertising must be monitored for its effectiveness, and care should be taken to include all elements of effective advertising design be included.

Sources

There are many advertising sources available to an apartment community, including:

1. Direct mail
2. Signage: billboards, directional, bootleg, bandit
3. Newspaper: city or neighborhood
4. Apartment directories, guides, magazines, or other specialty publications
5. Radio
6. Television
7. City magazines
8. Locator services
9. Realtors

10. Paid resident referrals*
11. Trade shows
12. Yellow pages
13. Merchant referrals*

*Paying resident and merchant referral fees is illegal in some states. Please consult legal counsel prior to implementation.

Most of the above will require a sizeable chunk of your advertising budget, but there are alternatives. There are many excellent low- to no-cost advertising sources at your disposal. This is not to say that unpaid advertising is free to the community, because in fact a great deal of staff effort is required; however, the benefits far outweigh the footwork required. Low- to no cost advertising sources include:

1. Co-op, shared, exchanged, or bartered advertising
2. No-cost referrals, residents, merchants, other apartment communities produced by off-site marketing
3. Press: television, radio, or newspaper
4. Resident activities

No matter what advertising vehicle you employ, you will have to check for any pre-established rates that your community may be eligible for, and the advertising rate card in calculating the total production cost.

Elements of Effective Ads— Writing Ads That Sell

Lets face it. None of us can afford to waste money on advertising that doesn't work. We only run ads to generate traffic. Sure, we've all laughed or smiled at cute ads, or marveled at clever ones. Do those ads sell? All the cuteness and cleverness in the world won't generate a response, unless the ad represents a well conceived and delivered idea.

You don't want a laugh, or a smile, or to just convince someone that you're clever. All you really want is a RESPONSE. You'll know immediately if your ad is good or a dud. A good ad generates signed leases. A bad ad costs you money that you can't afford to lose. Following are nine rules that will help you gain the maximum attainable amount of traffic from your advertising dollars. They won't guarantee the perfect ad, but they will prevent you from making mistakes that could make your ad a dud.

Rule #1—Know Your Apartments, the Community, the Residents, and Your Competition.

At first this may seem obvious, and it is, but the obvious is often overlooked. Go to your model or to a vacant unit and look around. You might be surprised at what you'll learn. Make a list of all the benefits in the apartment as well as your community's benefits. Your next step is to find out what kind of ads your competitors are running.

An apartment community in Orlando, Florida, once ran an ad campaign called "Think Pink." It was that simple. They had billboards, bootlegs, and newspaper ads covered with just those two words and the community's name, and it was a huge success! A very smart manager down the street started an equally successful campaign: "Pink Stinks, Blue's Better." Sure, this type of advertising depends strongly on the target market and won't work for just any property. The point is that by simply getting to know what your competitors are saying and doing, you can, and probably will, improve your ad campaign.

Before you go any further, you absolutely must know why your residents leased in your community. Even an informal survey of 10 of your residents can provide a world of information. Every good manager gets out and talks to his/her residents anyway.

Rule #2—Grab Their Attention with a Good Headline.

David Ogilvy, an advertising specialist says, "On the average, five times as many people read the headline as read the body-copy. It follows that unless your headline sells your product, you have wasted 90% of your money."

Your future resident will spend perhaps a fraction of a second deciding whether to read your ad or go on to the next one. Make your reader stop long enough to notice and start reading your ad. A headline has four major purposes.

1. *Attract the future resident's attention:*
   ▶ Appeal to the future resident's self interest—"Save Money."
   ▶ The word "free" always gets attention. Steer clear of free rent specials. Give them something that you already have but don't charge for, such as "Free View" or "Free Service."
   ▶ Make a provocative statement that is outrageous enough to make them start reading your copy just to satisfy their curiosity.
   ▶ If your community has something new, state it in the headline. Words like "new," "announcing," "at last," "now," "discover," and "introducing" always catch the reader's eye. People are interested in what's new.

2. *Target your future residents:*
   ▶ Aim at the right profile for your community. For example, "Attention Families" will attract future residents with children and discourage inquiries from singles.

▶ Let them know that your community has something special just for them. "Important News For Women Who Live Alone" is excellent if your community has security gates, availability in upstairs apartments, or security alarms.

3. *Deliver a complete message:*
   ▶ Summarize your copy in one complete statement. If David Ogilvy's estimate is correct, then for every future resident who reads your ad in full, there will be five future residents who read only the headline.

4. *Your challenge is to draw the future resident into the body copy:*
   ▶ Few apartments can be leased with a single headline. Use the headline as a lure that will hook the future resident and draw them into the body copy. If your headline hooks their interest, make sure the body copy reels them in with information they'll be looking for.
   ▶ Write your headline in the form of a news story headline, as in "Apartments Now Less Costly Than Buying a House."
   ▶ There are seven basic types of headlines:
      1. *The Reason-Why Headline:* lists the reasons why the future resident should lease at your community. (Example: "Seven Of Fifty-Seven Reasons Why You Should Call Our Community Today")
      2. *The Testimonial Headline:* uses quotations marks. Studies have shown that the use of quotation marks increases readership. (Example: "Someone Whose Opinion I Respect Has Told Me To Visit ABC Apartments. He's A Resident, And Has Been Living There For Four Years.")
      3. *The Provocative Headline:* grabs attention by making a provocative statement, dramatic challenge, or an outra-

geous claim. (Example: "If Other Apartments Could Run This Ad, They Would... But They Can't")

4. *The News Headline:* catches the future resident's eye by telling them that you're offering something new. (Example: "Announcing A Tennis Pro For ABC's Residents")

5. *The How-To Headline:* says that the reader will get useful information from reading this ad. (Example: "How To Lease Your Next Apartment And Have A Cup Of Coffee In Only Ten Minutes")

6. *The Benefits Headline:* states an important benefit that your community offers. (Example: "ABC Apartments Leases At A Value" or "Extra-Large Closets in Extra-Large Rooms")

7. *The Command Headline:* tells your future residents what to do. (Example: "Don't Go To Strangers When You're Looking For A New Home")

Rule #3—Write Body Copy That Will Hold the Future Resident's Attention.

Begin with a list of the benefits of living in your apartment community, in order of importance. (Save this list, you'll find it has many uses.) Start your body copy with the most important reasons for leasing at your community. Keep in mind what your residents said when you surveyed them. The body copy must support the idea presented in the headline. There are seven basic steps to writing body copy, many of which are also useful in developing headlines.

1. Define the objectives.

2. Obtain product knowledge. Know your competitors' style of advertising as well as your own.

3. Create a feature/benefit checklist. This is also a great exercise that will assist you in leasing apartments.

4. Select the key features/benefits. This will attract the greatest number of residents to your community.

5. Organize the ad's layout.

6. Write the ad.

7. Edit and polish the ad, as many times as necessary! The checklist below will help to ensure that your body copy is successful.

> ▶ Is the body copy clear?
> ▶ Have you used the simplest words? Words that sell? Paint a picture?
> ▶ Are the sentences too long?
> ▶ Is the headline as strong as it can be?
> ▶ Does the ad make sense?
> ▶ Does the copy flow smoothly?
> ▶ Is the ad complete? Does it tell the whole story? Does it contain all necessary information?
> ▶ If you were the future resident, would the ad persuade you to visit or pick up the telephone?
> ▶ Is the copy interesting? Will it hold the future resident's attention?
> ▶ Is the ad built around the needs, concerns, and desires of the targeted future resident?
> ▶ Does the copy talk to the future resident person-to-person?
> ▶ Is the copy enthusiastic?

Rule #4—Write in a Natural, Clear, Simple, and Conversational Style.

This one speaks for itself.

Rule #5—Make Sure That Graphics, Photographs or Drawings Work with the Headline.

Make your visuals simple. Between the visual and the headline, you should be able to get your point across. As a rule, simple visuals that show your community or illustrate some aspect of it are better than unusual, creative concepts that tend to hide what you are selling. A well placed visual can enhance the selling power of your ad; however, remember that the visual only plays a supporting role. The following five tips will help to ensure the successful use of visual accents in your ad.

1. Don't force yourself to include a visual in your ad if it's inappropriate. An ad does not need a picture to sell.

2. The simple visual is usually best. A floorplan or a black and white photo of your clubhouse are two examples. You can take your own photos by purchasing black and white film. Most media sources allow for enlargement or reduction.

3. If your ad is 3" x 4" or smaller, consider a small, simple visual... or no visual at all. Try an attention grabbing border instead.

4. Ask your media representative what visuals they have to offer. Make use of what's already at your disposal. Creating new artwork or illustrations is expensive.

5. Photos are usually better than drawings. Future residents find photos more credible because they are "real."

Following are seven types of visuals and tips on how to use them:

1. *Show a picture of a staff member.* If you offer a service-oriented type of community, the power of this visual builds people's trust in you and your community. This

way, they can see the face behind the statement or promise. Try a picture of a happy resident, leasing professional, or maybe the service technician, depending on the focus of your ad.

2. *Show the community or apartment.* The use of a floorplan can be beneficial if you have large square footage, a unique layout, or even lots of closet space. Studies have shown that future residents like to see floorplans in ads.

3. *Show your community's amenities and benefits.* Depict residents playing tennis, picnicking, swimming, working out, or just relaxing.

4. *Use "before and after" visuals.* This is particularly effective for depicting a good location. The "before" visual would show a person sitting in traffic at 6:00 p.m. The "after" visual would show that person sitting in a chair by your pool with a drink at 6:05 p.m.

5. *Depict a lifestyle.* Allow the visual to create a setting in which the future resident can see himself. An ad that would appeal to a busy executive might show him working late at night in his office, surrounded by a blizzard of paper. The body copy and headline simply states: "When you have time to relax, try ABC Apartments... etc."

6. *Show the person.* When you use a testimonial headline, use a picture of the person and their own words. This gives the future resident someone to identify with, especially if the person is an existing resident.

7. *Use special typesetting effects.* In ads that don't contain a visual, use different styles of letters (fonts), and different text sizes to emphasize key points.

Rule #6—Layouts Draw the Future Resident into the Ad.

Avoiding the use of too much copy in a small space will make your ad easy to read, and won't discourage the future resident from reading further. Leave plenty of white space. Create a focal point. More often than not, your focal point will be your headline or visual. Remember that your goal is to draw the future resident's attention to the ad and invite the future resident to read your message in a logical sequence. Keep the following in mind when designing the layout of your ad:

1. *Typeface*: Get to know the different styles of lettering in which your copy will be printed. Ask to be shown samples of several typestyles that the medium you are using offers. Type falls into two basic categories: serif and sans serif. Serif type lettering is the kind with little curves and lines at the ends of letters. Serif lettering is commonly considered easier to read, as the reader's eyes are more familiar with the shape of the letters. Sans serif is a more sterile looking type, is devoid of the "serif" lines, and is generally easier on the eyes, as it allows a little more "white space" in the copy. It is most commonly used for headlines.

2. *Color*: A "two-color" ad is created by simply taking a black and white ad, and making it stand out by adding a second color, such as blue or green. Adding the second color can be expensive in major newspapers, but when the apartment section is crowded with display ads, it will make a difference. Blue, green, and yellow tend to provoke a better response than red. Blue evokes a feeling of sincerity, security, and peace. Bright green evokes vitality and life. Avoid lighter shades of green, as they tend to have a calming effect and won't draw attention.

Yellow is the color for attention, and will immediately draw notice against a black and white background. Avoid red if at all possible, as it conveys a subliminal stop, danger, or anger signal. Don't use the second color in your headline.

3. *Visuals*: It is better to have one large visual than a series of photos or graphics. When the future resident sees a layout with two or three visuals, he doesn't know where to look first. Never print the body copy above the visual.

4. *Copy*: For the copy to be most legible, it should be printed in black on a white background. Copy should be set in type large enough so that it is easy to read. "Point" size is what typographers measure copy in, with one point equal to 1/12 of an inch. Most newspapers are set in 8 or 9 point type. Ad type should be set in at least 8 or 9 point, and preferably 10 to 12 point, with the headline up to 32 points.

5. *Logo*: The community or company logo, if you use it, is generally placed in the lower right-hand corner of the ad, below the last line of copy. If you use your company logo, make it small. You want the attention on the apartments, not on the company.

6. *Slogan*: If your company or community has a slogan, it generally should appear directly below the logo.

Rule #7—Know What Your Future Residents Want, Not What You Think They Want.

This is the most common mistake made. You have to give the information that's important to the future resident above all. Good ads 1) focus on the future resident and how your apartment community fits his/her needs and desires; 2) allays fears and concerns; and 3) provide the benefits that he/she wants.

This is where a resident survey is invaluable, unless you want to change the resident profile of your community. In that case, you'll want to go to a community that already has the profile that you want to establish. Knock on a few doors (remember the first knock is always the hardest), and say "Hi, my name is _____. I'm the marketing representative for a neighboring apartment community. Could I just take a minute of your time to ask you a couple of questions?" Your ads will certainly reflect the difference. Who knows, you might just find a new resident!

Rule #8—Decide What You Want the Future Resident to Do—Whether it Is to Call or Visit.

Decide which you prefer, then ask the future resident to call or visit, and make it easy. If it's a call you want, make sure the phone number is easy to see. If it's a visit you're after, give directions and the office hours. Make it easy for the future resident to get in touch with you or to find you. Once you've decided, and given appropriate direction in your ad, write your ad to draw the maximum number of future residents. The following tips will help.

1. Ask for action. You must tell the future resident to visit, phone, or request a floorplan.

2. Offer free information, e.g., a color brochure. This may sound ridiculous, but it works.

3. Describe your apartments and community.

4. Show a picture of your community or floorplan.

5. Give your floorplans names. A title implies value.

6. Include your address in the last part of your copy, under the logo, in easy-to-read type.

7. Include your phone number in bold-face type.

8. Put a small telephone next to the phone number with a phrase like "Call Now" or "Call Today."

9. Create a hotline. For example, future residents call the hotline for more information or to set an appointment. Track the response.

10. When using a full-page ad in an apartment publication, use a coupon for more information. It can increase response from 25% to 100%.

11. Make the coupon large enough for the future resident to write their name, address, and telephone number.

12. Give the coupon an action headline: "Yes, I would like additional information about ABC Apartments!"

13. For a half page ad or less, put a heavy dashed border around the ad. This gives the feel and appearance of a coupon, which in turn stimulates response.

Rule #9—Small Ads Pull Traffic if They Are Well Written and Properly Laid out.

It's commonly believed that small ads don't get noticed, yet there are apartment communities that refuse to use display ads and phones keep ringing.

Small ads do get noticed, but they are harder to write than big ones! You're limited to the space available and very few words, and you must still explain what you are offering. Linear ads (simple text without visuals) are a great value, and can still generate plenty of traffic. The following guidelines will help ensure successful linear ads:

1. Use a short, direct headline, like X-LARGE, 1 BEDROOM, HUGE, JUMP, etc.

2. Use telegram-style copy. Don't write in full sentences. Write in sentence fragments using bullets to separate sales points.

3. Put a dotted or dashed line around the ad.
4. Use bold, 32-point typeface to grab attention in the headline.
5. Ask for action: call or visit, etc.

Many communities have actually stopped using display ads, not because of cost, but because of the response generated by linear ads. You can spend the same amount of money on an in-column ad as you would on a display ad, and pull up to 100% more traffic, because you'll have more lines to tell your story, and it will be different from everyone else's.

Production of Ads

To prepare an ad or collateral piece for final production, follow these three steps to make sure you're really ready to proceed:

1. Carefully re-read the copy that you have written, and make any changes that are necessary prior to typing. Have several others read the copy and make comments.
2. Type the copy as you want it to appear in the advertisement, and have someone else proofread it for typographical errors.
3. Attach any additional visual elements that you want shown, in camera-ready form, such as the community logo or map. You may want to add written notes on any ideas that you have for graphics or photos.

Placement of Ads

When you're finally ready to place an ad, follow these simple steps:

1. Select the medium (newspaper, apartment publication, flyer, etc.), and contact the media representative with whom you will be working.

2. Determine the ad size, amount of time or number of times you want to run the ad, and the budget for your ad. Show the ad to your media representative for an actual cost quote. Check to see if this media placement is within your budget. The representative may also be able to suggest alternative sizes that will be just as effective, but more economical.

3. Review the content of the ad and then give the representative the typed copy and any artwork or logos.

4. Ask your media representative for a proof of the ad. Make any necessary changes prior to publishing. If changes are made, ask for a second proof.

Printing of Additional Support Materials

If additional support or collateral materials are used, take the following steps:

1. Proof the promotional piece and make any changes prior to printing. Again, if changes are made, proof the piece a second time. Take the time to have several people proof the ad. Mistakes are costly.

2. Determine the total number of pieces that you need to have printed.

3. Select printers from whom you wish to receive proposals. Contact the representative at each printing company that you'll be working with when they submit quotes or bids on your materials.

4. Determine the type of paper to be used, and the ink color(s) to be used. Keep in mind that to bid fairly, each

printer's bid should be based on the same type of paper and ink colors.

5. Ask each printer to quote their price for the job (if you've decided to offer the opportunity to more than one printer). Choose the printer based on their quote as compared to the quality that they can offer.

6. Check the budget and get any necessary approvals.

7. Give the printer all of the materials necessary for the job (copy and artwork).

Legal Guidelines for Apartment Advertising

According to the federal Fair Housing law, advertising for the sale or rental of property may not state a preference for any person or an intention to exclude any person because of the person's race, color, religion, sex, handicap, familial status, or national origin.

The prohibition of discriminatory intent applies to the use of media, such as newspapers, radio, television, or billboards, and any written material produced in connection with the sale or rental of a dwelling, such as application forms, brochures, flyers, signs, posters, or banners.

To comply with the law, *AVOID:*

▶ Using words or phrases describing the dwelling, landlord, or residents. Examples are: "white private home," "colored home," "Jewish home," "Hispanic residence," "adult building," or other words indicative of race, color, religion, sex, handicap, familial status, or national origin.

▶ Conveying preference for one group over another or exclusion due to race, color, religion, sex, handicap, familial status (children under 18), or national origin.

- Using catchwords, such as "restricted," "exclusive," "private," "integrated," "traditional," "board approval," "membership approval."

- Using symbols or logos that imply or suggest discrimination because of race, color, religion, sex, handicap, familial status (children under 18), or national origin.

- Writing out directions to the property that refer to well-known racial, ethnic, or religious landmarks or to any other major landmark that could signal a preference for a specific type of person.

- Targeting advertisements to one particular segment of the community.

- Using only adult or white models over a significant period of time.

- Using prohibited words or phrases with respect to handicapped persons or families with children, including the following terms:

crippled	mature persons
deaf	restricted community
retarded	exclusive
adult building	blind
mentally ill	singles

- Advertising in limited geographic area; in particular editions of newspapers to reach a particular segment of the community; in small papers that cater to particular ethnic or religious groups rather than general circulation papers; and only in selected sales offices.

The Fair Housing Act *PERMITS:*

- Indicating that a rental community is accessible to handicapped individuals or intended for and operated as housing for older persons.

▶ Indicating age restrictions for occupancy as long as children are not excluded. Local law may prohibit discrimination on the basis of age. Check your local statutes.

▶ Using the Equal Housing Opportunity logo, statement, or slogan in all advertising.

▶ Using human models who represent all races and age segments of the population in the area, including families with children and handicapped persons; vary periodically so that diverse groups in your community are featured— majority and minority in the metropolitan area, both sexes, families with children (when appropriate); portray persons in an equal social setting; or indicate to the general public that housing is available to all persons, regardless of status.

Localize your efforts to abide by the law by doing the following:

▶ Know the guidelines in the area where promotional materials are seen. Laws vary according to the location. Local laws forbidding discrimination in real estate ads not only repeat the federal categories, but add prohibitions against discrimination based on age, parental status, sexual orientation, political ideology, or a renter's qualification for rent subsidy support.

▶ Learn about each publication's guidelines or criteria before placing an advertisement.

▶ To avoid both civil and criminal liability, don't use words that obviously connote any of the forbidden categories. Other words that are not so obvious have also been interpreted liberally by the courts to violate the categories. Check with your local Fair Housing Office for a complete listing of words to avoid. For example, the following terms may, in the context of an ad, be considered in violation of federal, state, or local laws.

private (as in
  private community)
bachelor
integrated
couple
membership approval
family (perfect for family)
mentally ill
mature
no children
religious landmark
  (near St. Marks)
one person
sex (may be OK if
  advertising for
  roommate)

single
religious
two people
race
christian
restricted
executive
senior discount*
exclusive
adult
handicap
older persons*
retired*
senior citizens*
physically fit person
  (ideal for)

*Housing for the elderly may be exempt from the Fair Housing Act if specific criteria have been met. A letter from the advertiser stating that the requirements of the Fair Housing Act have been met in one of the following ways must be on file prior to publication: The dwelling or housing community must either 1) be designed and operated to assist elderly persons under a state or federal program; 2) be occupied solely by persons 62 years of age or older; or 3) have at least 80% of its occupied units occupied by at least one person 55 years of age or older per unit AND have significant facilities and services designed to meet the physical and social needs of older persons. Retirement communities do qualify as housing for older persons exempt from the Fair Housing Act.

The above list is by no means complete. If you have any questions about this matter, please contact your attorney.

PLANNING AND IMPLEMENTING PROMOTIONAL ACTIVITIES AND EVENTS

By Jennifer A. Nevitt, RAM®

When you're working on an activity or event for your community, there are two variables that will affect the choices you have and the decisions you make: time and money. You may find yourself short of either or both.

If you're short of time, you may have to spend more to get what you need. For instance, if you're short of time, you may have to purchase whatever you can get your hands on to decorate, you may have to pay extra for a rush order on invitations, and you may have to pay someone else to do some of the planning or implementation because you and the rest of the staff cannot jam so much into so few hours.

If you're short of money, you will need to be especially creative when looking for ways to get the job done. Ideally, you will have more time than money. If that is the case, you will be able to use effort and extra thought to get more from your tight budget.

If you are short of both time and money, you have to be even more creative and even better organized. You must focus on the job at hand, make your decisions, and keep going.

No matter what your situation regarding time and money, a thorough understanding of the process of planning and implementing activities and events and a good checklist that you use faithfully will put you well on your way to success.

What follows is an explanation of the many elements that are part of most activities and events. This will give you background and insight into those elements. You can use this guide to prompt your thinking when you are preparing a checklist for your event.

Note: For the purposes of this chapter, activities and events will be used interchangeably to mean any get-together, activity, or event that is sponsored by your community for its residents, the public, the media, or members of the housing industry.

First Things First

Who is your audience? Do the members of this audience have special needs? Interests? Are there subgroups within your audience? If the audience is residents, do you want them to bring guests? (This is a great way to introduce the community to more people.)

You must make certain that the event you are planning is appropriate for the audience. If it isn't, you may be wasting your time and your community's money. Throughout your planning, keep the audience in mind. By doing this, you will have an accurate and nearly automatic way to judge whether your choices are good ones.

Remember, the event you planned last year for an audience of mostly seniors may or may not suit a more mixed group this year. If last year's plans are on file, take them out and go over them and the postevent evaluation. Use what is useful, but be ruthless about altering what no longer works.

What is the purpose of your event? Are you staging a picnic to introduce new residents to the rest of the community? Are you holding a media conference to discuss the opening of a new phase of a multiphase building project or the innovative upgrading and reuse of an old building? Are you hosting an awards banquet given by the owner for the staff?

After you know why you are planning the event and who it is for, you are ready to begin making your plans.

Remember: Make certain you have approval from management for the event, the date, and the budget. Do not skip this step.

Timing Is Everything

Before you send out invitations, hire a caterer or schedule speakers; take about half an hour to check your chosen date and time against what else is going on in the community. Check with local sports teams, the community calendar, and the schedule of events in the Sunday newspaper. Although you will never be able to avoid all conflicts, you can do this quick check and avoid glaring ones.

The Event Coordinator

You will quickly realize that every event, large or small, needs someone who is in charge, someone who is "in the know" from start to finish. This someone is the Event Coordinator. This is the person who orchestrates, coordinates, and takes responsibility for the big picture and every related detail. He or she must be detail oriented, with a calm demeanor and good people skills.

The Event Coordinator must not be the person for whom the event is being planned. For example, if the event is a grand opening, do not make the coordinator the owner or the property manager. The Event Coordinator will be too busy to take part in the ceremony, make a speech, or greet guests. The Event Coordinator's job is to run the event, and that is all. (It is enough.)

Note: In this chapter, it is assumed that you are the Event Coordinator. Remember, you do not have to be the Event Coordinator, but you do need to choose one.

Before You Send Invitations

Before you have invitations printed and addressed, and long before you send them, make certain that any major variable that could affect the invitations has been checked: time and date, availability of the place for the event, availability of your chosen speaker, potential conflicts. As with anything having to do with the planning and implementation of events, have a Plan B, and possibly a Plan C and D if there is a possibility that you'll need one.

A Theme Is Mandatory

All events, activities and promotions need a theme. Without one, it is possible that the audience will miss the point. Without one, you will have to work harder to have an impact on that audience. A theme allows you to focus and intensify your efforts and makes it easier to pay attention to the details.

Choose a theme that reinforces the reason for the event or the point you want to make. What do you want your audience to know and remember? If you are emphasizing the magnificent lake view, choose a theme related to water, beautiful views, or lifestyle.

Your theme can be as simple as a choice of color or colors, or a bit more ambitious, although you will find that simplicity works in your favor.

If you find it difficult to be creative with themes, go to the library. Pull books on different topics that you think are appropriate to your event.

Remember: the simpler the theme, the more successfully you will be able to implement it.

Sample Themes

▶ Gone With the Wind
▶ The Fifties
▶ Star Trek

- All Star Celebration (could be sports or the night sky)
- Garden Party
- Almost any holiday
- Spring, Summer, Winter, or Autumn
- The Sky's the Limit
- Everything is Coming Up Roses
- The Living is Easy
- Taking it Easy
- Movies (in general, or choose a type, such as screwball comedies or westerns)
- It's Everybody's Birthday
- Italian Dinner Party
- Lazy Days of Summer
- The Good Old Days
- Splash: A Pool Party and Picnic
- A Magical Evening (entertainment: a magician)

Invitations

To be useful, an invitation has to be complete. Include, at a minimum, the following information:

- Who
- What
- When (day and time)
- Where
- Why (what is the occasion or purpose)
- Response card and/or telephone number(s) including area codes
- Directions or a map
- Any special information (there will be activities for children or there will be a drawing)

Double-check: Are the numbers in the address and phone listing correct? Are all of the names spelled and punctuated correctly?

After you have all of the information, you can put together the invitation. Stick with your theme for maximum impact.

You have the option to have the invitations printed commercially or to use desktop publishing to create your own. With the programs now available, you can turn out professional-looking invitations quickly and inexpensively on a computer.

You also have the option of printing the envelopes or of addressing them by hand. If the event is an elegant one, consider hiring a calligrapher to write each address.

Mail the invitations or have them delivered. For greatest impact, have the person who is delivering the invitations dress in a costume appropriate to the theme. You can also reinforce the theme by packaging the invitation in something other than a plain envelope. For example, roll an invitation to an Italian Dinner in a red-and-white checked paper napkin or wrapping paper and tie it with a bow.

The Mailing List

There is an adage in the events business that your event is only as good as your mailing list. Keeping in mind the event and its target audience, put together the list. Compile names from all of your senior managers' lists, not just the owner's. Cross-check the lists to avoid duplication. You don't want people to receive multiple invitations or mailings.

Double-check: spellings, addresses, spouses' names.

Give Each Participant a Chance to Look Good

Your event may include speakers or other participants, and these speakers or participants will probably include your owner. Do not assign any task to the participants other than their role as participant or speaker.

For the greatest possible success with the owner or other participants:

1. Get on the calendar with each person as soon as possible.

2. Be very, very clear about what you expect that person to do.

3. As each participant arrives to pick up a name tag, hand him or her a 3 x 5 or 4 x 6 card (small enough to slip into a pocket). On the card write:

   ❯ Participant's last name, first name

   ❯ Participant's itinerary, minute-by-minute. For example:
   10-10:30 Mingle
   10:30-11 At podium. Your mark is the red X.
   Script provided: left suit pocket.
   Joe starts. He will introduce you.
   When finished, leave the stage and sit in right-hand chair in front row next to Mary W.

   Be as specific as possible. The more precise you are about where each speaker or participant needs to be and what he or she is supposed to be doing, the greater the possibility of success.

4. Place colored chalk or tape marks on the stage or in front of the room, or use spray paint to mark the dirt or grass where the speaker or special guests are to stand. If there is a ribbon to cut, mark the spot on the back of the ribbon with two pieces of tape. The dignitary cuts between the pieces of tape.

Double check: Send a confirmation letter to any participant or speaker as soon as he or she has agreed to participate. The day before the event, call to reconfirm.

Speeches

Anyone who will be making a presentation should have a script prepared, double spaced, edited, and presented in final form before the event begins. This will help to keep speakers' comments brief and to the point and should minimize their going off on tangents. Establish maximum times for each speech and stick to them. This may require great tact on your part when negotiating with a long-winded speaker to whom you owe your livelihood, but it is necessary to save the audience from boredom-induced sleepiness. You want your guests to remember what a great event they attended and its purpose, not how long the speaker talked.

Props

If you are having a grand opening and ribbon-cutting ceremony, ordinary shears are not big enough. For real impact, hire an art person or the local theater department's scenery or props class to make giant, gilded scissors. The same resources can probably produce other one-of-a-kind props and simple sets should you need them for an event, from a bridge to enhance an awards ceremony to a setting for taking guest photos.

Name Tags

Use name tags at every event. Do not assume that everyone knows or will remember everyone else's names. Even at an internal company event, name tags are essential to eliminate awkwardness.

Because most people's handwriting is difficult or impossible to read on name tags, prepare name tags. Because people's handwriting on RSVP responses is just as difficult or impossible, have the capability to make additional tags on the spot.

Keep the PC Police at Bay

Considering the diversity of cultures in our country and the public's awareness of this diversity, it makes sense to be aware of all of your choices as they affect your audience as well as any media that may cover the event. Aim to be politically correct (PC). Check your menu. Are you serving roast pork or bacon to a kosher crowd? Don't do it. Did you put burgers and barbecue on the picnic menu for an event whose guest speaker is describing the virtues of a low-fat diet? The mistake will be glaringly obvious, funny to some, and very unfunny to others. Either way, the mistake will take attention away from the event and its purpose.

Don't limit your caution to the menu. Go over every aspect of the event with an eye to preventing a false step.

Make the Media Notice Your Community's Event

If you routinely send various members of the media—electronic and print—releases on company letterhead, you are probably wasting your time. Unless the story you're telling is brand new, offers great visuals, and dances across a desk, chances are the media won't be interested. Your release will look like everyone else's.

To improve the chances of having your story read and used:

❯ Submit stories with news value.

▶ Send or deliver your story to the correct person and/or department. If you're not certain where it goes, call and find out. Spend a few minutes to get the name and the spelling right, or you are wasting everyone's time.

▶ Get creative about the delivery. If you can, use your theme to guide your choice of vehicles. Should your media release come in a miniature basket attached to a bouquet of helium-filled balloons? In a pizza box? Wrapped around an arrow? Think: What will make the recipient notice the delivery and spend a few minutes with the release?

Warning: Don't go overboard with expense, even if your community can afford it. Some journalists feel compelled to reject anything that smacks of bribery. Some companies have policies about the monetary value of such vehicles. Your best bet is to get to know the people and the companies to whom you regularly send releases.

Dressing the Part

How do you want the staff to dress? Professional business clothes? Something in keeping with the theme, such as tropical shirts and straw hats at a luau or matching tennis shirts at a presentation highlighting the lifestyle of your community?

Whatever you choose, make certain that everyone on staff knows what he or she is to wear and has access to that costume. Send a reminder.

Professional Services

Do you want to record the event on video for promotional use or training? Don't do it yourself and don't let someone on staff do it unless that someone is highly experienced with videotape and recorders. You and every member of the staff have other duties. Instead, hire a professional. If it is important enough to record, it is important enough to record well.

The same holds true of photography. If you want to capture the moment for use in newsletters, a memorable gift to participants, or for the company archives, have a professional handle the camera. Don't trust an amateur.

Entertainment

Do you want and have the budget for live entertainment? Recorded music? Actors or mimes? Strolling musicians? Let your theme and your budget guide your choices. Just keep in mind the theme and whether the entertainment improves or distracts from your purpose.

Signage

Make it easy for guests and speakers to find their way. Depending on the event, you may need several directional signs to help people find the building and/or the room or outdoor area, parking, the coat check and the registration table. Other helpful signs include identification of restrooms.

Think it Through

How many people do you expect? This figure will change as you receive the RSVPs either by mail or phone. When you have arrived at a count based on the RSVPs, add 10% to 20% more, depending on your experience with the market and your expectations for attendance at the event. (Unfortunately, not everyone responds when requested to do so.) When in doubt, plan for more people rather than fewer.

Adjust the number of tables, table covers (skirted? plain? draped?), chairs and other equipment according to the number of people you expect and the function of the equipment. Do you need a cake table? A display area? Will your speakers need a podium as well as sound equipment?

Remember: It is better to have a bit too much space and food than not enough.

Plan a Drawing

If possible, plan a drawing or giveaway as part of every event, especially those events aimed at residents or future residents. As part of the invitation, mention that there will be a drawing and what the prize is.

Everybody Has a Job to Do

Each employee should have a job description for the day, and it should be specific. Ideally, you will rotate staff through the jobs every 30 minutes to keep interest and alertness high. List each person's job on a sheet with times and locations. Include a list of duties and/or a definition of the job. Jobs may include clean-up crew, lighting, cloak room, trash patrol, etc. Include one or more greeters. Put your most personable people to work making everyone else feel welcome.

Creature Comforts

People want to be comfortable, so anticipate their basic needs and take care of them. Have coffee and soft drinks on hand, and plenty of ice. Don't forget to offer a place for guests to dispose of dirty cups and napkins. Make certain that seating is plentiful and comfortable. If there are not enough restrooms, consider renting temporary facilities. These can be camou-flaged with screens, a tent, or potted greenery. Be certain that even the temporary facilities have plenty of toilet paper, soap, and paper towels.

Children

Arrange for activities, a separate space, or entertainment for children who are guests, or tailor the program to suit their interests and shorter attention spans.

One of the most effective ways to enchant children at an event is this: Go to a party rental company and see what is newest. Then rent it. Assign staff to the game or equipment.

Provide refreshments.

The Importance of a Telephone

On the day of the event, you must have access to a tele-phone. If necessary, rent a mobile phone for the day. And don't forget to bring a complete list of important telephone numbers with you. Include the caterer, equipment vendors, the entertainment, the media, and anyone whom you could possibly need to call on that day.

An example of a telephone's usefulness: You have prepared for 150 guests (120 sent RSVPs, but experience has shown you that there are always 10% to 15% more who show up.) Even so, it becomes obvious that there are not enough chairs. What do you do?

If you are in a hotel, tell the staff person assigned to you what you want. Make certain you get it immediately.

If you have rented chairs, get on your telephone and call the vendor. Tell the vendor what you want and that you need it immediately. (This is in the realm of Plan C.)

Prepare Plan B, at Least

Even when you've done everything right, it is the rare event that goes exactly according to plan. Always, always have Plan B for every major part of the event. At least. What will you do if the speaker doesn't show? What if it rains on a garden party? What if the field you have counted on for overflow parking turns into a muddy swamp just before the event? What if you have planned on 100 for dinner and 115 show?

If you have Plan B, you won't panic, overreact, or make an embarrassing mistake. You will be ready for just about anything that could happen. To come up with Plan B, imagine each step of the event, and then imagine each step going awry. Could the bulb in the projector burn out? Will the sound system screech? (Check it carefully before anyone arrives. Don't wait to say "Testing, testing, one, two, three" to a full house.)

Double-check: Review your plan and checklist and adjust as needed. Do not leave even the smallest detail to chance.

Follow-up

When the event is over, you still have work to do. You must supervise the return of all rented and borrowed items, then check vendor bills and pay them.

Write a thank you note to every speaker and guest. If there were photographs taken of the speakers and guests, send a print to each one.

This also is an opportunity to build your relationship with current residents and possible future residents. Send a note or letter to each person who attended. Include the theme and thank them for attending. Add whatever sales or other message is appropriate to your purposes. Keep in mind that you must have an accurate guest book or list of who attended to take advantage of sending a follow-up note.

Are there any postevent media opportunities? Was there an especially good photograph that could be sent out with a caption to local media? What about trade publications?

Finally, evaluate the event and its components: What worked? What didn't? Were there any emergencies or problems? How were they handled? Take detailed notes and file them for future use. This will help you to plan another successful event next time.

The Essence of Events Planning

In capsule form, this is events planning:

▶ Plan ahead.
▶ Put Plan A in action.
▶ Check everything repeatedly.
▶ Go to Plan B.
▶ Communicate to everyone involved.
▶ Check everything again.
▶ Go to Plan C as needed.
▶ Keep your sense of perspective and your sense of humor.
▶ Take notes, evaluate, and get ready for the next successful event.

Answers to "What if?"

What if a member of your management team is habitually late. You need him on the podium at 3 p.m. or not at all. What can you do?

Intentionally tell him the event starts 30 minutes earlier than it does. Do not let on that this is a fabrication to deal with his tardiness. In written memos, in the confirmation letter, and at the top of his speech, write the earlier time. He will undoubtedly show up on time, if not a few minutes early. Of course, he will think that he is running late, if he notices at all.

What if the speaker doesn't show?
Plan B:

If you haven't predetermined this (and you probably should have), the most articulate person on your staff who has knowledge of the subject matter wings it after a brief and upbeat introduction. Tip: Keep it short, relaxed, and to the point. If this person has been in the know regarding the event, he or she will, at the very least, understand the point of the event, and that is the point to make in the speech.

Plan C:

No one else can speak on the topic. In this case, choose someone else who is capable of public speaking, and announce that there has been a change of speaker. You have the option of announcing a change of topic if the previous topic had been announced. If not, let it be. Give a short but enthusiastic introduction, never mentioning the lack of preparation nor how unexpected this change in events is.

Items Most Likely Forgotten and Items You May Need on Hand

- Scissors
- Tape
- Guest list or book
- Ice
- Film
- Toilet paper in the bathroom
- Tissues
- Sanitary products in the women's restrooms
- Extra men's ties in basic colors
- Pantyhose in a neutral color
- An extra bulb for the projector
- Breath spray or mint

SUPERIOR PROMOTIONAL ACTIVITIES AND EVENTS
By Tami Siewruk

RESIDENT ACTIVITIES

Purpose and Types of Events

Community sponsored and promoted resident activities and social events, involving both residents and their guests, can have a significant impact on your marketing efforts. The key to using activities and events as marketing tools lies in including not only your residents, but also extending the invitation to their friends and associates. The idea is to create interest and involvement in the community and to promote a feeling of "what a great place to live."

There are many types of resident activities that your community can sponsor. They include lectures, classes, parties, sporting events and competitions, talent shows, art bazaars, flea markets, children's events, etc. Publicize events as thoroughly as possible, including a note in your monthly newsletter, special flyers, and posters. Don't neglect any opportunity to spread the news by word of mouth. Remind each resident as you see or speak to them, and invite all your new residents and future residents.

The only way to ensure that your residents will participate in a social event is to plan with their recreational preferences in mind. The easiest way to build a social or recreational profile of your residents is to conduct a survey aimed at determining their idea of a good time. Following is a sample leisure survey that will help you to plan successful resident events that are tailored to your residents' recreational habits.

WHAT'S YOUR IDEA OF A GOOD TIME?

Dear Resident,

We'd like to remind you that our #1 goal is to make this the best home that we possibly can! We need your help.

The attached survey is very, very important to us, because it tells us more about you. We intend to use the information that you provide us to develop a calendar of social events that is based on the leisure and recreational activities that you enjoy most.

We recognize the value of your time, and sincerely appreciate your willingness to participate. Please complete the following questionnaire and return it to the management office at your earliest convenience. We intend to return the favor throughout the year in fun and exciting social activities that both you and your neighbors can enjoy! Thank you for your valuable input.

Age Group:

[ ]	Under 25	[ ]	25-35
[ ]	36-45	[ ]	46-55
[ ]	56-65	[ ]	Over 65

Regarding our community, what do you like most?_____

_____

What one feature most attracted you to our community?____

_____

What would make you happier to live here? _____

_____

how to excel in leasing apartments

Do you participate in a sport?	Do you follow a professional sport?
[ ] No	[ ] No
[ ] Softball / Baseball	[ ] Baseball
[ ] Football	[ ] Football
[ ] Basketball	[ ] Basketball
[ ] Volleyball	[ ] Hockey
[ ] Tennis	[ ] Tennis
[ ] Racquetball	[ ] Golf
[ ] Golf	[ ] Auto racing
[ ] Bowling	[ ] Bowling
[ ] Soccer	[ ] Soccer
[ ] Other	What team(s): _____

In what organized sport would you be most interested in participating? _____

_____

[ ] Volleyball   [ ] Tennis
[ ] Softball   [ ] Bowling

If you are employed, how far do you drive to work?_____
How long does it usually take?_____

Where do you shop most often? [ ] Close to home [ ] On the way home from work

When do you have leisure time?

[ ] Sunday	[ ] Day	[ ] Night
[ ] Monday	[ ] Day	[ ] Night
[ ] Tuesday	[ ] Day	[ ] Night
[ ] Wednesday	[ ] Day	[ ] Night
[ ] Thursday	[ ] Day	[ ] Night
[ ] Friday	[ ] Day	[ ] Night
[ ] Saturday	[ ] Day	[ ] Night

How do you most enjoy spending your leisure time during the day? _____

How do you most enjoy spending your leisure time in the evening? _____

Please number the following in order of preference
(1=most fun; 6=least fun)

[ ]   Reading   [ ]   Cards/Board games
[ ]   Walking/jogging   [ ]   Arts/Crafts
[ ]   Movies/videos   [ ]   Other:_____

Which events would you most like to see held here at our community?

[ ]   Coffee and doughnut socials
[ ]   Health fairs
[ ]   Water aerobics
[ ]   Planned walks
[ ]   Bingo
[ ]   Card parties
[ ]   Business card exchanges/networking socials
[ ]   Lectures or seminars (please note your preferred subject and/or speaker):_____
[ ]   Other:_____

Which do you prefer? [ ] Going to a cinema [ ] Renting videos

What movie genre do you prefer?

[ ]   Drama   [ ]   Comedy
[ ]   Sci-fi   [ ]   Horror
[ ]   Action-Adventure   [ ]   Documentaries
[ ]   Foreign   [ ]   Art

How often do you rent videos?

[ ]   Daily   [ ]   About twice a week
[ ]   A few times a month   [ ]   Once a month
[ ]   Every few months   [ ]   Never

What night(s) do you most frequently rent movies or go to the cinema?

[ ] Sunday   [ ] Thursday
[ ] Monday   [ ] Friday
[ ] Tuesday   [ ] Saturday
[ ] Wednesday

Do you have children living with you? [ ] Yes [ ] No

Are your children involved in a structured summer activity?
[ ] Yes [ ] No

What are your children's special interests?

[ ] Movies   [ ] Board games: _____
[ ] Swimming   [ ] Arts/Crafts:_____
[ ] Sports: _____ [ ] Martial Arts:_____
[ ] Other: _____

Do you have a pet?

[ ] No   [ ] Fish
[ ] Bird   [ ] Cat
[ ] Dog   [ ] Other:_____

Planning the Event

The manager and team will be responsible for creating the event atmosphere, generating enthusiasm, and organizing the function. Make sure your team understands that they're not just throwing a party. They are involved in a marketing effort. The effectiveness of your team in planning resident activities can be gauged through reduced resident turnover and increased favorable word-of-mouth advertising.

In offering resident events, you are creating synergy between the resident's social life and the social life of your community as a whole. Resident social events should be designed to meet your residents' need to belong. The friendships created in a community will eventually lead to a reduced resident turnover, as those who feel that they are living among good friends will be less likely to move. Resident referrals will increase when your residents are encouraged to share their home with friends and associates.

New residents are often new to your area of the city. A resident may have special interests (i.e., sports) that require group participation, and will want to make new friends with similar interests. Additionally, people are also remaining single longer, which can create a sense of being alone in new surroundings. These factors will help draw your residents into social community involvement.

An effective social activities program doesn't happen without a great deal of effort. Each event must be carefully planned and executed. Resident activity committees can help you gather resident input, but realize that your team will bear the ultimate burden and responsibility in bringing social events to life. The use of an Event and Social Activity Planning Guide will help keep your team on track, and give you a place to keep track of or estimate your expenses while planning an event.

The first step involved in planning your social calendar is to determine your monthly social and recreational budget. Much of the cost of an event can be defrayed by asking residents to bring food and drinks where appropriate. Your budget will govern most choices in planning an event, but remember... NEVER lose sight of your resident profile when planning ANY activity!

Above all, remember that it is better to hold a well-produced party once a quarter than to hold a party monthly that is just thrown together.

Alternatively, you may choose to supplement your budget by charging the resident a nominal fee to participate in the event or activity. Another way to reduce expenses is to keep a list of supplies on hand following each event to make use of them at the next event.

Note: Never charge residents for drinks at community-sponsored events. Never ask them to pay cover or donation charges at events where liquor is served.

If you choose to serve liquor, provide plenty of coffee and snacks. You have a responsibility as the host to discourage overconsumption. Above all, make certain you are aware of your company and community policy regarding alcoholic beverages.

Some residents can become upset to constantly hear about free events; they know their rent is paying for community activities, and it makes any rent increases they may receive harder to accept unless they themselves enjoy and participate in the activities. It is a known fact that residents have moved from socially active communities because of their feeling of subsidizing community-sponsored activities. Keep this in mind, and don't be afraid to charge a small fee to fund your community's activity program, especially when the event provides entertainment. Your residents will feel as though they're really getting something for their money, and nonactive residents won't feel like their rent is paying for activities they do not attend.

With your budget in mind, the next step is to plan ahead with the use of a social calendar. This calendar is used for private clubhouse bookings along with community-sponsored events.

Before you begin planning in earnest, remember there will be changes, additions, and cancellations throughout the planning process. Keep a handle on the planning process, but don't attempt to do it all single-handedly. Some communities have had great success with activity committees composed of residents. Some committees are good for ideas only, but others will pitch in and help with decorations, bartending, shopping, and cooking.

Be Prepared for Successful Resident Events

The following planning guide has been designed to assist you in developing workable activity ideas and plans. You may consider establishing a Social Activity Planning Guide Exchange between your community and others within your company. This exchange will save everyone time when designing activities for the year. Keep all guides in a three-ring binder for easy access. Each time a new activity or event is designed, add it to the book. Before long you will have a complete book of activities that will last for years.

Be creative, enthusiastic, and prepared. You're certain to be a success!

Event and Social Activity Planning Guide

Community: _____

Designed by: _____Telephone: _____

Address: _____

Event/Activity Idea with Detailed Description: _____

_____

_____

Location (pool, clubhouse, etc.):_____

Time of Year (month): _____

Approximate number of guests: _____

Food		
Music		
Decorations		
Prizes		
Invitations, flyers (attach samples)		
Types of vendors/ sponsors needed		
	TOTAL BUDGET:	

How to Promote to Residents: Planning

6 Weeks Prior	
4 Weeks Prior	
2 Weeks Prior	
1 Week Prior	
Day of Event	

Additional Comments/Information:_____

_____

_____

Make a list of everything to do in preparation for the party well in advance of the party date.

Party preparation can take up to two to three months. You'll want to allow plenty of time to plan and spread excitement about the upcoming event.

Following are some of the major decisions that you'll have to make, and steps that you'll have to take as planning progresses.

Guest List

1. Residents and their guests, new residents, future residents, and suppliers
2. Determine method of arriving at approximate head count for the party:
   a. Ask residents to RSVP by calling or send back a return form indicating attendance.
   b. Have staff call residents to confirm their attendance (this method also encourages attendance).
   c. If there's no time for any of the above, guess!

Promotion

Announcement of the event is a major part of the preparation process. Use every medium at your disposal to generate interest and excitement, including your newsletter, flyers, posters, bulletin boards, and special invitations.

Announce events in your newsletter at least one month in advance. Make it a front-page item during the month of the event, and plan to have newsletters in your residents' hands by the first of the month. Make it sound like an event not to be missed.

Personally invite each resident as they pay their rent, call in a service request, or stop by the office to pick up a package. Ask questions such as: "Can we expect you at the party on Saturday?" This will increase enthusiasm, and will also give you a good idea of how many residents to expect.

Follow up two to three days in advance with a flyer on each door. A sign at your community's entrance and exit can also be used a few days in advance as a reminder. Keep reminding them. You'll get a better response.

Change the entrance and exit signs to read "It's Here! The Party Is Tonight!" on the day of the party.

Invitations

In many cases, your invitation will determine your event's success. If the invitation looks and sounds fun, they will assume that the party will be too.

1. Choose the type of invitation
   a. Flyer
   b. Flyer and newsletter
   c. Preprinted invitations
   d. Flyer
   e. Telephone call

2. Determine artwork style and copy. Obtain this information after the date and time are established and the clubhouse has been reserved.

3. Take steps that will result in the finished invitations being delivered or purchased.
   a. Assign artwork
   b. Allocate time for reproduction
   c. Allocate time for delivery

Use the following checklist:
- ❏ Name of printer:
- ❏ Point of contact:
- ❏ Phone:
- ❏ Pickup date:
- ❏ Deposit: $
- ❏ Ink/paper colors:
- ❏ Paper stock:
- ❏ # of invitations needed:
- ❏ Lettering styles:
- ❏ Date needed:
- ❏ # of response cards needed:
- ❏ Size of invitations:

Points to cover in the invitation copy:
- ❏ Type of party:
- ❏ Date:
- ❏ Time:
- ❏ Location:
- ❏ RSVP to:
- ❏ Suggested attire (costume, casual?):
- ❏ Bring:
- ❏ Who's invited:

Invitations may be informal or formal. An informal invitation can be printed on almost anything, with just the pertinent information. The informal invitation usually incorporates casual typefaces and illustrations. Formal invitations are usually printed on fine cardstock with black engraved lettering, and include a traditional message of invitation. Formal response cards are included, directing the recipient to respond regarding his/her attendance. Formal invitations are normally reserved for use on special holidays, grand openings, etc.

Remember that your invitation should reflect the character of your event.

Shopping List

Decorations	Dish soap
Prizes	Window cleaner
Glasses	Sodas
Napkins	Tonic water
Tablecloths	Soda water
Plates	Coke
Forks	Pepsi
Knives	7-Up
Spoons	Juice
Serving spoons	Grapefruit juice
Salt	Tomato juice
Pepper	Lemons
Tables	Limes
Trash bags	Ice
Toothpicks	Vodka
Scotch	Chairs
Whiskey	Prizes
Gin	Coffee
Bourbon	Coffeepot
Rum	Tea
Beer	Cream
Wine	Sugar
Snacks	Coffee cups

Professionally planned social activities can be presented on a low budget with a small selection of hors d'oeuvres and cheese trays. You may wish go to large discount stores or shopping clubs (Sam's, Pace, Price Club, Cosco, etc.). Purchasing in bulk will reduce the cost of food and drink considerably. Supplies such as cups, table coverings, napkins, silverware and plates are also best purchased in large quantities.

Setting the Stage

You may want to offer a door prize or hold contests where prizes will be awarded. Prizes could include movie tickets, wine, gourmet baskets, compact discs, gift certificates, sporting equipment, free dinner for two, etc. Merchants may offer a discount or even a free item in exchange for a promotional announcement in your newsletter, flyer, or move-in packages.

Creating the right atmosphere is important to the success of your social activity. It helps in developing a party mood. Use your imagination and sense of style. A sign greeting your residents is always a nice touch if you are not personally available.

Decorations can also be purchased quite reasonably from wholesalers. Often, catalogs from educational stores are available upon request, and looking through one will give you plenty of party ideas. Libraries will have a good selection on books published to give you low-cost party ideas. Many decorations can be easily made at low cost, but may require a lot of time to make.

Keep in mind lighting will also help you create a mood. The brighter the lights, the happier the mood. You may want to begin with bright lights, and then dim them as the night progresses, to create a quieter mood.

Note: Box up the decorations and props used for an event and offer it to another community. This not only saves money and time, but you will often get the box back with a few additions!

There are times when social activities call for added entertainment. There is a wide variety of entertainment options available to your community. Here is a partial listing:

- Rent a jukebox.
- Hire a disc jockey.
- Contact the concert bureau of a local conservatory, college, or music school.
- Contact the performing arts department of a local high school
- Look under "Entertainment" or "Music" in the yellow pages
- Rent a VCR and videos and prepare popcorn.
- Check with your travel agency. They can supply some interesting travel or video movies that may serve as a backdrop for scenery in your room.
- Put a video camera to work. Make your own movie with your residents. Let them write the script, be the director, producers and performers. (Teenagers enjoy this entertainment.)

Staffing

Although team members are encouraged to enjoy the social event, they should be aware that it is a working evening. Conduct should be friendly but professional at all times. Staffing might include:

1. Official hosts and hostesses: Hosts and hostesses are important to the overall success of your event. Being a good host or hostess is like being the producer of a Broadway play. You have chosen the actors (social committee, employees, hosts, and hostesses). You have set the stage and directed all the activities, arranged the props and raised the curtain. Now all you need to focus on is making certain the audience gives you good reviews. Here are a few quick tips to receive a "thumbs up" review and a standing ovation:

a. Welcome your residents and guests at the door. Take their coats, or inform them where they can be placed. Introduce your residents and guests to a few people by making a short explanation about the person that will help start a conversation. A good example is ... "Mr. Jones, this is Mr. Smith, who just moved here from Lakeland." You may want to try using name tags to aid you and other team members in these introductions. Keep in mind how you may feel when you enter a party and do not yet know anyone.

b. Keep plenty of carbonated water on hand. This will help remove spills on your clubhouse carpet or furniture. Remember, a good host or hostess never makes a fuss when something is spilled or broken. Chances are, the spill or breakage was not intentional and you do not want to upset a happy resident.

c. When a guest has had too much to drink and should not operate a motor vehicle, order a taxi, prepay the driver, and insist your guest leave their automobile. When they return to retrieve their car, you are certain to get a big "thank you."

d. When you are ready to wind down the party, you simply change the pace by turning the volume down on the music, turn the lights brighter or lower depending on the circumstances, and shut off a few lights. Wait a few minutes, and begin the clean-up process. The host or hostess should begin to thank everyone for attending and invite them back to the next event.

2. Cook—to replenish food supply, warm hors d'oeuvres

3. Bartenders

4. Clean-up crew for after the event. The manager and service technician should coordinate this effort.

5. If feasible, start decorating the clubhouse at least a week before the event. This serves as a great leasing tool to show the future residents you have an active social program. Show them how much fun it is to live in your community.

Everyone should have an assignment for the night of the big party so someone is bartending, and someone else is setting out hors d'oeuvres and replenishing the food trays.

Ensure That a Good Time Is Had by All

To be certain that residents enjoyed themselves and will want to attend your next event, send out an informal survey asking for their input. You can also simply call attendees at random. Whichever method you select, keep in mind that successful social activities can be a huge asset to your community.

Now that you're ready to plan a successful event, we've included some great party ideas that will help you with your event planning.

Recreational Activities

Volleyball or pool volleyball
Billiards tournament
Ping pong tournament
Swimming and diving contest
Camping

Scavenger hunt

Shopping trip to local outlet mall

Basketball, baseball, or hockey game picnic

Canoe lessons/trip

Challenge of the sexes olympics

Softball

Flag football

Ski lessons and a ski trip

Marathon/10-K race

Dancing lessons

Boating

Water skiing

Scuba lessons/scuba trip

Snorkeling trip

Ice/roller skating

Bicycle Race/trip

Game night (chess, checkers, etc.)

Backgammon lessons/tournament

Cards—poker, bridge, Uno, etc.

Horseback riding

Croquet

Badminton

Trip to race track

Basketball

Snowmobiling

Archery lessons/competition

Darts

Produce a play

Flea market

Chorus/choir

Street fair

Exercise class or aerobics

Tennis lessons/ tournament

Racquetball lessons/tournament

Self-defense/martial arts
Belly dancing lessons
Fencing lessons/competition
Guitar lessons
Decorating contests
Trips to local places of interest

Educational Opportunities:

(offer classes on the following subjects)
Foreign language
Cooking
Investment counseling
Literature
Bartending
Cake decorating
Weaving
Photography
Microwave cooking
Sewing
Crochet or knitting
Needlepoint
Tropical fish & aquarium maintenance
Films
Wine tasting
Candlemaking
Sculpture
Sign language
Art and music appreciation
Make-up and hairstyling
Computer literacy
Gardening

You may also choose to offer your clubhouse free to local colleges and universities for Continuing Education classes in the evenings. (You may want to consider charging a small clean-up fee.) Gourmet stores, wineries, craft stores, photography outlets, dance studios, the local YMCA, karate studios, health clubs, the city parks department, and local schools are the best sources for talented instructors. Obtain a copy of your community college's current catalogue, and look for local "free university" publications. Contact the instructors. You will find many of them willing to offer their services outside the classroom for a group rate, or even free of charge.

Theme Party Ideas

Successful community parties are usually based on a theme. Remember that the decorations, costumes, food, drinks, and activities will all play a part in developing a successful theme. The following calendar may offer some inspiration.

January:
1 New Year's Day, Rose Bowl Day
5 Wassail Eve
6 Twelfth Night, Epiphany, Three Kings' Day, Opening of Carnival Season
10 League of Nations Day
15 Martin Luther King's Birthday
16 Franklin's Birthday
19 Robert E. Lee Day, Confederate Heroes Day
24 Paul Pitcher Day
25 St. Paul's Day, Super Flush Sunday
26 Australia Day
29 Carnation Day
30 Franklin D. Roosevelt Day
Also: Handsel Monday, Inauguration Day, Plough Monday

February: 2 Candlemas Day, Groundhog Day, Presentation of Our Lord
3 Blaise's Day
6 Waitangi Day
12 Lincoln's Birthday
14 St. Valentine's Day
15 Decimal Day, Lupercalia Battleship Day, Susan B. Anthony's Birthday
22 Washington's Birthday, Thinking Day
23 Hobart Regatta Day
27 Majuba Day
29 Leap Day, Bachelor's Day
Also: Meal Monday, Presidents' Day, Washington-Lincoln Day

March: 1 St. David's Day
2 Texas Independence Day
4 Town Meeting Day
5 Mother-in-law Day, St. Piran's Day
6 Alamo Day
8 International Women's Day
12 Girl Scout Day
17 St. Patrick's Day, Evacuation Day
18 Sheelah's Day
21 Earth Day
26 Lady Day, Annunciation, Maryland Day, Greek Independence Day
30 Seward's Day
Also: Commonwealth Day

April: 1 All Fool's Day/April Fool's Day
2 Taily Day
12 Halifax Day

	14	Pan-American Day
	15	Swallow Day
	19	Primrose Day
	22	Arbor Day
	23	Shakespeare's Birthday
	24	Secretaries' Day
	30	Walpurgis Night
	Also:	Geranium Day, A Patriot's Day
May:	1	May Day, Labor Day, Beltane Day, Lei Day
	3	Crouchmas
	8	Furry Day, VE Day, Harry Truman's Birthday
	9	Liberation Day
	12	Hospital Day
	24	Commonwealth Day, Empire Day
	25	Flitting Day, Dismal Day
	29	Royal Oak Day, Oak Apple Day, Restoration Day, Shick-Shack Day
	30	Memorial Day, Decoration Day
	31	Republic Day
	Also:	Armed Forces Day, Cup Final Day, Fishin' Day, Early May Bank Holiday, Late May Bank Holiday, Mother's Day, Victoria Day
June:	1	Corpus Christi, State Foundation Day
	3	Jefferson Davis's Birthday
	6	D-Day
	11	Long Barnaby, St. Barnabas's Day, King Kamehameha Day
	14	Flag Day
	15	Pioneer Day
	16	Bloomsday, Dismal Day
	17	Bunker Hill Day

18 Waterloo Day
19 Emancipation Day
21 Longest Day, Mumpint Day, Summer Solstice
23 Midsummer Eve
24 Midsummer Day
Also: Alexandra Rose Day, Ascot Sunday, Father's Day, Lanimer Day

July: 1 Canada Day, Dominion Day
4 Independence Day, Fourth of July, Old Midsummer Eve
5 Tynwald Day
12 Orange Day
14 Bastille Day
15 St. Swithin's Day
25 St. James's Day
26 St. Anne's Day
Also: Diamond Day, Spinning Wheels Day, Watermelon Days, Wrong Days

August: 1 Lammas Day, Gule of August
5 Oyster Day, Grotto Day
6 Transfiguration
12 Glorious Twelfth, St. Grouse's Day
15 Assumption, VD Day
27 Lyndon B. Johnson's Birthday
Also: Nut Monday, Picnic Day, Victory Day, Walking Sunday

September: 1 Partridge Day
3 Cromwell's Day
9 Admission Day
10 Air Force Day, The Tenth of September

12 Defender's Day
14 Holy Cross Day, Holy Rood Day
17 Citizenship Day, St. Lambert's Day
23 Autumnal Equinox
29 Michaelmas
Also: Kid's Day, Labor Day, Pig Face Sunday, Sunflower Daze, Thamesday

October: 2 Old Man's Day
6 German Day, Ivy Day
10 Kruger Day
12 Columbus Day, October the Twelfth
14 The Fourteenth of October
18 Alaska Day, Lukemas, St. Luke's Day
21 Trafalgar Day
24 United Nation's Day, Pioneer Day
25 St. Crispin's Day
27 Big Bang Day, Day of Peace
30 Devil's Night
31 All Hallows Eve, Duck Apple Night, Dookie Apple Night, Halloween, Nevada Day
Also: Apple Tuesday, Fall Harvest Day, Fraternal Day, Good Thief Sunday, Punkie Night

November: 1 All Saints' Day, All Hallows Day, Hallowmas
2 All Souls' Day, Day of the Dead
4 Mischief Night
5 Guy Fawke's Day, Bonfire Night, Ringing Day
9 Lord Mayor's Day, Sadie Hawkins' Day
11 St. Martin's Day, Martinmas, Remembrance Day
17 Queen's Day
22 St. Cecilia's Day

23 Repudiation Day, St. Clement's Day
25 Cathern Day, St. Catherine's Day
30 St. Andrew's Day
Also: Grey Cup Day, Melbourne Cup Day, Raisin Monday, Recreation Day, Thanksgiving Day

December: 6 St. Nicholas's Day
11 Indiana Day
13 St. Lucy's Day
16 Day of Covenant, Day of Vow
17 Aviation Day, Saturnalia
21 Forefather's Day, St. Thomas's Day, Gooding Day, Winter Solstice, Shortest Day
24 Christmas Eve
25 Christmas Day
26 Boxing Day, St. Stephen's Day, Day of Good Will
28 Childermas Day, Holy Innocents Day, Proclamation Day
31 New Year's Eve, Hogmanay
Also: Advent Sunday

Other Party Suggestions

Sunday Brunch
Hobo Party
50's, 60's, or 70's Party
New Resident Coffee and Donut Gathering
Summer or Winter Sports Club
Come As You Are Party
Come As You Were Party
Wine and Cheese Party
Before Sporting Event Party

Scavenger Hunt
After Sporting Event Party
Travel Club
Chili Cook-off or Dinner
Ski Club
Pizza Party Movie Night
Toga Party
T.G.I.F.
Style Show, Male & Female
Old Fashioned Picnic
Funny Hat and Glasses Party
Punk Rock
Western Theme
Monday Night Football
Week Breakers
Pig Roast
Cookout
Luau
Dinner Theater
Clambake
Over 30 Party; Over 40 Party
Parents Without Partners
A Night Under the Stars

You may also find a nightclub willing to treat your group to a "discount" hour in that establishment. This provides a free place to hold a resident event with no clean-up responsibilities.

Here are a few additional ideas and details, many of which can come alive with an approximate investment of $250. Management companies may choose to produce one theme, and split the cost among several communities who can make use of the props and decorations.

20's Prohibition Speakeasy

The "roaring twenties" was a time when people flocked to the illegal and well-concealed speakeasy clubs in the warehouse districts of every major city. There, they danced away the blues while enjoying a spot of much-coveted local moonshine, or "bathtub" gin. Your residents will enter the secret jazz club through the back alley door of an old warehouse, and find themselves amidst the covered crates and boxes of a storage room-turned nightclub. Silhouettes of thugs and a bathtub filled with bottles of gin will create the seedy, secretive ambiance of the Prohibition speakeasy era. Photos of jazz players can be used for mood setting.

30's Cotton Club

Take your residents back to the 1930's for an evening of lively music and dancing during the relaxed decade following World War I. Clubs were no longer hidden in the warehouse districts, but became bright, elegant places where people could throw their cares away and celebrate the end of Prohibition in high style. Brick columns supporting an awning and lamp posts create the entrance to this decadent theme event. Inside the clubhouse, Art Deco-style ostrich plumes and blue neon sconces set the mood for an evening of carefree entertainment in the elegant style of "The Cotton Club."

50's Blast to the Past

Blast back to the innocent, fun-filled days of the 50's with this colorful theme event. Create a time tunnel filled with memorabilia from the era, and take your residents back in time to where they will once again experience the drive-in diner, the soda bar, the old-fashioned juke box and the vintage car that took them to their first high school sock hop. A 50's band or DJ playing all the old favorites can complete the transformation into a nostalgic memory lane.

60's Psychedelic Scene

Groove on back to the 60's for an evening of listening to the still-fantastic music of Motown. Bright colors in psychedelic patterns can give this theme design a unique look, and will inspire your guests to "cut loose" and "get down" for an evening of high-energy dancing and fun. Use a stage design straight out of "Laugh-In" to set the mood, while graphics of Peace and Love symbols bring out the flower child in everyone.

Into the Future

Beam "Into the Future" for an evening of high entertainment and fun. A futuristic "time tunnel" moves guests into the clubhouse. Geometric shapes suspended from the ceiling in bright neon colors create a galactic effect that will keep eyes darting from place to place throughout the evening. Star Trek characters and the Starship Enterprise give residents plenty to talk about.

Batman Bash

The mysterious "Bat Cave" entrance will set the mood for this ominous theme event. "Batman" theme music will play and the Joker's menacing laugh will add drama. Once inside, your residents will be awed by the decor that creates the interior of the cave. Gothic arches, hanging moss, blinking computer panels and life-size stand-up Batman and Joker cutouts will create the mood.

Sports-a-Thon

This event is perfect for team-building sports lovers, as it takes you into a stadium where America's favorite pro sports are represented. The four corners of the clubhouse are transformed into sports bars that represent either a specific sport or team location. Posters, pennants, and other sports paraphernalia are displayed. Run game bloopers on a television or big screen. For the competitive side in each of us, the game board gives residents the opportunity to compete for prizes and recognition. Pop-a-shots, football tosses, billiards, and other games of skill are found around the perimeter of the room, and will provide hours of entertainment and fun at this all out, high-energy sports-a-thon!

Toga-Toga-Toga!

This is the perfect theme if you want an all-out crazy party. Ask your residents to dress in Greek togas or as their favorite "Animal House" character. The theme is based on the movie Animal House recreated, and is ideal for any group that is ready to cut loose and party with the "Greeks" in this recreated frat house. Rent the "Animal House" video and play it on a big screen TV.

Let's Dance

Come dance 'til you can't stand up at this party designed specifically around music and dancing. Decor elements include oversized records, black glittered music notes, instruments, and perhaps a Karaoke talent contest to spotlight your guests' singing talents! Everyone is sure to leave their cares at thedoor and join in with the fun and merriment for an evening spent dancing and singing along with the crowd.

Sun 'N Surf

Not all states have surf, but all have at least some sun. Incorporate ocean waves, palm trees, beach characters, etc., to provide the surf. Do it any time of the year, but it's especially great in the dead of winter. When it's cold and dreary, everyone would like to take a vacation—real or imagined—to the Bahamas, Hawaii, Caribbean, Mexico, or wherever your fantasy paradise happens to be. Bars will be found under bright cabanas, and buffets include an extra special surprise of a person buried up to his neck in the sand! A volleyball net over the dance floor with suspended seagulls and beach balls will continue the theme in a whimsical fashion. Finally, posters from your travel agency keep the imagination traveling.

Mardi Gras

Your residents will feel as if they have actually been to New Orleans for the famous celebration called Mardi Gras! Invite them to put on their favorite costume and come party the night away to the jazz sounds of Bourbon Street recreated. Bright lamé fabrics, confetti in purple, green, and gold, and Mardi Gras masks and beads form the basics of this theme's decor. A huge dragon can be suspended over the dance floor amidst kites and luminaries to bring in the illusion of parade floats, common on the streets of New Orleans during this annual celebration.

Hooray for Hollywood

The glitz and glamour of Hollywood come directly to you in this spectacular theme event that is perfect for your community awards program. White lights on a black marquee, red carpet treatment, crowds cheering, and elegant contemporary staging set the tone for an evening reminiscent of the Oscars. Live video cameras can be incorporated into the decor for an upscale presentation. Life-size cutouts of the stars complete the theme and offer an excellent photo opportunity for the guests to have their pictures taken with their favorites.

Cajun Wharf

Join us down on the Bayou for some eerie, mysterious swamp action, where there's always danger lurking near the festive wharves of Louisiana. A suspended wooden bridge will guide your residents over the dangerous croco-dile-infested swamp waters, through the entwined branches of the cypress trees hung with Spanish moss, out onto the brightly lighted docks. Residents can find refreshment at the tin "Moonshine Shacks" where bootleggers still make their own whiskey. Be warned—this brew is stronger than the legal stuff! All created with painted refrigerator cartons, blow-up crocodile pool floats, and a few silk trees.

It's a Jungle Out There

This outlandish theme event will take your residents deep into the jungles of Africa or South America. Ruins, over-grown with vines and tropical foliage, stand guard at the entrance of the clubhouse, and the only way in is to traverse the suspended rope bridge. Sounds of screaming birds calling to one another accompany your residents into the clubhouse. The huge face of a gorilla stares ominously out over the crowd from his place of honor. The perimeter of the room is transformed into a tropical world using paradise bird panels and tropical leaf patterns. Vines hanging from the ceiling amidst various colorful birds carry the design throughout the room. All these items can be purchased at a party store.

Champagne and City Lights

Red carpet between fake marble pedestals, topped with exotic leaf arrangements, leads the way to an elevator facade that will carry your guests to this apartment penthouse suite for an elegant, formal affair. The twinkling lights of the city skyline gleam through your clubhouse windows.

PROSPECTING FOR TRAFFIC
by Anne Sadovsky, RAM®

Are you sitting around waiting for prospective renters to parachute into your office?

That day is over. With so much competition today, consumers have so many choices that they may never make it to your property. So put on your marketing hat, and get out and make it happen.

Drive-By Gets Credit for 50 Percent or More

If drive-by is anywhere near your greatest source of traffic, look for ways to attract even more. IMPROVE CURB APPEAL with seasonal color, perfectly groomed grounds and flower beds, and spotless parking areas. Colorful and interesting SIGNAGE helps clients find the property, then the office after they arrive. RESERVED PARKING for office guests/future residents lets them know that they are important to you. Where permitted, FLAGS AND BANNERS that are tasteful and strategically placed help attract attention and guide customers to your door. If the office is difficult to find or needs added color, AWNINGS over the door bring attention to the entry.

What Can You Do to Create More Traffic? Outreach

Calling on local employers and area businesses does pay off, perhaps not with immediate leases, but the residual effect can be powerful. Start with companies within a 10-mile radius of the community, dress for success, and gather an appropriate number of collateral materials. Brochures and other materials should be professionally designed and printed and must represent your property well. Most employers will refuse an appointment with you by asking you to mail the literature, so don't call first, just drop by. The front desk person can make you or break you, so win them over immediately. Try taking a small gift (a coffee mug filled with candy) and give it to the person who greets you. Ask for the owner or the human resources director. Promise to be brief, then do so.

Never tell the employer how much you need their employees to live on your property; rather, tell them how their employees will benefit by living there. Follow up with a letter, send more brochures, and ask them to let you know when they need more. OUTREACH is not a one-time effort. Develop a relationship so that when the company hires in the future, they will refer new employees to your community. Be sure that the companies you call on have employees who can afford the rent at your property.

Resident Referrals

The real licensing agencies in some states prohibit the paying of referral fees to unlicensed people/residents. Some states do allow referral fees. Either way, resident referrals are a critical part of the success of the property.

Having a resident referral program in place but not promoting it gets few results. Having a column on referral programs in your newsletter is great, but it may disappear in all the other features. Make it stand out. Coordinate it with posters in the clothes care centers (laundry rooms) and mail box areas. Change the theme regularly; for example, do a seasonal promotion four times a year. A "Choose Your Own Neighbors," "Bring a Friend"-type theme should run through promotions, as should the rules where fees are being paid.

Resident referral programs are totally ineffective on properties where service is poor or nonexistent, so if you expect results you must first deliver the finest service your residents have ever had.

Other methods of CREATING MORE TRAFFIC are monitoring the success of your advertising methods, writing editorials and getting them placed in newspapers, increasing community/ public awareness by hosting events like art shows and charity events on site, and generally being a public relations/marketing representative for your property. It takes extra effort to read newspapers and send information to newly engaged couples, newlyweds, new businesses moving to the area, and personnel agencies advertising for employees who might move to your area, but it really pays off.

When you experience the results of marketing your community, you'll wish you'd done it long ago.

OUTREACH PROGRAMS TO BUSINESS, INDUSTRY, AND OTHER ORGANIZATIONS
By Tami Siewruk

Why and When

Marketing calls can be one of the most effective means of generating qualified rental traffic to a community. The purpose of a marketing call is to introduce the community to the merchant or corporation and offer some type of incentive to send qualified rentals to the community. There are three types of marketing calls: blitz marketing calls, merchant, and corporate. Keep a record of off-site marketing calls. A sample log sheet is provided at the end of this section.

Marketing Calls and Referrals

Blitz and Merchant Marketing Calls

A blitz marketing call usually takes a minute or two to complete and simply involves a brief greeting to the merchant and giving out several referral cards or flyers. You will ask the merchant to send qualified future residents to your community. This type of call is extremely brief, but is effective because of the number of merchants who can be contacted in a relatively short period of time. It would not be uncommon to make 20 to 30 blitz marketing calls in an hour. Merchants to visit on blitz marketing calls are limitless. Consider visiting shopping centers, shopping malls, restaurants, grocery stores, gas stations, furniture stores, sporting events, health clubs, beauty salons, doctors' offices, and more. These sources are ones which should be exhausted as a part of the marketing program. Each community differs, and marketing sources must therefore be developed accordingly.

A merchant marketing call is the same as a blitz marketing call, only more time is taken with each call.

Follow these very simple steps:

1. Call the merchant and ask for the manager. Say why you are calling and ask if he/she has some free time; you would like to share your new merchant referral program. Make sure they understand that there is no cost involved. Set up an appointment.

2. Bring a portfolio of merchant referral flyers. Show specific examples of what their personal coupon referral will look like.

3. Tell them again, and repeat several times, that this program is free. All the merchant has to do is to pass the coupon flyers out to every customer who purchases from him. Customers should not be asked whether they would like the flyer or not. It should automatically be put into their bag with their purchase. EVERYBODY KNOWS SOMEBODY WHO NEEDS AN APARTMENT.

4. Reassure the merchant that the leasing consultants will be keeping track of validated coupon flyers. You will purchase a gift certificate from the merchant for a specified amount in the future resident's name when they lease and move in. Note: Gift certificates should only be given to the new resident on the day of move-in, in case of cancellations.

5. It is important that you shop the merchants to see if they are passing out the flyers. If they are not, follow up with a personal visit and explain the program to the merchant again.

6. Revisit or call each merchant once a month to restock flyers.

7. With each referred future resident, call the merchant immediately to let him know that the program is working.

The items listed below, with promotional cards attached, have been distributed on blitz calls with great success:

- A package of microwave popcorn with a card reading "Things are really popping at our community. Pop in and see why!"
- A stick of gum with a card saying: "Chew on this idea. Visit our community and see why our residents stick with us."
- A small bag of red hots with a card reading "Red Hot deals are available at our community" or "Come visit us for a red hot value!"
- A small bag of nuts with a card saying "We must be nuts to offer such a great value. Visit our community and you'll go nuts over our apartments" or "Visit our community and see why our residents are nuts about us!"
- A lollipop with a card saying: "Lick the high cost of living. Move to our community."
- A fortune cookie with a card (or a custom message inside) saying "You'll save a fortune when you move to our community."
- A ball with a card reading: "You'll have a ball at our community. Bounce on over and see why!"
- A balloon with a card saying: "Don't blow up over high rental rates. Visit our community today!"

All cards should be professionally typeset and printed on card stock. Attach it to the item with staples or tape. This will make your blitz marketing calls fun, easy, and, most importantly, MEMORABLE.

Corporate Calls

Corporate calls take more time and preparation than blitz marketing calls; however, they can yield an excellent pay-off if conducted professionally. This type of marketing involves the cultivation of employment centers for current and future residents. Whether a hospital, local industry, military base, government agency, or school, these can be excellent sources of rentals over an extended period of time. Following are some guidelines for making professional corporate calls.

Apartment Communities—Recruiting referrals from other apartment communities can be another source of traffic. This works best when used with communities that are not in direct competition with yours.

Note: Keep in mind that presenting this opportunity to another community works well when your community offers to do the same. Follow up a visit with a hand-written thank you note. A telephone call should be made every 30 days, unless a future resident has been generated. In that case, you should always thank them immediately for the referral, by telephone and by mail, even if they don't result in a new lease. When a community or individual has gone out of their way to send you referrals, you should try to do something extra-special for them, like sending a plant, book, or even taking them out to lunch.

The local Chamber of Commerce is a credible business source for all targeted resident profiles and should not be overlooked! Newcomers to a city turn to the local Chamber of Commerce for answers to housing and employment questions. Employment agencies, too, can be extremely valuable in the referral business. Keep every place supplied with all current information and brochures.

Credit Unions—Develop an ongoing relationship with a service-based credit union(s). These associations are generally amenable to putting your informational inserts in the direct mail they send to their membership.

Employee Associations are independent of companies. This is a plus when dealing with companies who often have strict policies about recommending anything. A discussion should be held with the president of the association to determine the best way to make the offer known to the membership. Most of these associations also have publications in which the community may advertise.

Hospitals and Military Bases—They usually have housing sections within their personnel departments. Keep them supplied with current information and brochures. These two establishments also utilize newsletters with advertising inserts for local and community advertisements and activities. Also, see if they will use your brochure in the employee orientation packets they send to employees prior to their relocation to your city.

Hotels and Motels—Immediate rentals are the norm with this marketing opportunity. Personalize your presentation so as to be unique and remembered by the high-energy people whom you usually encounter. Follow-up is of the utmost importance here and bimonthly visits are recommended. When a lease is executed, a personal delivery of the referral bonus is in order. Note: Generally, large hotel facilities are quite strict regarding solicitation. These facilities should be contacted once to establish a procedure and then considered obsolete if a "no solicitation" policy is stated. Paying resident and merchant referral fees is illegal in some states. Please consult legal counsel prior to implementation.

Create a Corporate Rental Program

Simply telephone major employers in your area to find out the name of the personnel director. Then, mail him/her a letter, along with several Corporate Rental or Guest Suites flyers. A sample letter is provided below.

Give Your Members
A Housing Discount at NO COST
to Your Company!

Dear Ms. Director,

Please allow me to introduce our Corp-Rent Program. This program, designed to be of NO COST to your company, offers a discount on housing to your employees.

Magic Apartments is located five minutes from your office at 1623 Bent Tree Road, just across from the new SuperMart. We are offering special discounts to employees of your company when they choose to lease one of our apartments. We hope you will pass this information on to your employees so that they can take advantage of our offer.

This program also provides you, the employer, with a recruiting aid, because you can offer future employees an opportunity to live near your place of business.

Enclosed you will find information about Magic Apartments, as well as flyers about the special Corp-Rent Program.

I am available to answer any questions that you may have, and will be glad to assist any of your employees that may be relocating to our area.

I am sure that both you and your employees will benefit from this program.

Sincerely,
Sue Smith
Leasing/Relocation Consultant

Here are a few ideas to help you design your Corporate Rental Program:

- No application fee
- Reduction in rent
- Reduced security deposit
- Gift certificate to dinner for two
- Move-in day pizza party
- Free location upgrade (a pool view for the same rental amount as a parking lot view)
- Installation of their choice of mini-blinds, a ceiling fan, etc.
- On the flyer, be sure to include addresses, telephone number, office hours, and this statement: "This Corporate Rental discount offer is available to employees of pre-approved businesses."
- The flyer can be a full 8 1/2 x 11 sheet or smaller if you need to conserve. Mail this program to the same corporations at least two to three times over a two- to three-month period. Re-mail flyers to those corporations from which you receive response.

Personnel Departments—Human resources/personnel departments are helpful to keep your community's information and brochures distributed to their employees via personnel lounge and word-of-mouth. Department store personnel departments are especially worthwhile to keep in contact with, as their floor personnel can provide good word-of-mouth information to their customers and usually are quite helpful in general community/neighborhood conversation.

Real Estate Associates and Relocation Services—Real estate associates are an excellent source of qualified traffic! Direct contact with the more active associates and at the general membership Board of Realtors' meetings enables you to present your community information and brochures and obtain attendees' business cards for specific follow-up. An open house specifically for real estate associates can then be hosted by your community. Relocation referral services are excellent sources for future residents. Generally, they visit your community and completely tour your apartment homes, as well as the immediate area, so as to compile a file with specific information for their future residents. There is often an unusually high referral rate from these relocation specialists.

Resident referrals are always the most effective type of advertising for any community. Existing residents are the best salespeople because they know the community and they are happy living there. Chances are also good that their friends will be of the same approximate income bracket, profile, etc. This results in qualified future residents. To help ensure the success of your Resident Referral Program, follow these guidelines:

1) Publicize the program with a flyer or door hanger. Don't combine it with other flyers or information that could cause it to be overlooked.

2) Post a reminder of the program on resident bulletin boards, and in strategic locations in and around the leasing office.

3) Publish a quarter-page ad in your community's newsletter.

4) Issue reminders periodically to maintain interest.

Note: In many states, paying a resident referral fee is ILLEGAL. Please be absolutely certain about your state laws before implementing a resident referral program.

The ideas listed below will help you to implement an exciting and productive resident referral program. For best results, don't use any single one alone. You will be able to reduce your outside advertising costs, but you must already have a well-managed and -maintained community in order to gain the full benefit of a resident referral campaign.

1. Send flowers to the resident's place of employment, thanking him/her for a referral who ends up leasing. If the law prohibits this, then send the flowers on Resident Appreciation Day. Think for just a moment what happens when you receive flowers at the office. Does everyone ask, "Who sent the flowers?" or "What's the occasion?" This is a great way to spread the word about your community. Flowers aren't the only thing that can be sent. Try balloons, a plant, or a tin of popcorn. Be creative... remember, it has to be noticed.

   Note: Your local florist often discards flowers that are still fresh but close to fading, to prevent disappointing a customer with short-lasting blooms. Most would be happy to give them to you instead, free of charge or in exchange for mention in your newsletter.

2. Have a new move-in pizza party. With each new move-in, provide pizza and beverages to the new resident and their friends who helped with the move. This is a great time to get the new resident's friends and associates interested. Plus, the resident will be thrilled that you cared enough to give them lunch on such a busy day. Make sure you have the pizza party in the clubhouse or someplace where the guests will have access to your floorplans, etc.

3. On the back of your business cards, have printed some type of referral message. Example: "Please remember to refer a friend" or "If you liked our community, please refer a friend." Future residents can be a good source of referrals as well as your residents.

4. Make a rubber stamp with your referral message. Stamp everything that leaves your office that could potentially

lead to a referral (Example: service requests, messages to the residents, future residents follow-up, etc.)

5. On a snowy morning, have your maintenance team arrive a couple of hours early to clean the snow off your residents' cars. Leave a brief note saying, "Please refer a friend today." This is also a good resident retention program.

6. When you have community activities, always invite residents to bring their friends and associates.

Like marketing plans and resident retention plans, you should have a resident referral plan that your staff can refer to periodically. Keep your staff aware that happy residents are your most effective referral agents.

Schools and Universities generally all have housing departments for students, so they should be contacted frequently and in person. Your community information can be sent with their recruitment packages, as well as in direct response to inquiries from their students. Some will actually provide you with their student relocation inquiries list! Universities utilize their professional associations for associate professor and professor relocations. Direct communication with one of their staff generally results in a direct line of communication to their relocating personnel. They are quite helpful in the university system to their "new to the area/university" professor and will specifically direct these staff relocations.

Training Programs require short-term housing, and if the community can help solve these housing problems, a good working relationship with the company may be developed. Many hospitals have programs where nurses are brought in for two or three months of training. A hospital's training program may lease an apartment on a long-term basis and utilize it as a guest suite.

Generating Traffic Through Cross-Marketing

When performing marketing calls and establishing a cross-marketing program, you have to realize that your efforts aren't going to give you immediate rentals, or even traffic. Your marketing calls program will bring in some traffic and rentals, but it is the accumulated results over a longer period of time that will make your program worthwhile.

If you are looking for immediate traffic and rentals, the programs in this section are not for you. On the other hand, if you give these programs the time and effort they need, you'll get the traffic and rentals that you want.

Where marketing calls introduce your community to a merchant or corporation with the goal of obtaining referrals, cross-marketing involves a reciprocal exchange of advertising between yourcommunity and a business.

A cross-marketing program is virtually free when compared with radio, television, apartment guides, newspaper, and locator services. In most cross-marketing programs, your cost will include the typesetting and printing of certificates.

The most common mistake made by management companies when performing marketing calls or establishing a cross-marketing program is setting up these programs with merchants and corporations that are within their area of geographic control.

The most effective means of determining your area of geographic control is the creation of a pin map. This will help you to identify the geographic area from which you pull the majority of your residents. This area is where you should perform your marketing calls or cross-marketing programs to attract new residents.

Many companies perform cross-marketing within a two- to three-mile radius of their community. Unless you find that the majority of your residents have moved in from just around the corner, you are, in effect, spending most of your resources marketing to your current residents!

To gain the maximum benefit of a cross-marketing program, focus on promoting to future residents by setting up promotions with corporations and merchants that are outside your geographic control area.

A strong advantage in using cross-promotions is competitive control. Let's say that you can't afford disclosure by direct mail (when you direct mail, your competition knows exactly what you are doing, allowing them to react). By using cross-promotions in the geographic control area of your competitor, you can achieve results similar to that of a direct mail campaign. This will give you control over your competition because you are systematically defining your market area.

If you perform your cross-marketing programs in your geographic control area, and offer an incentive, discount, or gift, you will be unable to protect your price credibility because you are marketing to your own residents.

An example of protecting your price credibility is the ONE MONTH FREE promotion. As an example: Your occupancy rate isn't keeping pace with the rest of the market, and everyone else seems to be advertising ONE MONTH FREE. Rent is a major expense for your residents, and the savings involved are extremely attractive, so you end up with approximately 30 lease expirations in one month. Of course, these residents have seen your newspaper advertisement for free rent, so they come in to renew their lease, and guess what they want? FREE RENT. So you either give it to them, or stand the possibility of losing the resident. If you lose the resident, you've gained the cost of painting, cleaning, maintenance, leasing, payroll, carpet cleaning, rent, and advertising.

There is an alternative approach to offering free rent that will allow you to protect your price credibility at the same time.

1. Start by advertising in the newspaper, apartment publications, and anywhere else that your advertising budget allows, but do not advertise the offer as a free rent special.

2. Set up a cross-promotion to offer one month free to a select group of people. Transfer the responsibility for the free rent to the referring corporation or merchant. When you transfer the responsibility, you are also giving the corporation or merchant a big benefit. Have your free rent coupon or certificate printed to state that the offer is a complimentary offer from the merchant, and entitles the bearer of the card to one month's free rent at your community with a one-year lease (make sure your card/certificate states that certain qualifications will be necessary). Present your proposal to the merchant with a letter that presents the program as a benefit that can be offered to his/her employees, without costing the merchant a cent. All the merchant has to do is to distribute the cards or certificates to his/her employees.

There is still a chance that a current resident who is ready for renewal will be affiliated with the merchant, and come to you with a free rent certificate. Honor the certificate.

As a result of this type of promotion, the majority of your current residents who are ready for renewal won't know about the promotion, and therefore won't feel cheated when it isn't offered to them.

Reverse cross-marketing can work to your advantage as well. This includes special deals that you hand out to your residents and future residents in exchange for advertising the services of local businesses. This offers current residents an added value at the low cost of printing the promotional materials involved. This serves several purposes, including maintaining a vital local economy and increasing awareness of local resources. Most important to you, it will increase resident retention as your residents become more actively involved with local businesses in a mutually beneficial way.

Try to target merchants who will assist your future residents on move-in day (moving companies, local restaurants that deliver, etc.).

Maximize your cross-marketing efforts:

1. Target cross-marketing coupons to renewals, future residents, and residents with separate campaigns designed to most effectively meet their needs. For future residents, package the coupons in an envelope printed with the total value of the coupons inside, if redeemed. Come up with extra-special offers for your renewals. For residents, print coupons in your community newsletter.

2. Design a basic coupon layout, so that you will only have to change the merchant's name and logo. This will help you to avoid repeated typesetting and publishing costs.

Rejection-free cross marketing:

1. Introduce yourself in a friendly way. Establish a rapport without being overbearing. Start with a merchant who does business for your community. It will help to break the ice.

2. Show the merchant an actual sample coupon, personalized to his business. Don't use copies, drafts, or sketches. This is a professional presentation, so prepare for it as such.

3. Explain why this is a good deal for his/her employees.

4. Agree when the program will start. Allow plenty of time to have certificates printed and deliver them personally. Use the merchant's logo.

5. Agree when the program will end. Three months is a typical duration, but allow an equal amount of time off before starting another promotion. You don't want future residents to expect special offers from your community. (Example: three months on, three months off.)

6. Give the merchant something in exchange for his cooperation. Establish a friendly bond (i.e., a community T-shirt, coffee mug, etc.).

7. Make sure your entire staff (bar none) has personally seen the coupons, understands their use, and knows the duration of the program.

Remember that careful planning and kid-glove treatment of your merchant partners will help to ensure the success of any community and local business cooperative marketing effort.

Corporate Marketing Call Log

COMMUNITY:_____

Company: _____

Type of business: _____

Address: _____

General location / directions: _____

_____

_____

Phone: (____)_____ Fax: (____)_____

Contact person(s): _____

1. Name _____

   Title_____

2. Name _____

   Title_____

Date telephoned for an appointment: _____/_____/_____

by: _____

Results of telephone conversation: _____

_____

_____

_____

_____

First visitation date: _____/_____/_____

Spoke with: _____

Community spokesperson: _____

Results: _____

_____

_____

_____

Date and type of follow-up: (Thank you notes or cards, phone calls, or visits) _____/_____/_____,

_____

_____

_____

Referrals Generated: (Names, dates, leased)

1. _____
2. _____
3. _____
4. _____
5. _____

Executive, Corporate, or Guest Suites

One way to add income to your community's bottom line is to have a successful corporate suites program. These homes away from home can add thousands of dollars to your community's income. Start out with one suite and continue to add suites as you consistently have the first one occupied. You need to plan:

1. Who is going to handle your suites and how.

2. Establish a system for reservations, payments (by credit card, etc.), check-in, and check-out procedures.

3. Maid service. How often? Are you going to add to your existing staff?

4. Marketing plan (where to advertise, whom to target)?

5. What to charge daily, weekly, or monthly based upon costs to operate your suites.

Once you decide you are going to have corporate suites, and how you plan to manage and market them, you'll need to contact your furniture rental company. Some companies can supply you with everything from linens and dishes to pictures and plants.

If you find that a full-service rental company is not available, here is a corporate suites shopping list for everything except the furniture.

Corporate Suites Shopping List

LIVING ROOM:

Telephone
Ashtray
Plants (silk for easy care)
Telephone pad and pen

Television
Books/magazines
Throw pillows
Pictures

KITCHEN:

Silverware and tray
Cooking utensils
Coffee, creamer, sweetener
Dish towels
Salt & pepper shakers
Glasses
Waste can
Can opener

Pots and pans
Coffee maker
Dish soap and dishwasher
 soap
Potholders
Salt & pepper
Coffee mugs
Toaster

BATHROOM:

Hotel size soaps
Towels and face cloths
Toilet paper & tissues
Waste can

Shower curtain and hooks
Floor mat
Disposable cups

BEDROOM:

Pictures	Hangers
Sheets & pillowcases	Mattress pad
Bedspread	Pillows
Alarm clock	Plants (silk for easy care)
Telephone (this can be an extra)	

EXTRAS:

Microwave	Answering machine
Sodas for the refrigerator	Small snacks
Extra blanket for bedroom	Iron & ironing board
Kitchen mat	Entry mat

You'll want to put together a Corporate Suite Information Package that contains:

▶ An area map

▶ A listing of local restaurants, nearby churches, and shopping areas

▶ A reservation request for future dates

▶ Check-in and check-out procedures

▶ A couple of community postcards or sheets of stationery and envelopes

You need to supply a telephone book and an explanation on how they will be charged for any long-distance telephone calls.

Note: Your telephone company may be able to put a hold on all out-going long distance calls. If this is not possible, it is recommended that a credit card slip or deposit be taken in advance.

Ideas and Things to Remember About Corporate Suites

1. Create a Frequent Guest Program. The concept is much like a Frequent Flyer Program in that the more often your guest stays, the more your guest will earn. Example: Stay seven nights, get one night free.

2. Guests will come back if their stay is comfortable and hassle-free.

3. Guests do become residents. Treat them like you want them to stay forever.

4. Ask for referrals and establish a referral incentive program for them if they refer.

5. Make certain every advertisement that your community places says "Corporate Suites Available."

6. Make certain your residents know about your suite program. They'll refer friends, family, and associates who are coming into town.

Attracting Future Residents to Fill Your Executive Suites

1. The key to keeping your suites full is consistently keeping your community's name in front of potential customers (just like in long-term rentals, except to a different market). Start a mailing list of major corporations, real estate brokers, apartment locators, and convention centers or bureaus. Mail your information, brochure, or flyers to them at least once a month.

2. Contact the following organizations for information to see how your community can become a member or assist in supplying housing needs:

The Employee Relocation Council
1720 N Street, NW
Washington, DC 20036
Phone: (202) 857-0857

National Interim Housing Network
6117 Twin Oaks Circle
Dallas, TX 75240
Phone: (241) 385-7356

Your local Chamber of Commerce: Check to see if it can provide you with a list of companies moving into the area. The Chamber will also have a listing of major corporations that you'll want to add to your mailing list.

3. Conduct a fax marketing campaign. Purchase a fax telephone book and fax your advertisement to local businesses. If you have trouble locating such a book, call your telephone company or long distance affiliate.

4. Run a small ad in the local business magazines or trade newspapers.

5. Advertise your executive suites to your residents. They may have family or friends coming to town or have an associate or vendor who will be visiting.

6. Market your executive suites to residents in other company-owned or operated communities all over the United States. Your company may even want to put together an Executive Suites Directory.

The Press
Press Kits

Press kits often offer the media their first impression of your community when you're trying to get free publicity. With that in mind, it's important to present your community's information in a succinct and interesting manner.

The first step in developing your community's press kit is to think like a reporter. Ask yourself, "What basic information is needed to understand the company, community, and industry? What impact does this community have on its residents, future residents, employees, and the public? What makes this community different from its competition?"

Avoid information overload. The key to an effective kit is to deliver the necessary information without going overboard. A frequent tendency is to fill a kit with materials until it is chock-full—and the reporter loses interest. The following guidelines will help to ensure the success of your press kit.

1. Depending on your budget, the outside cover can be very simple: a glossy white folder with your community's logo and name, or you can have it designed by a graphic artist for a more elaborate look.

2. The contents may vary depending on who is receiving the information. It's best to prepare a variety of basic information, limiting each aspect to one page. Here are some traditional types of information to include:

   ▶ Historical perspective
   ▶ Corporate background
   ▶ Biographies of key people
   ▶ Fact sheets
   ▶ Photos—black and white 5 x 7 shots

3. To build a relationship with reporters and the media, give them a reason to keep in touch with you over the long term. Include your business card by clipping it to the outside or inserting it into a ready-made cut that's part of the kit.

A useful press kit forges friendly relationships. Reporters will look to you as a source of information on the industry as your credibility rises. Your community or company will benefit from positive public opinion.

Tools—The Marketing Call Kit

A professional marketing call kit, or a presentation book, should be created prior to presenting your community to a corporation. The idea is to go armed with a polished, professional, and informative package that will present your community in its best light. This kit should include:

1. Information regarding the size and rental range of your apartments, with floor plans.

2. A current copy of your community's newsletter.

3. Photographs of:
   ▶ your community during different seasons
   ▶ the clubhouse, pool, tennis courts, and other amenities
   ▶ the model(s)
   ▶ exterior views of lakes, woods, etc., and any view that would show your community in a positive light.

4. A map with your community's location clearly marked.

5. A fact sheet containing helpful information regarding neighborhood conveniences.

6. Invitations to your upcoming community social events.

What Impacted Me Most about this Chapter:

_____

_____

_____

_____

_____

_____

_____

_____

_____

What I Need to Work on:

_____

_____

_____

_____

_____

_____

_____

_____

_____

My Strengths Discovered in this Chapter:

_____

_____

_____

_____

_____

_____

_____

_____

_____

CHAPTER 10

Resident Renewals & Retention

"The Renewal Process"-*Blake Cline*

"Resident Retention"-*Chasick*

THE RENEWAL PROCESS
by Toni Blake Cline

The renewal process begins the day the apartment is leased. One of the newest concepts in resident retention is to create a sense of ownership for the apartment resident. Building a relationship that is long-lasting often starts with ownership and personalized apartment decor. By providing residents the opportunity to purchase minor decorator services through your office, you allow them to personalize their new home. They may want a blue wall in the bedroom, a cherry wood trim chair rail in the dining room, or a Southwest border added to the living room. Their cost would be for supplies, labor, and a removal charge. Encouraging residents to spend money and decorate the apartment gives them the perception of ownership. Instead of offering just another vanilla box, they can have one with Southwest borders that match their sofa. With your help, they have made this investment and will probably settle in for a longer stay in your community. Do you believe they will move due to a rent increase when they have spent their own money in this location?

The friendship and trust that are developed between the leasing consultant or staff member and the resident build the foundation for good resident relations. It is very important to follow through with all promises given to your new resident. Above all, give them everything they are expecting. Don't expect great appreciation from them, however, when you have met an expectation. After all, they were expecting it. If you want to build appreciation into the relationship you have to provide them with the unexpected. The best time to do the "unexpected" is on move-in day.

First, I recommend you separate the lease explanation from the move-in. This allows the tenant to really concentrate on the business at hand. You may want to consider holding a New Resident Orientation Night. You could hold two or three programs with light refreshments in the early evening, i.e., 6:30-8:00. New residents can come by and meet the staff, sign the lease, and go over community policies. Not only does this type of function get the resident off to a good start, it can also help reduce possible future complaints. Outside litigators report that most ethical complaints brought against our industry stem from misunderstandings about the lease and community policies. Build good resident relations by starting out on the right foot.

Today's customers want us to help them take the stress out of moving into an apartment. We can do this by making things easier. Completing the paperwork before the move-in makes things easier for the new resident. On move-in day when they arrive with their U-haul and have a million things on their mind, all you need to do is exchange rent for keys. This attitude can set the stage for a future full of happy days (and rent increases).

In addition to making the move easier, you might also consider adding some extras to the day. Several companies sell items such as "First Day Kits" which include bandages, coffee & cups, toilet paper, dish towel, light bulbs, and more. You can leave the package in the apartment with a welcome note or give it to the new residents when they pick up their keys. You might consider children's puzzles and pet toys when appropriate, or small nonperishable food items. Be sure to put a bow on anything you leave in the apartment to let the resident know it is a gift for them and not something left behind by the old resident.

Another no-cost extra you can provide is setting the appropriate temperature in the apartment. Or, make fresh ice and leave a note and date so the resident knows they are fresh. You may want to have a stamp made that says "Enjoy Fresh Ice" and a place for the date. When thinking about extras, remember that little extras are wasted if you haven't done the basics. Be sure to have their paperwork ready if you haven't already completed an orientation.

Some properties have even begun to offer a "Resident Services Move-in Gift" from maintenance. These include small nails, picture hangers, a box opener, a small plunger, a paint brush and a small jar of touch-up paint, a notepad with information on how to write a service request, a refrigerator magnet with the service slogan and the phone number to call for assistance. If they have a pet, you may want to include a pooper scooper. You might also include maintenance instruction cards explaining the operation of any complex appliances in the apartment, along with a note from your resident service technician inviting them to call if they have any problems understanding the information or appliances. I have even seen a card left on the counter by the service technician assuring the new resident that everything has been checked out on their new apartment.

Anything you can do to educate residents about the importance of preventive maintenance and help them avoid maintenance problems will save you money in unreported and unnecessary service requests. Repairs that are done weeks, if not months, after the problem first appeared are much more costly and time-consuming. Make sure you continually reinforce an open-door communication policy. A good resident retention will help achieve this. Surveys have shown that up to 95 percent of move-outs reveal unreported service requests. How many times have you found problems in your vacancies that should have been taken care of before the move-out?

Maintenance plays a very important role in the resident renewal process. It is difficult to get the renewal or implement a rent increase if the customer has had problems with the apartment. Yet, we often don't hear about those problems. How many times have you had residents move out and leave an unreported service request in their apartment? This means that sometime during their stay, something went wrong and they did not tell you about it. The two most common times for hearing complaints are when rent payments are due or when you increase the rent. The best time to discuss such problems is not during the rent renewal, even though many management teams send out the renewal without checking with the resident to see if everything is all right in the apartment. This is like asking someone to reorder a product without first checking to see if you are truly happy with their first order.

The first effort aimed at renewal of a lease should be a visit to a resident's apartment 10-14 days after they have moved in. They have just completed the move, and now is a good time to find out if they need any service. At the same time you could bring them your newsletter and even a handwritten invitation to the next social event. People love to feel like they are wanted, and a little note that says you'll be looking for them may be just the incentive they need to show up at your party. This is important, because the more friends they make within the community the better your chances of renewing them.

The next contact with the resident should come 30-40 days after the move-in. This welcome letter should include information on the local community. Now is a great time to introduce your new resident to the activities and businesses in the area and give out some of those local discount coupons you've been saving. Cross-marketing is a proven tool for resident retention. When your customer also becomes a customer to the other businesses in your area, another move becomes less attractive. This letter could include a map, list from the Chamber, and some rent payment envelopes. Another small gift idea for the welcome letter is welcome labels. For just a few dollars you can purchase personalized change-of-address labels. These labels are produced on a single sheet in two colors with the resident's name and new address.

Rent payment envelopes are a wonderful way to communicate and serve your residents at the same time. Simply have card-size envelopes preprinted with a place for them to fill out their apartment information. You could also print on the envelope:

1. "For your convenience, we have provided you with complimentary rent envelopes. Please feel free to either mail it in or bring it to our convenient rent drop-off by the manager's office."

2. "Thank you for paying your rent on or before the first."

3. "Is everything all right in your apartment?"

4. Ask for the names of anyone they know who might be interested in your New Resident Packet for referrals.

The next contact with the resident should be either midway through the lease term or 60 days prior to the renewal letter. The purpose of this contact is to clear the way for a productive and easy renewal procedure. Call the residents and speak to them personally about their satisfaction with the community. I like to present this to them as a management survey. Have a series of questions available for them to answer concerning their likes and dislikes about the community and their apartment. Be sure to preview their file before calling and acquaint yourself with any service they may have requested and other events that may have occurred during their residency. Do your best to discover any problems and solve them now before the renewal process begins. The time to be handling the residents' problems is before, not during, their renewal. One of the most important questions in your survey is your request for a testimonial. Tell the resident you are always looking for great testimonials about your community, and would they mind telling you the top five reasons why they love living at your community. These items should be carefully documented in their file for the renewal. People don't renew for your reasons, they renew for their own, and it's a good idea to know what those reasons are before you go into the renewal.

Today, many properties are beginning the renewal invitations much earlier than before. This allows time to communicate with the resident without using a formal letter of intent to renew with the legally required rent increase notification. If you are required to sent rent increase notices 30 days prior to the renewal date, you might send a renewal invitation between 31-60 days prior to the renewal date. You can use some creative marketing ideas to effectively use this additional communication opportunity, such as a long-stem rose with a note attached that reads: "We would like to extend an invitation for you to reserve another six months in your apartment home." There are several companies that provide preprinted cards and gifts ideas if you don't want to design your own.

Now you are ready to renew! Just as in closing the sale, your success in this situation is not solely based on your renewal performance. It depends greatly on everything you have done up to this point. I find that the most successful properties don't offer incredible renewal gifts, they offer a lifestyle people grow accustomed to and do not wish to leave. Customer dedication and loyalty are earned by consistently practicing good management principles. In talking to residents about why they love their community, you often hear about dependable service technicians, reliable management, good follow-through, clean grounds, and a disciplined, controlled environment.

Here are some helpful do's and don'ts for getting the renewal lease signed:

▶ Do talk about everything you are giving to them and all the things they love about the community. This is a renewal of their commitment and you should share your enthusiasm about your community now as you did back then. The only difference is now they have experience with you that will either lead them to believe or disbelieve what you say.

▶ Don't talk about what you are taking away from them in rent dollars. If you do have to talk about it, try to refer only to the amount of the increase and not the total new rent amount. You may even consider breaking the increase down evenfurther to an amount per day or week. By presenting it in this manner you help to minimize the amount of the increase. Another technique is to use a "Cost of Moving" card to show the resident how much more expensive and time-consuming it would be to move. You can demonstrate that they will actually come out ahead by staying where they are and they will avoid the extreme stress of a move. This can be a very convincing argument to sign the lease.

▶ Make it easy and convenient for them to sign by creating special renewal appointment times, visiting their work place or apartment, or even arranging a quick lunch for the renewal. You pay the check, they sign the lease, and everyone is happy (especially you because you actually got lunch)! Today's national consumer marketing trends indicate that customers desire things to be simplified and made easy. I like to refer to the renewal process as WOO,

COO, and PURSUE! First, you woo them with great daily management skills and extraordinary service. Then you send them cards and flowers in an attempt to COO them. Finally, you let them know they are wanted by an aggressive renewal pursuit. People are very flattered to know they are wanted. The ego is your greatest avenue for successful renewals.

Don't justify the renewal! It is a mistake to tell residents that they are paying higher rent because of capital improvements. They are looking for someone to blame for this extra expense and if the cause is a spending decision you made, they are going to want to advise you about your spending decisions. It is always best to point in the direction of cost-of-living expenses affecting you as well as them. Point to Washington, the electric company, and the price of goods. This puts you in their court, as a victim of the same increase, and allows them to vent their anger elsewhere.

I hope you have gained some exciting new ideas and gentle reminders of the many facets of resident relations. I find the very best way to reduce your turnover cost is to keep them from leaving! Good luck!

RESIDENT RETENTION
By Douglas D. Chasick, CPM®, RAM®

It's a well-known fact that the most cost-effective method of maintaining a high occupancy is to renew the leases of your current residents instead of continually moving people out and re-renting apartments. Turnover costs average between $200 and $300 per unit, before calculating vacancy, advertising, marketing, and leasing or referral commissions—often yielding total costs of more than $1,000 per re-rented apartment.

High turnover can also create apprehension for your other residents, who often wonder "What's wrong with this place? Why are so many people moving in and out all the time?" After several months of constant turnover, otherwise stable residents may move as well, in reaction to the perceived problems of the property.

Increasing resident retention is an on-going process—a process that involves all members of the on-site team on a daily basis. When residents renew their lease, they are, in effect, telling you, "I like living here. I feel I'm getting good value for the rent I pay, service is delivered professionally and in a timely manner, the office staff is friendly and helpful, my neighbors are nice, the property and amenities are clean and well maintained, and I'm not embarrassed to invite my friends and family to visit me. Of course I'll renew my lease!"

Merely sending a card or letter, perhaps with a gift of candy, flowers, or cookies, to your residents will not produce the above-described reaction. In order to make your residents feel comfortable, welcome, and taken care of, you must consistently take care of your residents and property on a daily basis.

Since most residents have lived in at least one apartment community prior to living at yours, they are accustomed to speaking with the manager or "office" only when the rent is late or the lease is expiring. They know that we will do almost anything to initially lease the apartment to them, and that we will pretty much ignore them once they've signed the lease (until the rent is late or the lease is expiring!).

You can break this cycle by regularly contacting your residents, throughout the lease term, for no apparent reason. These "warm calls" are made by you or your staff simply to speak with the resident and find out if they need anything. If they need service, get it done as soon as possible. Call them back and make sure everything was done to their satisfaction. It's not enough to talk about caring; you must demonstrate caring—that's what will separate you from your competitors.

Your renewal program should be in writing, organized in a checklist format. There are too many variables to trust your renewal program to memory, ad-libbing as you go. Each step should be detailed on the checklist, answering the questions "who, what, where, when, and how." This ensures consistent delivery of quality service, and simplifies training new on-site staff. For example, one of the items on your checklist would be "Resident Lease Orientation." Under this heading, you would include:

"The manager or a trained designee must review all lease documents with each person signing the lease. This review is done in the management office prior to physical move-in, and is designed to educate residents about their obligations under the lease and answer any questions they may have concerning the apartment or the community."

❯ Review all lease provisions with resident.

❯ Highlight and initial rent payment clause.

❯ Review community rules and regulations.

❯ Review other lease addendum: Pets, Boat Storage, etc.

❯ Execute all lease documents.

A separate checklist should be prepared for each step in the move-in process, such as Lease Package Preparation, Lease Orientation, Apartment Walk-Thru and Completion of Move-In Inspection Checklist, etc.

The formal renewal process starts on the day of move-in. Proper resident orientation and move-in procedures set the tone for the new resident's stay at your property. A perfectly prepared apartment, timely response to resident problems, and maintenance requests and periodic "warm call" contacts will enhance your chances of renewing the resident's lease.

Prior to extending a renewal invitation to anyone, evaluate the resident's payment history and behavior. Make certain that your maintenance workers note any poor housekeeping, unauthorized pets, or other irregularities discovered while performing routine or preventive maintenance in the resident's apartment.

Renewal contacts should follow a definite schedule, and should be tracked. When setting your schedule, allow enough lead time to contact the resident four times before reaching the 30-day point prior to lease expiration. This is an important date because most leases provide for an automatic conversion to a month-to-month lease if the lease is neither renewed or canceled. In order to assess month-to-month fees and raise the monthly rent commencing with the first day of the month-to-month lease, most areas have a legal requirement of a written notice sent to the resident 30 days prior to the lease expiration date.

The first formal renewal contact should be a personalized letter sent to the resident 90 days prior to lease expiration. The letter should express your appreciation that the resident lives at your community, inform them that their lease will be expiring soon, and that you would like to meet with them at their convenience and in their apartment, to discuss their new lease.

Why meet with them in their apartment? You are selling them—you want something from them—so why make them come to you? Many people feel trapped or pressured sitting in someone else's office, and meeting them in their home will allow them to feel comfortable. It also gives you the opportunity to inspect their apartment, and make immediate decisions about offering them an incentive for renewing—a ceiling fan, carpet shampoo, or other apartment improvement.

Speaking of incentives, it is imperative that all residents be offered the same incentive to renew their lease, so as to avoid any inference of discrimination. This doesn't mean that you have to offer a carpet shampoo to everyone, but rather that you establish a dollar value of incentives for each resident. If you establish a $100 incentive for lease renewals, then you can offer the resident a choice of services or improvements totaling $100. Consider a sliding scale of incentives based on how soon the resident renews their lease. For example, $150 of incentives if the lease is renewed 60 days prior to expiration, $100 of incentives if the lease is renewed 59-45 days prior to expiration, etc.

After the first letter is received by your residents, some will simply call the office and request a new lease—no appointment, no discussion, just "send me my new lease!" Most residents, however, will not make your life so easy, and will require additional contact.

The second contact should be a phone call placed five to ten days after the resident has received the letter as a follow-up. Make certain they received the letter, and set an appointment to meet. If no appointment is set, send a second letter to the resident, written in a more "urgent" tone, that should arrive 45 days prior to lease expiration. This letter is also followed up with a phone call.

Remember that the purpose of these letters and phone calls is to set an appointment to meet the resident, not to renew the lease over the phone. Although some people will tell you to send them a new lease at each point of contact, most will want to meet with you personally.

The final letter should be a more formal, business-like letter that reminds the resident that their lease is expiring, and serves as your notice to them of what the new rental rate and charges will be if the lease is allowed to convert to month-to-month status.

All letters to residents should be personalized with the resident's name and address, and should be signed by the writer. Avoid signing letters "The Management" because it sounds impersonal. Your letters should be in plain English: Avoid long sentences and long words! Write as you speak, in a casual, professional manner. Keep your sentences under 12 words, and limit your paragraphs to four sentences, five at most.

Many of your lease renewals will involve a rent increase. If you have stayed in communication with the resident throughout the lease term, provided good service, and have made the resident feel at home, you will encounter minimal resistance as long as your rents are within the market rents for your area. If you have ignored the resident, expressing interest in them only when their rent is due or their lease is up, the resistance will be greater.

Market rents are determined by the rental rates charged at the properties most like your own. These properties, often called "comps" or comparables, are selected based on their ability to attract prospects in the same profile group as your property. Comps may be located near your property, but location is not the only factor. Amenities, unit sizes, and rent levels also must be similar to qualify a property as a comp.

Since most properties are not completely alike, adjustments must be made to their rents when comparing them to your rents. Comp properties should be shopped monthly, in person, to keep track of what your prospects see and hear before/after they see your property.

What Impacted Me Most about this Chapter:

_____

_____

_____

_____

_____

_____

_____

_____

_____

_____

What I Need to Work on:

_____

_____

_____

_____

_____

_____

_____

_____

_____

My Strengths Discovered in this Chapter:

_____

_____

_____

_____

_____

_____

_____

_____

_____

CHAPTER 11

Personal Growth Messages

"Self Motivation" *-Cardella*

"Your Continuing Growth"
-Cardella

SELF-MOTIVATION
By Carol Ann Cardella, RAM®, MIRM®, GRI®

Self-motivation is really a matter of personal experience. It varies for each individual, and it can vary within a lifetime as we mature and modify what's important to us at life's intervals.

My career in apartment marketing began in 1969, since which time I've repeatedly heard people equate self-motivation with a positive attitude. The context usually implies that if you adopt a positive attitude, self-motivation and positive results will follow. It sounds like good copy and learned advice except that I haven't found one begets the other.

You can't wear a positive attitude when it's convenient or because someone tells you that your attitude isn't in the right place to bring you or them the results they want and expect out of you. A positive attitude evolves from within. It isn't outerwear.

Self-motivation has more to do with *reality, commitment,* and *follow-through* than with something you do. An attitude is a consequence of how you really feel about a subject, your belief system. You can't sustain a positive attitude for a meaningful period of time if you're faking it.

Reality

By the very nature of the words "self-motivate," the implication is that you are in control of your own thoughts, actions, and results or consequences. Even inaction is a form of action. Once you accept the reality that you are in control, that you are responsible and accountable for your thoughts, deeds, and results, the rest is relatively easy.

A good way to begin examining your own personal reality is to refer back to the previous chapters that address personality traits and characteristics needed for success in a chosen endeavor. You need to discover if your personality matches up with the task at hand and if you possess the character traits to succeed. Of course, there are varying degrees of ability, but do you have what it takes to go beyond just getting by and basic survival? Can you produce above average to reap the recognition and rewards?

The point is, if you aren't well-matched to the situation, you'll feel uncomfortable and inadequate in ways which seem beyond your control. Square peg, round hole. Nothing is wrong with the square peg and nothing is wrong with the round hole. They just don't match and interface well. Wrong fit. Don't beat yourself up, re-examine where you are and if you belong there. Put yourself into situations that make you feel good because you derive enjoyment from the process and the environment. That's a sure way to turn yourself on. And when you're happy, others around you will get caught up in your positive light.

The *prerequisite for reality* is to *identify, clarify,* and *reposition* as needed.

How Goals & Objectives Turn Into Reality

There is often so much ado over goals that many people are intimidated by them and, consequently, they avoid them. Goals are nothing but a list of things you need or want to do that are good for you. Goals change as you change.

For that reason, you need to revisit your goals to modify them so they can keep up with where you're going and help you get there. Helping you get there is where objectives enter your field of vision. How can you get "there" if you don't know where "there" is? Without a clear understanding of your destination, or objectives, you will surely take a circuitous route and lengthen the journey unnecessarily.

To determine where you're going, you don't need to bear the burden of trying to figure out where you want to be ultimately. Think in shorter terms that are more tangible and clearer in your vision than those long-term dreams.

First, examine your short-term and long-term goals and objectives to learn if they really are your goals. Or were they planted by someone else in your life such as a parent, mate, teacher, or role model? Did you just adopt them because it led to approval or because of your desire to please another or be part of someone else's dream? Or do your goals really belong to you because that's what you want and it's good for you— they make you happy or give you some measure of peace, comfort, or contentment?

Remember, you can change your goals—your list of things to do that are good for you. And you should, whenever they are no longer inspiring you or making you do whatever you must do to accomplish your objectives.

Goal setting should be done in various increments of time. Establish where you want to be in one or two years, five or ten years, depending upon how experienced you are in recognizing what you want or need. There's nothing wrong with planning an objective no more than one year in advance.

Now, let's see if your objective and timeframe are realistic! Create another list that breaks down your objective into what you must accomplish each month to achieve that objective in one year. Then repeat the process for each week and eventually break it down into what you must do daily to get you "there." This process is an action plan, perhaps better named a "recognition" plan because, so far, all you're doing is acknowledging what you must do if you want to realize your goal. Goals are achieved one day at a time. And your goals can only be achieved by you, they can't be achieved by anyone else.

Commitment

By now the message is probably loud and clear that you are responsible for your own success or failure. Anyone who acknowledges that degree of accountability is going to get what he/she wants. And it's going to happen sooner rather than later. An accountable person doesn't wait for others to initiate plans or actions that affect his/her progress or outcome. If you can't get it done one way, you'll look for another way to get it done, whatever "it" is. It's amazing just how creative you will be when you really want something specific. This is especially true of a sales personality.

That brings us to "thrust." Once you've identified what you want, you need to put enough thrust behind yourself to do whatever it takes to accomplish your objective. Your degree of thrust and commitment determines your degree of success.

Along the way, don't be afraid of making a mistake. Someone, although I don't know who, said, "A man who never made a mistake never made anything." Over the years, I've made a lot of mistakes and was consoled by these words. Perhaps you will be also. Taking risks is a part of moving forward. It's also a part of stepping backwards, but two forward and one backward is still a net gain that places you ahead of where you were before you tried.

Fear wastes time and expends energy in unproductive places. So do intrusions and invasions of emotional, mental, and physical space. But these interruptions are a reminder to renew and revitalize your commitment to yourself and others along your journey.

The most effective technique for staying on track is to maintain your focus. And you accomplish that by blocking intrusions, invasions, and diversions. Self-imposed blinders will insulate you whenever you have the need, as long as you have the self-discipline to follow through to fruition.

Follow-through

We have explored terms such as "productivity level," "energy level," and "thrust" either in this chapter or in previous chapters. But we need to tie these terms to relevancy. They need a destination or objective.

What purpose will it serve to increase your productivity level it if isn't related to an objective of increased effectiveness? What purpose will it serve to improve your energy level if it isn't related to resolving priorities? What will "thrust" accomplish if it isn't related to achieving a specific objective?

Salespeople by nature have "starter-upper" type personalities. But it's the completion that actually reaps your rewards. So, often you generate a lot of activity that you know will bring eventual rewards but you expect some recognition and gratification from others before they see the results. If praise is not forthcoming, we feel a bit let down and deflated, which impacts our resolve. People around you just want results; although the process and technique are important, your performance is measured on the basis of results more than process. Sometimes you need to let the results sink in for awhile before anyone credits you with the achievement. And it takes results to collect rewards.

Strong salespeople (good closers) aren't known as a very patient or tolerant group. They tend to want instant gratification. You need to learn to stretch your attention span long enough to follow through with whatever it takes to achieve your objective. Otherwise, you'll fall just short of success because you didn't take it as far as you could. It's nice to go out with a flare but why go out at all? Cash in on your efforts before someone else does.

In the interim, develop your habits so they will establish a pattern of consistent production. That's what it takes to assure upper management that you can and will deliver results again and again. That's accountability. You're in a wonderful position being an "income generator." You yield a lot of power but don't know it just yet.

Follow-through is where success is measured and won. Be a winner. Choose success. You may only be passing through this career on your way to somewhere else, but that shouldn't prevent you from enjoying the moment to the fullest and taking from it all that you're entitled, provided you gave it all you could.

Self-motivation begins and ends with you. You're in charge of your own destiny just as sure as the next moment is the beginning of the rest of your life. Go on, turn yourself on!

YOUR CONTINUING GROWTH
By Carol Ann Cardella, RAM®, MIRM®, GRI®

Now that you've completed reading this book, we hope you've taken pleasure, knowledge, practical applications, and positive energy from each of us in the spirit of sharing and networking. As you learn and grow, we ask that you pass the same along to others coming up behind you who will be hungry for a place where they too can self-fulfill.

Just in case you came upon our book at a time when your job was just a vehicle to get you where you're going, or was a means to pay your bills, perhaps we've had enough impact on you to enlighten your vision of your own potential and the possibilities within our industry. Because you happen to be in an industry where opportunities abound.

Well, whyever or however you chose our world of apartment marketing, we're glad you're here.

The next most obvious question is: Where do you go from this point forward? What are your options? Some of you may be ready to move on to tougher challenges in other positions within your organization, or different sites, or more demanding companies. And some of you may want to just try putting more of yourself and what you've learned into practice in your present situation.

Whenever you're ready for more input and greater personal and professional rewards, here are some suggestions that may provide guidance and stimulation to make your journey more fun and interesting:

▶ If you have read this book independent of the accredited course curriculum to be a "Certified Leasing Professional," then it's time to inquire about where the courses are offered and how you can obtain accreditation for future credibility.

▶ If you have a local Multifamily Council, get involved; take an active role to shape it into whatever you want out of it. It's surprisingly rewarding to network with your peers and have a sense of what's happening around you, especially if you are a part of the happening.

▶ Share your experiences and your perspectives with your peers at a national level by writing articles or letters to the *RAM Digest*, a national magazine that serves our industry and is published six times a year. *RAM Digest* is available at the National Association of Home Builders (NAHB) through the National Council of the Multifamily Housing Industry (NCMHI). You can subscribe to the magazine as you would any national publication, or you can receive the publication automatically as a member RAM (Registered Apartment Manager). Without national input, your world view could be a bit narrow and somewhat dull.

▶ Watch for local seminars and attend them whenever a program of interest to you is available. Don't wait to see if your company is going to pay for admission. It's nice if it does, but your career can't wait or shouldn't be postponed pending a response. Treat it like a concert or a play you want to attend. Go for it. It's your future and your career. Besides, you never know who you'll run into who will do you some good.

▶ There are lots of books and tapes available through NAHB's Bookstore or through RAM that may be helpful to you. Also, some of the contributors to this book have tapes, books, and seminars that they offer independently. Don't hesitate to contact them.

▶ If you're looking for a change of pace and need an injection of enthusiasm, why not save your pennies and attend the Multi-Housing World Conference (MHW) held each spring in a different great city? Contact Miller Freeman in Dallas for a conference schedule. It's a hoot! Lot's of fun people who do what you do, just looking for more people like themselves. It's a fun, growing, sharing experience.

There's also the annual convention for NAHB each January in conjunction with a wonderful exhibition of products and services for the building industry. During this conference, many educational programs are held on marketing, design, architecture, management, etc. Contact NAHB in Washington, D.C., for the convention schedule. It isn't unusual for 60,000 people to attend this convention, so you'll be in great company!

If you are interested in either or both conferences/conventions, know that you need advance reservations (six months is great, three months is okay) if you want a good hotel experience. Turn yourself on and join others who are already turned on!

Most of us who have contributed to this book began by working on-site and got more involved in any way we could as our careers progressed. The same opportunities that existed for us also exist for you, only more so. We broke ground and paved the way. It wasn't always easy but we're glad we're here and invite you to come along. Capitalize on every opportunity before you. It all happens one day at a time.

Brenda McClain

Cynthiann King

Anne Sadovsky

Tami L Siewruk

Shirley A. Robertson

Kay Green

Nicki Joy

Jennifer A. Newitt